EXTREME
TRUST

EXTREME
TRUST

[Honesty as a
Competitive Advantage]

Don Peppers and

Martha Rogers, Ph.D.

PORTFOLIO / PENGUIN

PORTFOLIO / PENGUIN
Published by the Penguin Group
Penguin Group (USA) Inc., 375 Hudson Street, New York, New York 10014, U.S.A.
Penguin Group (Canada), 90 Eglinton Avenue East, Suite 700, Toronto, Ontario,
Canada M4P 2Y3 (a division of Pearson Penguin Canada Inc.)
Penguin Books Ltd, 80 Strand, London WC2R 0RL, England
Penguin Ireland, 25 St. Stephen's Green, Dublin 2, Ireland
(a division of Penguin Books Ltd)
Penguin Books Australia Ltd, 250 Camberwell Road, Camberwell, Victoria 3124,
Australia (a division of Pearson Australia Group Pty Ltd)
Penguin Books India Pvt Ltd, 11 Community Centre, Panchsheel Park,
New Delhi – 110 017, India
Penguin Group (NZ), 67 Apollo Drive, Rosedale, Auckland 0632, New Zealand
(a division of Pearson New Zealand Ltd)
Penguin Books (South Africa) (Pty) Ltd, 24 Sturdee Avenue, Rosebank,
Johannesburg 2196, South Africa

Penguin Books Ltd, Registered Offices:
80 Strand, London WC2R 0RL, England

First published in 2012 by Portfolio / Penguin,
a member of Penguin Group (USA) Inc.

10 9 8 7 6 5 4 3 2 1

LIBRARY OF CONGRESS CATALOGING IN PUBLICATION DATA
Peppers, Don.
   Extreme trust : honesty as a competitive advantage / Don Peppers and Martha Rogers.
   p.   cm.
   Includes bibliographical references and index.
   ISBN 978-1-59184-467-9
   1. Business ethics.   2. Customer relations—Management.   3. Trust.
4. Honesty.   I. Rogers, Martha, 1952– II. Title.
   HF5387.P434 2012
   174'.4—dc23   2011045730

Printed in the United States of America
Set in Adobe Garamond Pro
Designed by Jaime Putorti

CONTENTS

[3]

TRUSTABILITY: CAPITALIST TOOL 59

[4]

SHARING: NOT JUST FOR SUNDAY SCHOOL 87

[5]

TRUST AND THE E-SOCIAL ETHOS 107

[6]

CONTROL IS NOT AN OPTION *128*

[7]

BUILD YOUR TRUSTABILITY IN ADVANCE *166*

[8]

HONEST COMPETENCE *195*

[9]

TRUSTABLE INFORMATION *221*

[10]

DESIGNING TRUSTABILITY INTO A BUSINESS *240*

EXTREME
TRUST

TRUST: NOT JUST A GOOD IDEA.
INEVITABLE.

Immediately after the first Gulf War in 1991, USAA—the insurance and banking company based in San Antonio, Texas—sent out refund checks to several thousand customers, called "members" by USAA. The idea was that since the men and women who had been serving at the front couldn't drive their cars back in the United States during the several months they were posted in the Middle East, USAA suspended the charges for the premiums during the time soldiers were overseas, and sent out unsolicited refunds once the military personnel got home. USAA consistently comes out as the most trusted financial services organization in the United States, and customers believe USAA will always do what's right for them, never oversell them, always be there when a member needs the company. The company was originally established to serve current and former U.S. military officers, but today USAA serves everyone, although not everyone is eligible for every product offered. Once you become a member, however, your children can also become USAA members, and USAA's loyal customer base now runs into the third generation. The employee culture at USAA is based on a simple idea: treat the customer the way you'd want to be treated if you were the customer.

And as for those refund checks? Nearly 2,500 of them were sent back to USAA by grateful customers who told USAA to keep the money and just be there "when we need you."

Imagine for a moment that you run any other bank or insurance company in the United States.

How will you compete against a financial services institution that customers love so much they sometimes refuse to accept refunds and are loyal into the third generation and counting?

[Yesterday, Trustworthy Was Good Enough.
Today, Only Trustability Will Do.]

What's the difference between USAA and the other financial services companies we all know about? Many of those companies, with names familiar to customers around the world, are not bad companies. On the contrary: Their officers are ethical. Their legal departments make sure they don't break any laws. They issue privacy policies and policy statements of all kinds, and then for the most part they do exactly what they say they're going to do. And yet none of us—not even the executives of these well-run institutions—could imagine customers refusing to take refunds from those companies. The companies are lucky if a customer keeps doing business for several years, and they don't even think about multigenerational loyalty. *What is the difference?*

Most businesses today consider themselves to be trustworthy, and by yesterday's standards they are. They post their prices accurately, they try to maintain the quality and reliability of their products, and they generally do what they say they're going to do. But that's as far as most businesses go, and by tomorrow's standards it won't be nearly good enough. Not even close.

The fact is that far too many businesses still generate substantial profits by fooling customers, or by taking advantage of customer mistakes or lack of knowledge, or simply by not telling customers what they need to know to make an informed decision. They don't break any laws, and they don't mean to do anything wrong. But think for a minute about the standard, generally accepted way some industries have made money for the past several decades:

- To credit card companies, a marginally sophisticated borrower who can never resist spending, rolls his balance from month to month, and often incurs late fees is considered a *most valuable customer.* The common industry term for a credit card user who dutifully pays his bill in full every month is "deadbeat."

- Mobile phone carriers profit from customers signing up for more expensive calling plans than their usage requires, and from roaming and data services accessed by accident.

- Retail banks make a substantial portion of their operating profit from overdraft charges and other fees assessed for what are usually just simple customer errors. (Many standard bank processes are explicitly designed to *encourage* overdrafts.)

- Some merchandise offered in pop-ups and on late-night TV is worth very little, but hooks buyers into paying a little money to have their names and contact information loaded onto a mailing list, which is the truly profitable product sold by the direct marketing company.

- The overwhelming majority of companies even today don't allow customers to post product or service reviews on their own Web sites.

- Does it drive you crazy when a company offers you a product and you refuse it, and then they offer it to you again? And pretty soon, *again*?

Despite the best intentions of good people running companies large and small around the world, is it any wonder that customers don't trust companies?

In this book we'll show that lots of traditional, widely accepted, and perfectly legal business practices just can't be trusted by customers, and will soon become extinct, driven to dust by rising levels of transparency, increasing consumer demand for fair treatment, and competitive pressure. A business can continue to try to keep things out of its customers' sight, but technology now makes it more than likely customers will still find out, one way or another. Things that companies, governments, and other organizations never meant for people to know, they *will* know. Any business that fails to prepare for this new reality will soon be competed out of business by rivals who figure out how to do a better job of earning the trust of their customers.

Transparency will increase because of technological progress, and progress is inevitable. It cannot be avoided, averted, or slowed down. But what makes this particular aspect of technology so different is the degree to which it will heighten and magnify our connectedness, as people. We are all social by nature. We like being with others, telling stories, whispering rumors, playing games, laughing, entertaining, and being entertained. We like to share ideas, get feedback, discuss nuances, and sharpen our own thinking with other people's perspectives. We even look to others in order to know what our own true feelings should be. Being social is an essential ingredient of human nature. The term "antisocial" is an indictment, implying that someone is unfriendly, cold, or misanthropic. If you're antisocial, something's wrong with you.

As important as our social nature is, however, social media and other interactive technologies have injected it with steroids. Before our very eyes, we are being transformed into a dynamic and robust network of electronically interconnected people in a worldwide, 24/7 bazaar of creating and sharing, collaborating, publishing, critiquing, helping, learning, competing, and having fun. The volume and speed of our interactions with others grow in lockstep with Moore's law, which specifies that computers will get about a thousand times more powerful every fifteen to twenty years. But this also means that every fifteen to twenty years we will interact a thousand times as much with others—by voice, phone, text, e-mail, status update, and other means we don't even know about yet. The steady march of technological progress brings us steadily better devices, better online tools and platforms, and better mechanisms for managing. What it adds up to is *more* interactions that are faster, cheaper, and more convenient. At this rate we are destined to interact everywhere, all the time, with anyone anywhere.

You've probably observed this yourself. It's been hard to miss. Just think about how your own interactions with friends, family, and business colleagues have increased over the years, as the tools to connect have been increasingly computerized. How often did you send out pictures of your kids or just interesting tidbits to friends or family members before Facebook? And how often did you keep up with your old high school buddies? Remember life before cell phones? How about before e-mail? If you're a baby boomer, try to remember what business communications were like before fax machines, when letters were often dictated to a secretary using shorthand, typed out, and then sent with stamps through snail mail (or sent to foreign countries via cable). Or think back to when phones were just landline phones, without voice mail or answering machines.

We have all been living through this revolution in communication and interaction. But while we are often fascinated by the rapid innovations we encounter, it's easy to overlook the broader, more general implications of these new technologies. Technology has now changed the landscape of competition so much that a new, more extreme form of trustworthiness will be required in order to be successful. Simply doing what you say you're going to do and charging customers what you say you're going to charge them will no longer be sufficient. Instead, businesses will be expected to protect the interests of their customers *proactively*—to go out of their way, to commit resources, and to use their insights and expertise in such a way as to help customers avoid making mistakes or acting against their own interests simply through their own oversight.*

We've coined the term "trustability" to encapsulate this new form of Extreme Trust, and what we mean by trustability is very simple: "proactive trustworthiness."

> Trustability is nothing short of "proactive trustworthiness."

---

*An important issue beyond the scope of this book is the idea of companies "doing right for the community." We believe a company that is proactively caring for customers will also treat its own associates well, will genuinely care about the environment (and not just slap on a "green" initiative), and will be good citizens of the towns and countries where the company makes money. See C. B. Bhattacharya and Sankar Sen, "Doing Better at Doing Good: When, Why, and How Consumers Respond to Corporate Social Initiatives," *California Management Review* 47, no. 1 (Fall 2004).

$$\left[\begin{array}{c}\text{Trustability: A Higher Form} \\ \text{of Trustworthiness}\end{array}\right]$$

Most businesses and other organizations operating today *think* that they're already customer-centric and that they are basically trustworthy, even though their customers would disagree. Seventy-five percent of CEOs think "we provide above-average customer service," while 59 percent of consumers say they are somewhat or extremely upset with these same companies' service. In one infamous study reported by Bill Price and David Jaffe, 80 percent of executives thought their companies provided superior customer service, but only 8 percent of the customers of those companies thought they received superior customer service. Being "trustworthy" is certainly better than being untrustworthy, but soon even "trustworthiness" won't be sufficient. Instead, companies will have to be *trustable*.

Take a minute to look at Table 1 on page 7 and tick down the list of policies a genuinely trustworthy company might implement, or the actions it might take. Most of these probably apply to your own firm, and all of them are clearly honest and straightforward. It's isn't hard to imagine a customer-oriented company adopting these policies, and even being celebrated for them. Go ahead, do your own "self-assessment," and count which of these statements apply to your company.

Each of these statements represents the kind of policy or action that would normally be undertaken by any company trying to do business honestly and professionally, right? Above board. By the book. For the most part, they are customer-friendly actions, tempered only by a company's own need to manage its brand and make a profit.

But *trustability* is a higher standard still.

Rather than simply working to maintain honest prices and reasonable service, in the near future companies will have to go out of their way to protect each customer's interest *proactively*, taking extra steps when necessary to ensure that a customer doesn't make a mistake, or overlook some benefit or service, or fail to do or not do something that would have been better for the customer.

TABLE 1

	A trustworthy company:
1	Carefully follows the rule of law and trains people on its ethics policy to ensure compliance
2	Does what's best for the customer whenever possible, balanced against the company's needs
3	Fulfills all its promises to customers and does what it says it will do, efficiently
4	Manages and coordinates all brand messaging to ensure a compelling and consistent story
5	Uses a loyalty program, churn reduction, and/or win-back initiative to retain customers longer
6	Focuses on quarterly profits as the most important, comprehensive, and measurable KPI*

To see the difference yourself, turn the page and take a look at Table 2. Compare the principles of a merely "trustworthy" company with those of a company that can be designated as having high "trustability." How will the higher standard of Extreme Trust be applied? Now try another self-assessment.

---

*Key Performance Indicator.

TABLE 2

	Twentieth Century **A trustworthy company:**
1	Carefully follows the rule of law and trains people on its ethics policy to ensure compliance
2	Does what's best for the customer whenever possible, balanced against the company's needs
3	Fulfills all its promises to customers and does what it says it will do, efficiently
4	Manages and coordinates all brand messaging to ensure a compelling and consistent story
5	Uses a loyalty program, churn reduction, and/or win-back initiative to retain customers longer
6	Focuses on quarterly profits as the most important, comprehensive, and measurable KPI

Although most of today's successful companies implement many if not all of the policies and actions on the left side of Table 2 (above)—that is, trustworthy policies—the vast majority of companies' actions would still *not* be considered *trustable*, and only a very few companies have implemented the policies found on the right side of Table 2 (facing page). Trust, yes, but *Extreme* Trust? No. A company might be scrupulous in its ethics, completely honest in its brand messaging, and highly involved in tracking its customer satisfaction, but will it be *proactively* watching out for its customers' interests? If it wants to succeed in the Age of Transparency, yes. Because we will all be more and more interconnected—never less—we will live in an increasingly transparent world, and trustability is the only competitive response a company can have. Trustability is not a fad. It will outlive all of us and our children.

Twenty-first Century **A trustable company:**
Follows the Golden Rule toward customers and builds a corporate culture around that principle
Designs its business to ensure that what's best for the customer is financially better for the firm, overall
Follows through on the spirit of what it promises by proactively looking out for customer interests
Recognizes that what people say about the brand is far more important than what the company says
Seeks to ensure that customers want to remain loyal because they trust the firm to act in their interest
Uses customer analytics to balance current profits against changes in actual shareholder value

An affluent friend's wife realized one day that the credit card he had been using for three years carried no bonuses—no miles, no points, no cash back. (Scott Adams's Dilbert would have referred to him, despite his many talents, as a member of "the stupid rich" market segment.) Since he charged at least $100,000 a year on this card, the couple had forfeited significant benefits. The wife called the large, well-known issuing bank and complained, pointing out that since our friend was a client, his relationship with the bank was supposed to get a regular review. The client manager who took her call explained that the card did carry a benefit—a very low APR/ interest rate. The wife practically spat at them. "So what? Check your records. He pays off the entire balance every month. He doesn't need a low APR." So they answered with what they thought was a surefire

*defense of their behavior: "Well, this is the card he picked out." The
wife's reaction? "Not good enough!" Her point? He just grabbed a
card one day to get out of their office as fast as he could; if this bank
couldn't be trusted to make sure he's carrying the right credit card,
then they can't be trusted with any banking and investment oversight. The wife has since closed out all their accounts and moved
everything to a bank where she believes the company would rather
have a legitimate long-term customer rather than a little short-term
cash. The couple has never heard from the old bank, where her husband had been a customer for over two decades.*

[Why This Book Is Different from Others You've Read on "Trust"]

Everybody's talking about trust these days, and many use *trust* as a syn-
onym for what we might call "reputation," or "regard," or "popularity,"
or "familiarity." Brand equity like this is valuable and worth pursuing,
but it's not the same as "trustworthiness," any more than fresh paint
and a freshly mown lawn can reveal whether or not a house has a solid
foundation.

Some of the best books on business and personal relationships have
been written on the broader subject of trust. These books—even just the
really good ones—are too numerous to mention here, but we do want
to acknowledge the works of Stephen M. R. Covey, Charles H. Green,
and a host of others, and we suspect you've read at least some of them.
We also appreciate the work done by the Edelman Trust Barometer. In
this book we will focus on why simple trustworthiness is no longer sufficient, and why a more extreme form of trust—trustability—will soon
be the new standard by which consumers measure the businesses and
brands they buy from. And then we'll talk about *how* companies must
respond to this demand, if they want to remain competitively viable.

For the most part, the business authors who've written about trust in
the past have developed their own taxonomies to catalog the various elements that make up trustworthiness, ranging from dependability and

reliability to honesty and authenticity. In synthesizing these ideas and joining them to our own, we're going to suggest that the most direct way to think about trust is in terms of a combination of *good intentions* and *competence*. In other words, being *trustworthy* requires:

Doing the right thing. And doing things right.

Peter Drucker referred to doing things right as "management." (That's the competence piece.) Doing the right thing? He called that "leadership," and that's the piece that's all about good faith, playing fair, best intentions. We'll be talking a lot more about these elements as the book progresses, as well as about the underlying foundations of organizational production, the sharing economy, rethinking managerial "control," the difference between intentions and actions, the mandate for hassle-free customer experiences, and a new way to think about what it means when a company creates value—and how that drives the need for Extreme Trust. Mostly, if you want to succeed, you will need your customers to see you as reliable, dependable, credible, helpful, respectful, open, responsive, and honest. Whether you're any of these things or not, they'll still be telling their friends about you. You'll succeed when you generate ease of mind in helping your customers succeed.

Ultimately, our goal is to help you figure out how your business should adapt, as technology inevitably ushers in an age of extreme transparency. Extreme Trust is our answer. Being proactively trustworthy. Treating your customers just the way you would want to be treated if you were in their shoes.

As Interactions Multiply, Trust Becomes More Important

Trust has always been touted as important, certainly. But one of the most important implications of a more highly interconnected world is the increased level of trust and trustworthiness we expect from others. The fact is that trust is becoming a more essential attribute of human culture, for several reasons, as people connect with one another more efficiently. First, of course, is the simple fact of transparency. The more interacting we do, the more transparent things will inevitably become. From WikiLeaks and the Arab Spring to a cable TV repairman asleep on your couch or an airline's luggage handlers mistreating bags, people will find things out.

It's important, however, not to confuse transparency with trustworthiness itself. Transparency increases the importance of trust because if something can be transparently exposed to the light of day without causing undue embarrassment then it must be considered inherently trustworthy and ethical. On the other hand, *the reverse is also not true.* Keeping a secret might be valid for reasons of discretion, privacy, or competition, and not exposing everything all the time does not necessarily imply unethical or untrustable behavior. Businesses and governments have legitimate reasons for keeping secrets, and often these reasons are even enforced by laws and regulations. If your marketing department, for instance, were to voluntarily release its confidential pricing plans for a new product, tipping off your competitors, your executives could be jailed for collusion.

But this doesn't change the fact that the world *is* becoming more transparent, and that this *is* raising the stakes when it comes to trying to keep secrets!

> Transparency increases the cost of hiding the truth. More efficient interactivity exposes truths that used to be inexpensive to hide.

How will you compete when everything you say or write may be overheard immediately and everywhere? In addition to the issue of increased transparency, trust also plays an important role in helping people deal with the burden of information overload. We are all inundated with a cacophony of messages, information, data, and opportunities to engage with others. For most of us, trust is one of the most important filters for deciding what messages or interactions deserve more of our attention.

Which messages are from the most trustworthy sources? Which interactions involve the most trustworthy people? Which e-mails are likely to affect us the most or to contain the most reliable, useful information? In chapter 9 we'll discuss the issue of making sense of the flood of information being unleashed by technology, and how managers can make better decisions by deploying more reliable and trustworthy tools and analytical capabilities.

However you look at it, trust is probably the single most important ingredient in any personal interaction or relationship. After all, if what you learn from someone else can't be trusted, then it's not worth learning, right? And if you want to have any kind of an influence with others, then what you communicate to them has to be seen as being trustworthy. Short of threat of job loss or brute force, in fact, being trustworthy is the *only* way your own perspectives, suggestions, persuasive appeals, or demands can have any impact on others at all. Whether you're telling or selling, cajoling or consoling, what matters most is the level of trust others have in you.

So the technology steroids that are now supercharging our social nature are also supercharging our expectations for trustworthy behavior in others. Moore's law is not just driving technology; it is driving the trust we demand from friends, relatives, bosses, colleagues, sales reps, or spokespeople. It should be no surprise that every single business how-to book on dealing with social media emphasizes the importance of participating in an honest, transparent, and straightforward way.

> Transparency may be the most disruptive and far-reaching innovation to come out of social media.
>
> *PAUL GILLIN,* **THE NEW INFLUENCERS**

The penalties for untrustworthy behavior in a highly interactive and transparent business world will be severe and immediate—loss of credibility, for one, and the loss of social or economic value—while the benefits of sharing, collaborating, and cooperating in a more trustworthy way can be immense. The end result is that the more interactions we all engage in, the more trust will be demanded. The more social we are, the more trustworthy we must be if we want to participate credibly. Because everybody can now hear from everybody, the only ones who will be heard will be those who are *trusted* by somebody.

In the same way you've personally witnessed the technology-driven increase in your interactions with others, you've probably also witnessed an increase in your own personal expectations of trustworthiness in others. When cell phones first became generally available, for instance, do you remember how careful people were not to give out their numbers to just anyone? You didn't want some rapacious business bombarding you with unsolicited phone calls, using up your program minutes trying to sell you things. If your phone number fell into the hands of a profit-making business, then they might call you at all hours or sell your number to other businesses that would. And why shouldn't they? That's what businesses do. You couldn't fault a business just for wanting to make a profit. The same caution applied, initially, to e-mail addresses.

Today, of course, we no longer fear this kind of behavior from businesses (at least, not from "legitimate" businesses). We put our e-mail addresses and mobile phone numbers on our business cards now, and include them in articles and presentations for public consumption, distributing them just as widely as we do our postal addresses or business phone numbers.

Stop and think about why we can do this. Yes, increasingly efficient software is required to insulate us from the 90 percent or more of e-mail messages that are spam. But most spam messages come from fly-by-night operators and quasi-criminal outfits operating out of warehouses somewhere near Belarus, not from legitimate businesses. While there is certainly no less need today for companies to extract profit from every possible opportunity, the plain fact is that most real businesses don't abuse customers' and prospects' e-mail addresses or mobile phone numbers for reasons that have little to do with the patchwork of regulatory restrictions enacted over the last two decades. First, in the transparent world we live in, this sort of behavior would inevitably be exposed. So companies refrain from doing these kinds of things at least partly because *they would be found out.* Even if there were no regulatory penalty at all, to be found abusing any person's contact details would immediately tarnish a company's reputation.

Second, every organization and business requires *people* to make decisions and to carry out policies. Employees are people. They are social, like you, and they have empathy. They can be outraged at untrustworthy behavior. Sooner or later, outrageously untrustworthy behavior on the part of any organization is likely to be "outed" by an employee of that organization. And there are literally dozens of Web sites available to air such outrage—just try Googling "whistleblower."

But finally, and perhaps most important of all, *it is in a company's own economic self-interest to be trustworthy.* Companies cannot simply ignore the reputational damage they would do to themselves if they were to resort to spamming or rampant telemarketing, and as interactivity accelerates, and trustworthiness becomes even more important, it won't just be spamming that damages a reputation. Untrustworthy activities will cause genuine economic harm to a business, and its cost is likely to dwarf whatever short-term profits a business might have been able to generate. We'll take up the economics of trust in chapter 3 and then we'll come back to it more than once, so stay tuned. Economics may not be everything, but for a profit-making company with employees to pay and shareholders to satisfy it's *almost* everything. So it's extremely important that for most companies, acting in a customer's interest is nearly always going to be economically beneficial for the firm in the long run, even if it costs the firm money in the short term.

The security and stability of your life depend on people and things you can depend on. Trust is an important part of that: people and groups with whom you don't feel you have to watch your back all the time. Whether it's a true friend, the regular guy behind the deli counter at your local grocery store, your high school teacher who helped you get into college, your buddies at the club, your business partner, your spouse, your kids—if you're lucky, they're not just trustworthy; they are *trustable*. Someone who is truly on your side has your interest at heart, takes your perspective, won't manipulate you into doing something that you wouldn't want to do, and doesn't stay quiet while you mistakenly hurt your own interest or forget to do something important to protect it. A true friend empathizes and watches out for you. That's what trustability is.

As a business engages in back-and-forth interactions with its customers and employees, these customers and employees will increasingly come to expect not just trustworthiness, but *trustability*. They will demand *Extreme Trust*. And businesses will have to deliver on this demand for competitive reasons. Honesty, transparency, empathy—all the qualities anyone would associate with a true friend, a business will also need to demonstrate, just to stay in business.

It has never been possible to succeed for long with a business that offered substandard product quality or uncompetitive pricing. A business might generate extra profits for a brief period by cutting back on quality or raising prices above the norm, but as customers acquire the information needed to compare one company's offerings with others, it is inevitable that lower-quality, higher-price companies will lose out to higher-quality, lower-price competitors.

And one of the hallmarks of any free-market economic system is that price and quality information are conveniently available to all customers. Until recently, however, information about a company's service reputation, or about the overall customer experience at a firm, was not as conveniently available. Social media and mobile technology have revolutionized this, allowing customers quick and easy access, 24/7, to what other customers are saying about a brand or a business. Other customers' opinions on all aspects of their relationship with a company are widely available online, and growing even more available at the speed of Moore's law. And one key part of any company's overall service reputation has to do with whether it can be expected to act in the customer's interest. Is the firm really trustable?

Whatever your company does, good or bad, will be spread at Internet speed:

- Everywhere ("online" is ubiquitous)

- Immediately (news travels fast)

- Permanently (not enough lawyers on the planet to take stuff off the 'net)

As we all come to rely on and expect trustworthiness in others, the degree to which you can depend on a company to protect your own interests, proactively, will become an essential consideration in deciding whether to do business with it. In the e-social world, comparing companies for their trustability is not much more difficult than comparing them for their product pricing and quality.

[Making Whuffie]

Cory Doctorow's science fiction novel *Down and Out in the Magic Kingdom* portrays life in a future where the most precious asset a person has is social capital. Doctorow calls this asset "whuffie," and everyone's whuffie is easily visible to everyone else. You can build your whuffie up in three ways—by doing good things, by being well networked, or by being notable or famous. But when you lie, steal, cheat, whine, tick off your friends, or drop out of the social scene altogether, your whuffie account shrinks. In Doctorow's novel, the first thing anyone does when they meet other people is check their whuffie, which is the best measure of whether it's worth it to spend time with them.

This is actually not so far-fetched a future. We can already see parts of it beginning to materialize with respect to products and brands, as mobile technology increasingly puts product and service reviews at a person's fingertips, whether they are shopping online or off. And when we connect with someone on LinkedIn or Facebook or some other social network, the first thing most of us do is check for mutual friends or other signs of trustability. (How many times have you Googled someone either before or after meeting him?) Maybe you already do this kind of checking using your smart phone while meeting people at face-to-face social events, from business conferences and meetings to cocktail parties.

Social media commentator Tara Hunt has used Doctorow's sci-fi concept as a platform for dispensing advice on how a business (or a person) should approach social media. She suggests that a person's whuffie is "the culmination of your reputation, influence, bridging and bonding capital, current and potential access to ideas, talent and resources, saved-up favors, and accomplishments." Particularly striking is her description of the contrast between whuffie and traditional money:

> In the gift economy the more you give away, the more whuffie you gain, which is completely opposite from currency in the market economy, where when you give away money, it's pretty much gone. Saving whuffie for a rainy day doesn't work as well as saving money for a rainy day. Whuffie increases in value as it circulates throughout the community; for instance, when I use my whuffie to help you raise yours, there will be a net increase in whuffie for both of us. As it circulates throughout the community like this, it inherently connects people.

A company's trustability will operate in a similar way, and as it circulates throughout the economic system, it will inherently connect with people.

[But Hasn't Trust Deteriorated?]

Surveys do show that people's trust in governments, businesses, and other institutions has declined over the last several decades. According to a comparison of annual Gallup surveys from 1970 to 2010, American trust in institutions was at an all-time low in 2010. The 2011 Edelman Trust Barometer showed that even though trust in institutions measured worldwide showed a slight overall increase from 2010, the United States was the only country worldwide where trust in every institution was lower than it was the year before. For example, only 46 percent of Americans trust business to do what's right. That's only five points away from Russian respondents, who trust their businesses least of all in the world (41 percent). Trust in U.S. banks fell from 71 percent in 2008 to a witheringly low 25 percent in 2011. The government and the media fared even worse than business: just 40 percent of Americans trust government to do the right thing, while only 27 percent trust the media.

In part, at least, much of this can probably be attributed to the proliferation of television and radio news programs, with investigative reporting, twenty-four-hour news channels, news documentaries, and interview shows exposing misdeeds and screwups, many of which used to fade quietly away, unreported. Bad news has entertainment value, so that's what a free-market media industry delivers. Ratings are never higher than when a scandal or calamity of some kind is being covered, day by day, hour by hour. (We see you, Rupert Murdoch!) Moreover, as increasing transparency reveals more and more previously concealed untrustworthy activities, people's suspicions will go up and the degree to which they "trust" businesses or governments in general may decline even more.

Add to this the fact that political partisanship seems to have been facilitated and exacerbated by the proliferation of communication channels and interactive platforms. Twenty years ago, if you held extreme views, you might have found it hard to meet others who shared those views, while today it won't take more than a few mouse clicks to meet other racial purity advocates or back-to-nature anarchists, just like yourself.

The fact that people seem to trust institutions and companies less and less, even as the importance of trust seems to be on the rise, is something consultant and business author John Hagel has called "the trust paradox." He suggests that the very activities we undertake to improve our trustworthiness in the eyes of others have the perverse effect of undermining others' trust in us. When a brand promotes only its benefits (in order to earn the trust and patronage of customers), he says it defies belief, and asks:

> . . . *what is our reaction when someone presents an image of great strength and complete control, with no weaknesses? We don't trust*

them . . . If someone only presents strengths and accomplishments, we know they are not sharing with us the full picture. If they don't trust us enough to share their weaknesses and vulnerabilities, why would we ever trust them?

Hagel has a great point here, and throughout this book we'll discuss the importance of exposing your own vulnerability when it comes to earning someone else's trust.

However, a big part of the overall "erosion" in the general level of trust is almost certainly due simply to our very rapidly rising expectations. As the online economy has taken root, our collective tolerance for untrustworthy behavior has declined. Our standards are going up, so naturally we are more critical of the companies and organizations we deal with. Surveys show that even as technology improves, customers continue to have higher and higher expectations for how the companies they deal with should treat them. In one global survey, for instance, more than half of consumers said they had higher expectations for good service than they did five years ago, and about a third said their expectations had gone up in just the last year.

The declining level of trust we place in our institutions is somewhat analogous to the impression we all have that there is less and less free time available. Of course, technological advances continue to give us vastly more free time—way *way* more free time than our parents or grandparents had. But our desires have escalated even more rapidly. The more choices we have for interesting things to do, see, read, or play at, the more we have to give up when we choose just one option over all the others. Our attention span has remained fixed, but the things that clamor for our attention have greatly increased in number. In a similar way, the more we are well served by transparently honest companies, the more we will expect from our next encounter with any other company.

It doesn't really matter whether the general level of trust is actually declining, or our expectations are rising. Either way, the result is that businesses are going to have to radically improve their operations to satisfy their more demanding customers. In a hyperconnected world a successful business will have to be hypertrustworthy. Extreme Trust is what a firm earns by actively watching out for its customers' interests, and taking action when necessary to protect those interests.

[Our Goal Is to Help You Build a Solid Plan for Succeeding in the Age of Transparency]

Extreme Trust will require extreme change, and our book is organized to walk you through the basic elements of that change. In chapter 2 we'll take you through the basic principles of "good intentions," empathy, and the inherent conflict that these principles often have with traditional economic thinking. Companies that continue doggedly to follow the accepted business practices of maximizing short-term profitability and—sometimes—making money due to customer error will be outed and punished by the online mob. The tsunami of transparency will require companies to give top priority to building business models that align their interest in making money with their duty to look out for the best interests of customers. One of the most important tasks for any business trying to show empathy for customers is to "put on a human face"— that is, to try to behave with customers the way people would behave with other people. It's harder than it sounds, and we'll talk about how you can make it happen.

There is a strong financial case that can be made in favor of Extreme Trust. Your company, like many others, focuses on the measures that have made the most historic sense—measures that report and reward current-period numbers, based on costs and revenues. And even though we all know that companies must also build long-term shareholder value, the link between long-term value and the current-period numbers is not always clear. But customers are the most important part of that link, and in the e-social era the customer link will be even more critical to your success. In chapter 3 we'll dissect how customers actually create value for a business, and we'll show you both a philosophical and a quantitative method for demonstrating the business case for Extreme Trust.

One of the most profound effects of today's explosion in interconnectedness and transparency has been a massive increase in people's willingness to create, to share, and simply to help others, with little or no financial motive. Wikipedia, open-source software, customers solving other customers' service problems—these are just a few of the things that happen when people actually trust others enough to interact and collaborate voluntarily. As the standards for trust continue to rise, these forms of "social production" will become more and more important. In chapters 4 and 5 we'll describe this phenomenon and its implications for your business, including four strategies for influencing opinion-leading customers without using money, rebates, or other financial incentives which, more often than not, are perversely counterproductive in the social domain.

In chapters 6 and 7 we're going to reexamine the very definition of "management," not in the traditional business-book sense of leadership principles and best practices and all that, but from the perspective of what it really means to "control" events at all, as a manager. It's no longer possible to control outcomes the way managers used to, when the world was less technologically interconnected. Social interactions often generate dramatic and unpredictable cascades of sentiment, and you have to be prepared for a new and different kind of randomness. We'll first examine how some businesses have been buffeted and damaged by these cascades of sentiment, and then we'll discuss how they might have been able to succeed had they done things differently. We'll then show you six strategies for dealing with a more random world. But the bottom line is that if your business hasn't already established a reputation for trustability, then when the social media asteroid hits, your extinction may be imminent.

Competence is a topic we'll circle back to in chapter 8—including what it means to be "product competent" and "customer competent," and how to deal with the reality that not all companies can have the very highest quality products and services 100 percent of the time. The world may be less manageable or predictable than it used to be, but if you want to be trustable, you still have to be able to do the basics right, and we'll talk about how, along with strategies for dealing with mistakes and re-covering from a poor product or service execution.

One of technology's most thrilling and annoying effects for everyone is the sheer increase in the volume of information now available, and this makes the question of deciding just what actually constitutes a "compe-tent" decision all that much more difficult. We all use trust as our pri-mary "filter" for this data, but what does that really mean for a business? So in chapter 9 we're going to review what it means to "trust" different types of new information, and we'll consider how a trustable business *uses* information so as to make more competent decisions and be seen as more trustable in the eyes of its customers, employees, and other stake-holders. This is not as simple as it might sound, because the overwhelm-ing majority of today's businesses don't even apply the scientific method in evaluating data.

Throughout our book we'll consider at different points how various kinds of businesses, from credit card issuers to mobile phone carriers, might operate in a more trustable way. In chapter 10 we're going to put all our principles together and describe a few more hypothetical busi-nesses in a variety of other categories, the way they would operate if they were genuinely trustable. We say "hypothetical" because there are very few businesses today that operate this way, although we can find exam-ples in a variety of industries. But for the most part, what you'll be read-ing throughout this book, essentially, is a kind of "business science fiction." We are writing about the future of business competition, yes, but it is an inevitable future, because it is being shaped by technology's inexorable march toward more and more connectedness, and connected-ness generates trust.

Mere trustworthiness, fine until now, will no longer be enough to compete with companies that have figured out how to be genuinely trustable.

BASIC PRINCIPLES OF
TRUSTABILITY IN A BUSINESS

If you want your business to be trustable, and to succeed in a more transparent, hyperinteractive world, then you had best commit these three basic principles of Extreme Trust to memory:

■ **Do things right.** Be competent. Manage the functions, processes, and details right in order to make it easy for customers to do business with you. And pay attention to the customer's experience, not just the company's financial performance.

■ **Do the right thing.** Ensure that the way your organization makes money aligns with the needs and best interests of your customers. You can't be trustable if you're entirely focused on the short term. Customer relationships link short-term actions to long-term value.

■ **Proactively.** Knowing that a customer's interest is not being well served and doing nothing about it is untrustable. *Not* knowing is incompetent.

["You're Gonna Need a Bigger Boat"]

That's what actor Roy Scheider said in the movie *Jaws* as he got a good look at the immense size of the shark they were dealing with. And it's our advice for businesses now grappling with the rising importance of trust. You're gonna need a bigger boat. Earning and maintaining your customers' trust is a much bigger issue than you thought.

The demand that future customers will make for genuine trustability in the companies they deal with will have a dramatic impact on the structure, operation, and management of businesses. Businesses will need to think much more clearly about balancing their short- and long-term economic interests as they seek to maintain their own level of trustability. Untrustable businesses squeeze every last penny out of each immediate financial period, while trustable ones recognize that customer trust is a highly valuable—and measurable—financial asset, so they place more emphasis on balancing the short-term revenue from customers with the long-term value of their customers, their brands, and their reputation in the marketplace. The problem is that a great deal of money today is being made by *not* respecting customer interests. So the economic consequences of trustability are not going to be trivial.

Companies will also have to figure out how best to acknowledge and accommodate the spontaneous, user-generated customer communications that are likely to become the principal "voice" in the marketplace for any brand. Advertising and sales pitches are low on trustability, while collaboration and relationship building are more trustable. The ubiquitous availability of inexpensive tools for interacting with other people has given rise to a whole new way of creating genuine economic value: social production (see chapter 4). Open-source software, Wikipedia, online reviews, and other valuable information-based products and services are forms of social production, regularly made available for no exchange of economic value at all. In this burgeoning field of online activity, people volunteer, they create, they contribute, and (importantly) they *police* one another—all without formal remuneration. Instead, they take their compensation in the form of recognition, or pride of accomplishment, or general participation: they're makin' whuffie.

Yochai Benkler maintains that what we are witnessing represents a permanent change in the way human beings organize themselves, because (1) personal computers are inexpensive, widespread, and connected to one another on the Internet; (2) social tasks involve information, ideas, and intellectual property rather than physical goods; and (3) the Internet's structure allows large tasks to be broken down and accomplished in smaller steps. In other words, because it's made possible by technology, and because it generates progress and creates value, social production is inevitable. It's here to stay. So operating in a more trustable world will require a company to figure out how best to harness the forces that drive social production, a task greatly complicated by the fact that money just won't be the effective motivator.

And finally, we have to realize that social interactions are not as manageable as a company's marketing and other functions are. The social interactions you have with customers and other people can't be directed the same way advertising campaigns or cost-cutting initiatives can. Instead, in the e–social world what companies are likely to find is that top-down, command-and-control organizations are not trustable, while self-organized collections of employees and partners motivated by a common purpose and socially empowered to take action are more trustable.

These are *cataclysmic* changes for the business world. These changes will turn most businesses entirely upside down and inside out. We are not just talking about making nice with customers here. We are talking about a technology-driven revolution in human interaction that will wreak holy havoc with nearly every business principle taught in business schools today.

As with all disruptive change, it will be the new companies and start-ups that lead the charge against the established order. These rebels will be wielding honesty as a lethal competitive weapon to steal customers from their more established but less trustable rivals. By contrast, the firms that have already enjoyed the most success and profitability are the ones that will find it hardest to adapt. Some will try to become more trustable, but will only grudgingly relinquish the significant cash flows generated by untrustable business practices. Only those firms that see the issues clearly and make a more determined attempt at genuine transformation will succeed, and even for them the process will still be painful and difficult.

It won't be easy, but eventually our entire economic system will be transformed by this revolution, in the same way that interactivity itself has so dramatically transformed it over just the last twenty years. And while Extreme Trust may be the competitive motivation fueling the revolution, what you're going to find is that in order to use this fuel you'll need to change out your business's entire engine.

You're gonna need a bigger boat.

[2]

SERVING THE INTERESTS
OF CUSTOMERS, PROFITABLY

*We judge ourselves by our intentions and others
by their behavior.*
STEPHEN M. R. COVEY

Trust has been defined many different ways, but in the final analysis the trust you have in someone you interact with, or with a company you buy from, can be defined in terms of how you assess two different qualities in that person or company:

1. *Good intentions—Doing the right thing.* Do they intend to act in *your* interest, or do they appear more intent on their own self-interest? Selfishness manifests as the exact opposite of trustworthiness.

2. *Competence—Doing things right.* Are they capable of acting on these good intentions? Proficiency matters, and incompetence will destroy trust just as surely as bad intentions will.

Both these qualities are important if you want to be considered trustworthy; either one by itself is not sufficient. It does a customer no good, for instance, to deal with the best-meaning company in the world if that company doesn't have enough competence to deliver the product on time or in good condition. Even if your appliance manufacturer promises to look after your best interest with a three-year all-inclusive warranty, and even if they contact you to remind you when your warranty is nearly up, if they just can't figure out how to get a repairman to your house when you need it, you still can't trust them. And even if the airline's posted on-line policy is always to display the lowest fare available, if their Web site just can't access all the different fare combinations, then you still can't trust that you'll get what they promised.

We'll come back to both of these components of trust throughout this book, along with the important emphasis on being proactive, but it should be obvious that trust is a matter of degree, and that all of us will find some people or companies more trustworthy than others. In this chapter we're going to delve more deeply into the "good intentions" issue. What does it mean, really, when a business has good intentions with respect to a customer?

["You've Got Mail": The Wages of Untrustability]

"You've got mail" is a phrase made famous by AOL, one of the earliest and most successful Internet service provider (ISP) companies. Formerly known as America Online, at the height of its power AOL had some $5 billion in annual revenue, a market cap of $222 billion, and over 30 million paying subscribers, the vast majority of whom connected their computers to the Internet via AOL's toll-free telephone numbers. In 2000, AOL bought media giant Time Warner, in the largest corporate acquisition ever.

Over the last decade, however, AOL has been a business in decline. The company has once again separated from Time Warner (which remains reasonably healthy), and while it does earn some money from selling advertising and operating a few interesting and useful online properties such as MapQuest and Moviefone, today AOL is a mere shadow of its former self, with just 4 million paying subscribers, less than $2.5 billion in annual revenue, and a market cap of about $1.5 billion.

All this would be just another story about the meteoric rise and fall of an Internet company except for one thing: Throughout its history, AOL has reaped enormous profits by deceiving its subscribers, tricking them into paying higher fees than they needed to pay. It has raked in literally *billions* of dollars over the last twenty years essentially by ripping off millions of its own customers—customers who simply weren't paying enough attention, probably because it never occurred to most of them that a publicly held company with such a well-known brand name would actually stoop to such behavior. AOL would rank very high on any list of technically noncriminal companies earning the bulk of their profit by betraying the trust of their customers. The difficulty of quitting AOL as a customer is infamous on YouTube. Employee moles have sent training materials to customer activists exposing the call-center rep training that makes it hard to leave AOL and describes ways to "Think of Cancellation Calls as Sales Leads."

Despite AOL's more or less continuous controversy with respect to customer service, and its foray into advertising-supported businesses, the company still gets 80 percent of its profits from subscribers, many of whom are older people who have cable or DSL service but don't realize that they don't need to pay an additional twenty-five dollars a month to get online and check their e-mail.

> The dirty little secret is that seventy-five percent of the people who subscribe to AOL's dial-up service don't need it.
> *FORMER SENIOR AOL EXECUTIVE*

Given all this, it shouldn't be a big surprise when we say AOL is just not a firm you can trust. Even though companies have no minds of their own, AOL could serve as a poster child for consciously bad intentions. Suppose for a minute that AOL really were a person. Not a company, just a human being with a funny name. Would you trust Mr. AOL to give you the correct change at the checkout counter? If he offered you a used car for sale, would you believe him when he described its condition to you, hand over heart? If he ran a charity, would you contribute—confident that he wasn't pocketing a big percentage of your contribution as his fee and only sending a fraction of your gift to the cause?

[Banking on Customer Mistakes]

Untrustable business models thrive in our economic system today largely because being untrustable can be highly profitable—in the short term anyway—and many businesses are managed almost entirely for short-term results. If you've ever incurred more than one overdraft charge on your bank account in a single day, for instance, then you may be interested to know that this is exactly how some banks like it to work, and what they're doing is legal. Some retail banks clear the biggest checks and charges first, in an explicit effort to maximize overdraft charges. Let's say you have $250 in your checking account in the morning. During the day you withdraw $80 from the ATM, and then use your debit card to buy lunch for $20, then maybe a book for $25, then a new coat for $180. At the end of the day these charges won't be debited to your account in the order you incurred them, but in order of size, with the largest charges debited first.

Your charges, in the order made:	Charge	Balance		The bank's accounting:	Charge	Balance	
Initial balance		$250		Initial balance		$250	
ATM withdrawal	$80	$170		Coat purchase	$180	$70	
Lunch	$20	$150		ATM withdrawal	$80	$(10)	NSF!
Book purchase	$25	$125		Book purchase	$25	$(35)	NSF!
Coat purchase	$180	$(55)	NSF!	Lunch	$20	$(55)	NSF!

As a result, even though you only exceeded your account balance one time, with the very last purchase, ending the day with an overdraft of $55 in total, you will incur *three* NSF charges (bank lingo for "insufficient funds"), with fees totaling more than $100 at many banks.

> Miss Piggy—the famous Muppet—once pointed out that all you need to know about bankers . . . is that they attach little chains to their ball-point pens.
>
> *JIM HIGHTOWER, ON ALTERNET.ORG*

Now maybe—way back when the majority of retail checking transactions were physical checks that were cashed by merchants and then mailed in to banks in daily batches for clearance—just maybe this largest-charge-first policy was implemented as a service to customers, to ensure that the biggest, most important checks arriving in each day's batch of mail would be paid and not bounced. But this benevolent motive—if ever it was the real motive—has now been completely overtaken by the fact that real-time electronic transactions constitute a lot of retail banking activity. Most bounced-check fees today are incurred through ATM withdrawals and debit card swipes, with each transaction having an unmistakable date-time stamp.

Some banks' intentions can be called into question even more by the services they offer to ameliorate this situation, because many of these services are designed primarily to generate even more fees. Some banks offer their customers the option to cover an overdraft immediately with a credit card, for instance, but whenever such a transfer is made a cash-advance charge is applied to the credit card, and the minimum transfer may be $100.

Many banks also offer "courtesy overdraft" coverage up to some limit. But courtesy overdraft coverage doesn't mean what it sounds like—that you can overdraw your account as a "courtesy," for free. It just means the bank won't *stop* you from overdrawing your account, unless you exceed the coverage limit. A fee will still be imposed, but you'll be spared the embarrassment of having a debit charge denied. And while it used to be the case that you had to sign up with the bank to get this "courtesy" extended to you, increasingly banks are simply subscribing their customers to the policy automatically, so if you charge something with your debit card that exceeds the money in your account, the transaction will still go through—along with the NSF fee assessed to you later, often exceeding the value of the original charge! In a 2007 survey of the top five banks and savings institutions in each of the top ten U.S. metropolitan areas, the average "courtesy overdraft" charge was $29.

But at some banks it gets even worse. Suppose you only have $50 in your account but you also have courtesy overdraft coverage up to $250. And remember now, the bank may have even signed you up for this courtesy overdraft coverage without your knowledge. Not wanting to overspend, you use the ATM to submit a balance inquiry. The ATM will tell you your "available balance" is $300! This is of course an important figure to know, but the way it's presented by some banks will distract attention from your actual balance.

Even as new legislation suggests reforms in these areas, the result of all these policies is that while banking companies may not have real "intent," because a bank isn't a real person with a real brain any more than AOL is, anyone observing this behavior in a *person* would be likely to conclude that Mr. Bank *wants* you to overdraw, if it is at all possible for him to fool you into it. Mr. Bank *wants* to maximize those NSF penalties by reordering the daily charges to your bank account after they are made.

Still not convinced? Here's what one bank employee said with respect to promoting the use of debit cards, as reported by consumer-advocate blogger and MSNBC commentator Bob Sullivan:

> *Our focus is to get you to start using the debit cards so you can charge up those NSF fees, because the purchases that you make will not show in your account until many days later.*

When Martha signed up for a checking account at a large, well-known bank in New York, she was offered a debit card against it. She adamantly declined, commenting that debit cards are better for banks than for customers. Three days later, she received a debit card in the mail, with a letter that began: "Here is the debit card you requested." Does it matter whether the debit card sent to Martha after she refused it was sent on bad faith? Or (more likely) because the bank is not competent enough to meet the request of an individual customer? Either way, the customer starts looking for a way to jump ship because clearly this bank is not really trustable.

Not every bank behaves this way toward customers. But—like AOL—many that do would find it very hard to wean themselves off these perfectly legal practices. And if you are a customer, and you know enough to have your choice between two banks—one bank that looks out for itself and maximizes fees they can charge you and makes the most it can every quarter, and another bank that looks out for you and helps you maximize how far your money will go and makes a decent profit every quarter, *which will you choose?*

[Netflix: Bad Intentions? Or Incompetence? Or Both?]

Blockbuster, the original giant of the video-rental business, made a lot of money from late fees—so much, in fact, that its customers grew to detest them. Derisive jokes about Blockbuster and its late fees became regular fare for comedians on late-night television shows. But Blockbuster was addicted to the late-fee revenues, and rationalized that they weren't, themselves, to blame for their rampant customer dissatisfaction or the resulting abuse their employees had to take; all a customer had to do to avoid a late fee was bring the movie back on time. Blockbuster's business model was based on revenues that infuriated customers, and they weren't innovative enough to figure out any other way to make money that didn't include late fees.

But a newcomer did. In 1999 Netflix appeared with a completely different business model: customers got to choose their level of commitment to renting movies (different pricing levels for different quantities of movies out at a time), and paid a fixed monthly fee to enjoy each movie for as long as they wanted. Send them back fast, get more movies for the same price, but never pay a late fee. Furthermore, Netflix remembered what you liked, made recommendations, and allowed customers to create personalized "queues" that lined up the next movies they wanted to see. The way Netflix made money was aligned with the way customers wanted to do business.

After Netflix had siphoned off about two million customers, Blockbuster saw that to remain competitive with the most valuable movie renters, it too would have to adapt. In 2004 the company decided to eliminate late fees in its company-owned stores, despite the projected annual revenue loss of more than $250 million, although franchised stores were free to continue charging these fees, and many of them did. But the handwriting was already on the wall for Blockbuster's decline. Netflix had set up a low-priced, customer-friendly alternative in the form of mail-order DVD rentals, and disillusioned Blockbuster customers flocked to it. Hooray! They had found a business that valued customer service, made it super-easy to participate, remembered individual customer preferences, and didn't try to "trick" customers with fees that sometimes exceeded the value of the DVDs being rented. Netflix was *trustable*, reminding customers if they'd had a DVD for a very long time, in case the customer had forgotten it was lying around somewhere.

But even while it was still competing with Blockbuster, Netflix was occasionally accused of cutting costs by "throttling" its highest-volume, most frequent customers (that is, selectively slowing down the turnaround times on these customers' DVD orders). Nevertheless, its low-price market-entry strategy seemed successful enough on balance, and Blockbuster, which never lived down its reputation for rapacious late fees, filed for bankruptcy in 2010. By 2011 Netflix had established a growing business in live streaming videos as well as DVD rentals, with 25 million customers, and its market cap had soared to some $16 billion, as investors fought over the chance to own a piece of the victor in the U.S. video-rental war.

But then, in the summer of 2011, Netflix (like many companies) got so busy working on its "business" that it forgot the heart of its success: customers who liked Netflix, who valued what they had taught the company when they got good recommendations, and who trusted the company to provide good product and service at a fair price. Netflix benefited directly from Blockbuster's own self-inflicted wounds, and yet less than a decade after trumping Blockbuster's self-interested business model, Netflix put its own preferences for business structure and efficiency, as well as a desire for increasing prices, ahead of the loyalty of its customers. It may as well have started charging late fees.

Although its customers liked paying one fee and keeping one "queue" for streaming movies as well as DVDs by mail, Netflix wanted to anticipate the end of DVD rentals, which it predicted for 2018, and separate itself into two businesses—DVD rentals and streaming videos. This would be more convenient for Netflix, but not more convenient for the customers. In fact, the way Netflix reconfigured itself resulted in an effective price increase for customers, as well as a great inconvenience. Customers had to check movie listings on two Web sites (streaming Netflix and DVD-by-mail Qwikster), feeling as though they were dealing with two companies, and being ripped off in the process. Many customers felt betrayed by this company they once thought loved them.

In trying to navigate the difficult waters of its price increase, Netflix shot its own marketing foot off, soon (and ironically) antagonizing its own customers every bit as much as Blockbuster had. The structural siloing of the businesses, along with the resulting price increase, was announced by CEO Reed Hastings in a blog post on July 12, 2011, and the social media platforms lit up with protest instantly. Within just a few days Hastings's post had accumulated 81,789 comments, the vast majority of which were distinctly negative or overtly hostile (only 1.7 percent of the comments were positive). Adding fuel to the fire, in September Hastings posted an apology that just seemed to irritate people more. By the end of that month the company had lost millions of customers, and two weeks later announced it had canceled its plan for Qwikster.

If this was just a price increase, it certainly wasn't executed very skill-fully, especially for a high-visibility online company with what once seemed to be a strong talent for dealing with the e-social domain. The managers at Netflix were clearly aware of the power of the social crowd. The company had even crowdsourced its algorithm for recommending movies to people by offering a $1 million prize to anyone who could im-prove it by 10 percent. (It paid the million dollars out in 2009 and im-mediately began a new contest with new prizes, based on computing with a wider array of data.)

But this wasn't just a price increase. It was Netflix insisting on doing business the way it wanted to, without taking its customers' point of view into consideration as a key part of its competitive strategy (just like Blockbuster). Netflix did what would be good for Netflix and not what was good for customers.

Whether the company reverses its course, or follows Blockbuster into bankruptcy after opening the field to a new player who's more attuned to customers' sense of fair play, or something in between, Netflix pro-vides a parable about what happens when executives put their own busi-ness models ahead of how customers want to do business. By the end of October 2011, the company's stock market value had fallen to $4 billion, down 75 percent from its high in July, indicating that investors were still concerned about the direction of the firm's business, and CEO Hastings confessed that it would take more than a year for the company to claw its way back to the kinds of customer satisfaction levels it had enjoyed be-fore the debacle.

On one hand, we could argue that this is simply a case of incompe-tence on Netflix's part. It fumbled the ball during a complicated play, trying to shift its business model because of a legitimate and predictable technological change on the horizon. But we could also argue that it is a case of bad intentions; that Netflix never really thought of its customers first at all, but merely posed itself as a customer-friendly alternative to Blockbuster in a competitive strategy made attractive by the bigger com-pany's own prior missteps. Or maybe it was a bit of both?

[So What Are Good Intentions, Anyway?]

We can never really know someone else's intention. Any person's motive is internal to the person. It's in the mind. All we can do is observe their behavior—what they do, how they look, what they say out loud.

It is in our nature, however, to put ourselves in others' shoes, and to ascribe motives to people based on what we see them do. We know what goes on in our own minds, we know what *our* intentions would be if we were doing these things, and so we hypothesize about what must be going through someone else's mind to account for their actions. When we trust someone's intentions, we're really just making our own judgment based on their behavior. It may sound like a circular argument, but Henry Stimson had it exactly right when he said: "The only way to make a man trustworthy is to trust him."

Nor should it be a surprise that two different people, evaluating the exact same behavior in someone else, might make *different* judgments. Only a mind reader can be 100 percent confident when the subject involves someone else's intentions.

We make the same judgment calls when it comes to assessing the businesses we buy from, the companies we work for, and most other organizations we deal with. As Seth Godin has pointed out, a "company" doesn't really have intentions at all, because a company has no mind of its own. But this doesn't stop us from viewing a company's behavior through our own anthropomorphic lens, and asking ourselves what *we* would intend if we were to take the same actions. This lens may not explain how things actually happen in the world, but as a logical shortcut most of us still find it useful. And since we can't know someone else's actual intent anyway, the shortcut costs us nothing.

We've seen plenty of examples of bad intentions, or simply not caring. Assume that transparency, exposure, and the consumer thirst for retribution for unfair behavior will accelerate, and scare businesses straight. What does that mean for the way a business has to think about being deliberately trustable?

Figure out how to protect customer interests, profitably.

Understand that betraying customer interests will cost more than it has in the past.

If we've been looking at examples of bad intentions, how would we define good intentions? Without exception, definitions of "trust" require taking into account the other person's best interests when making decisions. This means treating someone the way you'd want to be treated yourself—it's the "Golden Rule" for Christians, and is a similarly revered principle in virtually every other world religion. When people describe "trust," they use words like "playing fair" or "following your conscience" or "showing goodwill." The academic term for this is "reciprocity," meaning that a trustworthy person must understand—have insight into—the best interest of "the other," and then reciprocate with his or her own actions. In order to be trusted by someone, a person must be seen to take account of and respect the other's interests.

The more you think someone else is only acting to further their own interests, the less trustworthy you're likely to think they are. One authority on trust, Charles Green (coauthor, with David Maister and Rob Galford, of the very well-respected and widely quoted book *The Trusted Advisor*), suggests that a person's trust in another is inversely proportional to the degree of "self-orientation" he perceives in that other person's actions. The more you think my actions are driven primarily by my desire to benefit myself or to achieve my own goals (say, making a profit this quarter), rather than by my desire to do what's in your interest (say, telling you the best prices available right now), the less inclined you will be to trust me.

In real life, it's easy to recognize the conflict between trust and self-interest. We don't trust transactional salespeople who have everything to gain from our purchase and nothing to lose from our dissatisfaction. We are *least* likely to trust someone who smiles and says, "Trust me."

We don't trust advertising and marketing messages because each is designed with a particular, self-oriented purpose in mind: to improve the bottom line of the company doing the communicating. Advertising costs money, and while no one holds it against a brand for trying to recoup this investment, it does mean that every ad carries a point of view—an inherent bias. Surveys show that consumers place far more trust in their friends' opinions, and even in the opinions of complete strangers whose reviews they read online, than they do in the claims made in advertising. They tend to trust "a person like me" or an objective expert the most. Ads have a bought-and-paid-for point of view, but your own friends—and even uninvolved strangers—have no such agenda. If you ask a friend his opinion, he's likely to give you his most honest assessment, because he's your friend. Right or wrong, his assessment is not going to be biased. If he's a true friend, his opinion will be delivered with no hidden agenda in mind at all. (Haven't you ever tried on anything at a clothing store and had a genuinely honest salesperson—one who really wanted to help you look good—say, "That doesn't really flatter you. Try this instead"?)

Being self-oriented, self-centered, or self-obsessed is simply not the way to earn someone's trust. Selfish people aren't considered trustworthy. Selfishness is antithetical to trustability.

[Is Your Company Trustable? Or Merely Trustworthy?]

A company can be trustworthy largely by doing what it says it will do. But it can only be *trustable* by genuinely considering the customer's interest and balancing it with its own. Obviously, a trustable company still wants to *make* a profit, but not by deceiving or fooling the customer, or taking advantage of the customer's lack of knowledge.

> Many companies, following their current business models, can be "trustworthy" in the sense that they are legally operated and do what they promise. But until they change their underlying strategy, which often depends on customers' not paying attention or not knowing enough to make the best decisions, they can't be considered "trustable."

Trustable companies do things right. A trustworthy firm will do what it promises, but may only do it in the most basic way. It will be competent enough to answer the phone when you call, but it may then measure the performance of its "service" reps solely by how many calls they can handle per hour. A *trustable* company not only means to do well, but cares enough about this objective to execute well also. Keeping its own profit in mind, a trustable firm is always trying to understand what it's like to *be* the customer, and then to make that experience as hassle-free and satisfying as possible. In most cases, of course, this will also create a great deal of value for the company itself, in the form of customer loyalty and additional patronage.

Trustable companies do the right thing. A trustworthy firm will do what it promises to do, but a *trustable* company, like a friend, will do what's best for a customer even if the customer isn't really paying attention or isn't as well informed or knowledgeable as the company is. Importantly, this means that a trustable company must find a business model that allows it to create shareholder value by acting in its customers' interests. It won't—and shouldn't—sell its products or services at a loss, but to be trustable it must be sensitive to the customer's point of view and try to deliver a fair deal. In the past, companies assumed a gap between what's good for customers and what's good for profits. The trustable company sees no such gap, but—starting from scratch if necessary—figures out how to use what works for customers as the basis for developing its business model and strategy.

> *A friend ordered a three-piece desk online. Two of the pieces were delivered without a hitch, but the third piece wasn't there a week later. Thomas called the company to ask about the missing piece, and discovered that the piece had been taken by the delivery company to the wrong delivery center and was in the wrong city. The online retailer's rep immediately solved the problem: "Sir, I am so sorry this happened. I'm going to sign you up for an even exchange, and send you the missing piece in overnight delivery so you will have it tomorrow."*

Our friend had been ready to express his annoyance but was disarmed by this completely fair treatment. When the rep said, "And we're going to credit your credit card an extra twenty-five dollars for the inconvenience," Thomas pointed out that it was not the retailer's error, but the transportation company's mistake. "Don't you worry about that," he was told. "We just want to make sure you are working at your new desk tomorrow." Is this good customer service? Good intentions? Competence? Who cares? This is a company you can count on, a company that is completely trustable.

[How Trustable Companies Use Customer Insight]

It's a reasonable bet that very few customers would *want* to pay $25 a month for a dial-up ISP subscription they don't need and never use, and don't really know they're paying for. And most likely no one would actually *want* to incur NSF (insufficient funds) charges by accident. There may be times a person would choose to incur such fees, and (who knows?) some people might simply choose to pay for AOL's dial-up service just so they can say they do, but on the whole, we don't think we're going too far out on a limb by saying neither Mr. Bank nor Mr. AOL is "doing the right thing."

Once we dispense with such obvious examples of untrustability, however, we will find that the task of acting in the interest of a customer is considerably more complex. Obviously, since I can't be any more certain of your motives and interests than you are of mine, it's possible my company might not respect your needs simply because I don't fully understand what your needs are. How can any company genuinely know what's in the best interest of a particular customer when customers clearly have different tastes and preferences?

Even though no company can ever be certain what's in any particular customer's mind, companies today do have much more capable technologies for analyzing their customers' needs and protecting their interests. Sometimes, all that's required is for a company to use its own processes to help a customer avoid a costly and preventable mistake.

Peapod, the online grocery service, for instance, has software that will check with you about a likely typo before you buy something highly unusual ("Do you really want to buy 120 lemons?").

And the best companies are also using their greatly improved IT capabilities to do a better job of remembering their customers' individual needs and preferences. A trustable company will remember what it learns about each customer, becoming smarter and more insightful over time, and then using this insight to create a better customer experience. Sometimes, all that's required is for a company to use its own database of past customer transactions for the customer's benefit. If you order a book from Amazon that you already bought from them, they will remind you before they process your order. Same with iTunes. These are examples of genuinely trustable behavior. In each case, the company's database gives it a memory that can sometimes be superior to the customer's memory. It would not be cheating for Amazon or iTunes simply to accept your money, thank you very much. God knows, Mr. AOL and Mr. Bank certainly would. Rather than using their superior, computer-powered memory to *take advantage* of the customer, however, Amazon and iTunes use it to *do the right thing*.

And note that "the right thing" to do, at least in this case, is mutually beneficial. Even as Amazon offers you the chance to opt out of a purchase you've already made, they also reduce the likelihood that you'll receive the book, realize you already have it, and return it. And when iTunes warns you you're about to duplicate a song you already own, they are making it less likely they'll have to execute a labor-intensive and costly refund process, or that you'll think badly of them aloud on Twitter. This is exactly how "reciprocity" is supposed to work—as a win-win.

Ironic—isn't it?—that some banks use their customer databases and analytics tools to craft highly sophisticated pictures of their customers' and prospects' value, profitability, and credit risk and then bombard them with two billion credit card solicitations every year. Why don't more of them do what Royal Bank of Canada has done? RBC uses its superior insight to extend automatic overdraft protection (with no fee!) to low-risk customers (that is, *most* customers). That way, the customer gets a break—and so does the bank; instead of having to pay a service rep to handle a call from a reliable customer who demands the fee be rescinded, the bank chooses instead to send a note explaining "this one's on us" and how to avoid this in the future, reducing their own costs in the process. Rather than incurring costs and resentment, and then netting no fee anyway, the bank saves the costs, builds goodwill, and *then* nets no fee. During the first ten years after instituting this approach, RBC increased per-customer profitability by 13 percent.

[Empathy, Self-Interest, and Economics]

One of the problems with the idea that trustability and selfishness don't mix, just in case you haven't already picked up on it, is that it calls into question the moral legitimacy of free-market economics itself, which is built on the principle that people acting in their own self-interest will, collectively, create a better standard of living for everybody. The "neoclassical" economic model assumes that people *always* act in their own self-interest, and that these independent, self-interested actions collectively create substantial economic value. As Adam Smith famously suggested in *The Wealth of Nations*, "It is not from the benevolence of the butcher, the brewer, or the baker that we expect our dinner, but from their regard to their own interest."

It turns out that neoclassical economics is flawed, however, in the way it defines human motives, because pure, absolute self-interest in any person is not the norm, but an aberration. Very few people are ever completely self-oriented, never doing anything that might undermine their own interest. People like this are called psychopaths, and what makes them aberrations is that they're completely immune to the feelings of others. The rest of us have empathy. Concern for others' feelings is hardwired in our brains. You don't have to "learn" empathy. Newborn babies, a few days old, will cry when they hear other newborns cry. Toddlers unable to speak will try to help adults in accomplishing tasks. So while Adam Smith's description of the baker's motive may be *generally* correct, if one of the baker's close friends was starving, or if the baker was contributing to a community dinner, or if he was particularly proud of one of his confectionary creations, then he would not be likely to look solely to his own financial interest in selling his goods.

Nearly all of us are born with such a strong sense of empathy, in fact, that we can barely tolerate the idea of killing or inflicting pain on others, even when dealing with outright enemies. During World War II, U.S. Army brigadier general S. L. A. Marshall surveyed several thousand U.S. troops immediately after they had been involved in combat. What he found was astounding: fewer than 20 percent of all American combat troops actually shot at the enemy, even when they were being attacked! In Marshall's words, "It is fear of killing, rather than fear of being killed, that is the most common cause of battle failure in the individual."

By the end of the twentieth century, social science had persuasively demonstrated that people have strong empathetic motives, and that these motives directly conflict with rational, economic self-interest. These findings are partly responsible for the rise of the entirely new discipline of behavioral economics, a field of study that combines psychological and emotional factors in human decision making, along with the rational calculations of self-interest posited by the neoclassical model. As one 2004 academic study summarized,

> *Over the past decade, research in experimental economics has emphatically falsified the textbook definition of* Homo economicus, *with hundreds of experiments that have suggested that people care not only about their own material payoffs, but also about such things as fairness, equity, and reciprocity.*

One of the most widely cited behavioral economics experiments demonstrating empathy is called the "dictator game." Designed to examine people's willingness to be generous with others—indeed, their *need* to be generous—it's not actually a game at all, in the strictest sense of the word. It doesn't involve any interaction between people, so there is no strategy to it, nor is there any decision making based on outsmarting or second-guessing some other player. Instead, in the dictator game two people are identified who don't know each other and are unlikely to have any future contact. The first is designated as the "dictator" and given a sum of money by the experimenters. The dictator then decides how much money, if any, he or she will give to the second person, and the experiment is concluded. The second person makes no decision at all, and the only role he or she plays is that of a passive recipient of the first person's largesse. The question being explored with this experiment, of course, is just how large a typical person's largesse is likely to be, under a variety of different circumstances. A purely self-interested, nonempathetic dictator would give nothing, keeping all the money himself. But repeated experiments under varying conditions show that a majority of people do not choose to keep all the money, but freely share some portion of it, averaging around 20 percent.

It's almost certainly an evolutionary advantage for our species that individual human beings have empathy, making it easier and more efficient for us to cooperate in finding food and preserving our joint lineage. Empathy plays a major role in the fact that we are social animals to begin with, and it is the fact that we are social that accounts, more than anything else (more, even, than our individual intelligence), for our civilization and technology.

In *How We Decide*, Jonah Lehrer reports on another dictator game experiment in which brain imaging was used:

> . . . *a few dozen people were each given $128 of real money and allowed to choose between keeping the money and donating it to charity. When they chose to give away the money, the reward centers of their brains became active and they experienced the delightful glow of unselfishness. In fact, several subjects showed more reward-related brain activity during acts of altruism than they did when they actually received cash rewards.*

Lehrer adds: "From the perspective of the brain, it literally was better to give than to receive."

So science has demonstrated fairly conclusively that empathy is a key motivation for human beings, having evolved in us for some reason almost certainly related to furthering our success as a social species. People have empathy not just because they expect to benefit themselves, per se, and not just because of some complex calculation or rational assessment of their own long-term self-interest, but also because empathy is a natural impulse. It is an *instinct*, hardwired into the human brain.

The same technology that is driving up our rate of interaction is almost certainly raising the general level of empathy we have for others as well. Concern for others increases as people become more interdependent and a society gets to be more advanced. In primitive societies, genuine empathy might be limited to blood relatives or maybe tribe members. With the Industrial Revolution and the invention of the modern nation-state, patriotism became a widely respected virtue, while tribalism was disdained as backward. And as we continue to become ever more electronically interconnected, with geographic boundaries declining in importance, we can already see that patriotism itself is losing some of its former luster. There can be little doubt about the direction of change. Some sociologists point out that modern advocates for animal rights are an example of empathy even being extended beyond our species.

Still, it will be a gradual and uneven process. Even today, tribalism weighs heavily in many African and Middle Eastern societies, while family ties remains the primary glue for many modern Asian business organizations—even giant ones. And we can't forget that for some reason about 1 percent to 2 percent of people get severely shortchanged in the empathy department. These are the people who are born with so little natural empathy as to be considered borderline personalities (that is, on the border between sane and psychopathic). It's interesting that when "normal" people encounter psychopaths and borderline personalities, they are usually astounded. They just cannot fathom how it could be possible for someone to show no feeling for the impact his or her actions have on others. They don't "get it," and so they don't believe it could be true. In *Evil Genes,* Barbara Oakley argues that "the worst of all human crimes—genocide—often occurs simply because people can't believe that heretofore noncriminal humans can perpetrate horrendous acts such as mass murder or gratuitous torture." Healthy, empathetic people fall into two classes, according to Oakley: those who have been personally victimized by a nonempathetic person, and those who have not. Only the victims, she says, truly grasp the ruthlessness and self-interested "evil" that a complete lack of empathy represents.

You don't have to be psychopathic to be a mobster, or a con man, or a drug trafficker. There are many gradations of empathy. Prior to the 2008 financial crisis there were some on Wall Street who cynically benefited from the financial bubble while fully expecting the party to end painfully for others, but this doesn't mean they were psychopathic, or even borderline. As an emotion, empathy is based on many nonrational inputs. Our empathy for someone else will depend partly on the closeness we feel to them and the type of action being considered. Taking home a big bonus for putting together a securitized bundle of subprime mortgages even though it's likely to go bad in the future is one thing, while raising your M-1 rifle, aiming at another human being's head, and pulling the trigger is another thing entirely.

The fact that empathy is a natural and increasingly important driver of human behavior overall doesn't change the fact that people are diverse, and some have less empathy than others. (We've been advocating customer differentiation for years. Perhaps now, instead of looking just at the ways customers are different in their values to the organization, and their needs from the organization, companies will eventually be looking for ways to predict which current and future customers have no conscience, in order to protect the organization's employees, other customers, and shareholders from these personalities!)

[The Social Role of Empathy and Trust]

Normal, empathetic people crave social connection and trust so much that they become upset, irritated, and sometimes outraged when confronted with what they perceive as lack of empathy in others, in the form of unfair or unjust actions. Most of us are not only willing to punish others who aren't trustable, but we take pleasure in it. Social, empathetic people derive a satisfaction from righting or avenging wrongs, and this human tendency contributes immensely to the success of our social structures. (We'll talk more about this later.) It's also one of the reasons trustability is going to emerge as the primary structural issue facing brands, marketing, and boardrooms.

As we'll see in chapter 4, the structure of a social network can be made more stable and trustable—and therefore more productive— when there is an appropriate mix of roles played by its participants, from producers of value or creators of content, to editors and curators, to punishers and enforcers. The right mix will ensure that cheaters and bad operators—the nontrustable few—never get too far before being restrained by the "system" or the network. In a stable social system, un-trustable participants aren't able to gain traction as fast as those who are trustable. Over time, as interaction continues to reinforce and feed on itself, empathy and trust will inevitably increase in value to everyone. The result is that the companies we buy from will be held to an ever higher standard, and this new standard will probably materialize much faster than most companies are prepared for today.

The world we live in and raise our children in just works better—for us, too—when we play fair in it. Here's how Martha explained it to her son when he asked how it could work at the newsstand where people paid $2 on the honor system and picked up a newspaper. She told him that if they just stole a paper this week, as they surely could, they'd get a free newspaper for a day or two. But in exchange for cheating the newsstand out of a few bucks, they'd pretty much guarantee that in the future, once they had to pay the $2 again, they'd have to stand in a long line to do it.

Although this book is about proactive trustability in business set-tings, we could have long discussions about the applicability to govern-ments, nonprofit organizations, schools and colleges, and other human institutions. Seattle often makes the list of top ten most livable cities in the United States, cited for having a high percentage of residents who recycle, volunteer, and learn CPR—all activities you engage in to make lives better for the collective, not just yourself. And Japan, one of the most socially cohesive of all national cultures, showed a remarkable spirit of community following the earthquake and tsunami in March 2011. Rather than the looting and the breakdown in civil order that often follows such a disaster, Japanese citizens actually returned wallets and safes that had washed up onshore, with the cash still in them! More than $48 million in wallet cash and $30 million locked inside some 5,700 safes were voluntarily returned by the finders to their rightful owners.

Our own well-being is wrapped up in the well-being of our society, and empathy for others is a social stimulant, a catalyst for collective welfare. As a result, the more technology facilitates the "social" aspect of our lives, the more selfless most of us will become. Being able to feel others' pain unconsciously is one of the most important building blocks of empathy, and for everyone but the psychopath it is a natural-born ability.

[Psychopathic Capitalism]

Human beings may seldom act out of purely "rational" self-interest, but what about companies? A corporation is legally chartered to create wealth for its owners, and failing to work on behalf of creating shareholder value would seem to be an abdication of management's fiduciary duties. However, in any modern economy a successful company is also a complex organization with multiple stakeholders, including not just shareholders but also employees, customers, and the communities in which it operates. From a practical standpoint, a company must be careful not to ignore the interests of its nonshareholder constituents precisely because doing so could threaten shareholder value. Abusing employees, the community, or the environment could easily lead to costly regulations or legal conflicts.

While there is no union movement or environmental group championing the rights of customers, the discipline of competition has always been considered a sufficient check. Fail to respect your customers' interests and you will be competed out of business, or so the argument goes. And for the most part it's proved correct. Case in point: AOL's steep decline, which as we've noted was almost certainly hastened by its aggressively self-interested dealings with customers. At the height of its fortunes several years ago, in an effort to overcome the looming technological obsolescence of dial-up connections, AOL tried to reinvent itself as an advertising-supported content company. Regardless of the technical merits of this effort, the initiative has not yet paid off very significantly, and the company certainly wasn't helped by the poor state of its customer relationships.

By contrast, consider how a trustable company might have fared, when faced with such an existential threat. Apple, for instance, has had no trouble at all moving its business into music retailing, interactivity, and even mobile phones. And Amazon's original bookselling business is now just a small part of an enterprise that includes all sorts of other retailing categories, as well as a considerable range of business services. It's doubtful that either of these companies could have made such transitions without having first earned the trust and support of their customers.

A trustable firm will find empathy returned by the customers themselves. You don't have to count your change when you're dealing with a real friend. When an untrustable company pursues immediate economic gain to the exclusion of all other considerations, however, we could make a direct analogy with the human psychopath, oblivious to how his actions affect the feelings of those around him. And while only a few of us may ever have been victimized by a psychopathic person, all of us interact regularly with at least a few "psychopathic" companies and brands. We have become so accustomed to nonempathetic customer "service," in fact, that we do not even consider it abnormal. But as standards improve, nonempathetic companies will become rare, then rarer, then endangered, and eventually extinct.

A trustable company with policies in place that demonstrate good intentions toward its customers is likely also to have those good intentions reflected in other domains as well—HR, investor relations, community participation, and so forth. The surest way to teach managers and employees to deal with customers the way they'd like to be dealt with themselves is to have them practice by treating each other in the same empathetic way.

Untrustable companies, on the other hand, see customers first and foremost as objects with pocketbooks, rather than as close business partners with individual needs. Customers are simply inanimate stepping-stones on the way to generating the immediate profits that feed the company's own interest. And in the psychopathology of an untrustable company, it's not too far a step from treating customers as objects to treating its employees or its communities the same way—or even, in extreme cases, the shareholders themselves.

Michael Schrage has recommended a litmus test for companies that are thinking about trustability. Are your best and most valuable customers dumb, uneducated, or not paying attention? (If the answer is "yes," then you should engage in a little self-analysis of your business model.) AOL may like 'em stupid, but no trustable company should.

Soon this kind of psychopathology on the part of businesses will just not be tolerated. Customers themselves will delight in exposing and punishing the unfair or nonempathetic actions of untrustable companies. According to one survey, more than 60 percent of those who read about a bad customer service experience online stop or avoid doing business with the company involved. Another survey showed that 79 percent of customers who had a negative customer experience told others about it, 85 percent said they wanted to warn others about their bad experiences, and 66 percent wanted to dissuade others from doing business with the offending brand. Some 76 percent indicated that word of mouth had influenced their purchasing decisions.

In the e-social world, companies will be expected to act toward their customers the way people act toward other people. With empathy. Violators will be prosecuted.

What do trustable companies look like?

- Jacquielawson.com, a clever e-cards site, invites you to sign up for automatic renewal with your credit card, but pings you before your credit card gets hit with the renewal: "Your membership of jacquielawson.com is due for renewal on 28 Jul 2011. When you last joined or renewed, you selected the option for automatic renewal, so unless you instruct us otherwise we will renew your membership using the same card details as before. The annual membership fee is $12 and this will be charged to your card on 28 Jul. For further assistance, including instructions on how to change the credit card details we hold for you, please go to http://www.jacquielawson.com/help_7.asp."

■ At Ally Bank (formerly GMAC Bank), customers are proactively reminded if they have funds in an account that could be earning higher interest, no depositor is ever charged for moving money from a savings account to a checking account in order to cover an overdraft, and the bank reimburses customers for ATM fees charged to them by other banks. According to Sanjay Gupta, chief marketing officer, Ally Bank's "three pillars" of customer service are to "do right, talk straight, and be obviously better," and it would hardly be possible to define a brand's positioning in a more trustable way. As a nationwide direct bank, without brick-and-mortar branches, Ally Bank doesn't take cash deposits, but provides postage-paid envelopes for mailing checks in for deposit, and it even allows customers to scan their checks and e-mail them to the bank for immediate deposit. Every page on Ally Bank's Web site has a toll-free 24/7 phone number clearly displayed, along with an estimate of "call wait time," and one of the very first options when calling in is to speak to a live person. In addition, Ally Bank has introduced customer reviews for all its various banking products and services. According to Gupta, the process had to be vetted in order to ensure that customer reviews were authentic, nonabusive, and so forth, but a "Customer Review" tab now shows on all product pages on the bank's Web site, and there are literally hundreds of reviews available. Asked how it was that Ally Bank seemed able to sustain its business following the implementation of new consumer-protection regulations without having to raise fees or introduce new ones, the way other banks had tried to do (including Bank of America's highly publicized $5 debit card fee, for instance, now withdrawn due to overwhelming consumer outrage), Gupta explained: "We just set out to build a business model that didn't depend on fees. We take deposits and we lend out money, and we make money on the spread. I guess you could say we have old school values but leverage today's technology."

■ A friend's daughter was moving a few blocks to a new apartment in Chicago. Her rental truck was due back to the garage at 5:00 P.M., but at 4:30 Amanda was caught in afternoon traffic, still needing to unload the last of her things and get the truck back to the rental company. Her cell phone rang. "How's it going?" asked the rental company. Amanda was dreading the need to pay another day's fee for being a few minutes late. "Don't worry," said the company rep. "Drive safely. Take your time. We'll be here till six and don't need the truck before then." Who does Amanda recommend to her friends who are moving?

■ At a speaking event we did in Mexico City, a teenager ran up to us and enthused, "I know what you're talking about! I got a text from my cell phone company that said my mom could save money if I were on a different plan since I send so many texts! Can you believe it? They helped us save money!" Telcel would have to really screw up to lose this customer, who tells everybody how fair they are and will be loyal to them for decades.

Customers who trust companies remain loyal to them. According to Forrester Research, the attribute that creates more customer loyalty than any other is: "the perception on the part of customers that the firm does what's best for them, not just for the firm's own bottom line."

[Putting on a Human Face]

And so we return to where we began this chapter: with the fact that trust is as trust does. Your ability to trust a company can only be inferred by observing its actions.

The argument we've been making about good intentions requires us to examine a company's actions as if the company were really a person, with a mind of its own, rather than just a legal entity. If a firm appears to demonstrate empathy for others, if it appears to consider their interests and not just its own, then people are more likely to conclude that the company is trustable. This means appearances do matter. No matter how good a company's *actual* intentions are, if no actions can be observed, there will be no basis on which customers can judge it to be trustable.

There is an important lesson here for companies trying to figure out how to appear to be more trustable to customers, so as to compete more successfully with other companies: In order to look trustable you must put on a human face. You have to behave in a way that demonstrates empathy, and this means your managers and employees have to behave this way. When thinking about customers, try thinking about them as your partners in a relationship that benefits both of you. When you make decisions for your company, you must ask yourself: What action would a friend take toward a friend in this situation, and is there any reason your company shouldn't proceed this way?

Rajendra S. Sisodia, David B. Wolfe, and Jagdish N. Sheth, authors of the book *Firms of Endearment,* suggest that one important aspect of demonstrating your firm's essential humanity is not to shy away from showing vulnerability when that's appropriate. We don't normally expect companies to talk frankly about their own problems, or to admit to their own vulnerabilities. Nor can we blame companies for being reluctant to do so, because exposing a weakness in the wrong context can sometimes lead directly to a lawsuit. But as direct interactions between companies and consumers increase in number, with blogs, Twitter, Facebook, YouTube, and other mechanisms, consumers have shown an increasing willingness to give the benefit of the doubt to those companies that do show a more "human" face to their customers.

Arguing that a willingness to admit error and take responsibility is absolutely essential to the idea of transparency, Sisodia, Wolfe, and Sheth admit that in most companies the legal department, and probably the PR folks, will be dead-set against it. Nevertheless, if you want others to participate in a genuine, empathetic dialogue—if you want to *demonstrate* your company's trustability—then it's essential to be vulnerable. Hiding your vulnerability reduces your stakeholders' willingness to show theirs, greatly diminishing the authenticity and value of any interaction or dialogue.

There's a bonus to putting on a human face. When you do, your employees will be proud to be part of your organization. Your employee turnover will go down, since your employees, for the most part, *prefer to do things in a trustable way*, and as you expect them to behave more trustably toward customers, your employees will trust your company more.

And finally, if you've kept up with the gist of our argument so far, you may be itching to object to the utter implausibility of it all, financially. Companies will never be able to afford to be *so* kind to customers, you might be thinking. No company can afford simply to give its products away at a loss, even though this might be the ultimate form of "trustability." So before going further we want to address these financial concerns directly. In our next chapter we will demonstrate that trustability is not only competitively necessary, but far more financially attractive than the current, psychopathically self-oriented service that many companies—even respected, successful companies—render.

TRUSTABILITY
TEST

Think about how you'd answer these questions based on how things work at your company, institution, or government agency. Talk about your answers with your colleagues. Visit www.trustability.com to see how other visitors' responses compare with your own for these and other questions.

▶ Would you say that your company's financial success is generally aligned with what's good for customers? Have you identified conflicts between how your firm succeeds financially, and how it does what's good for customers, individually?

▶ Overall, would your company make more money from an uninformed, unknowledgeable customer, or from a well-informed, knowledgeable one?

▶ If a customer is well informed, knowledgeable, and paying attention, would he choose to do business with your company or would he be more likely to choose a competitor?

▶ Does your company make more money when customers forget to claim what they're entitled to?

▶ Does your company make more money when a customer commits a minor error—an error that's easy for the customer to make and would be easy for your company to fix, such as an inadvertent push of a button on a cell phone?

▶ Do your employees proactively prompt customers to avoid errors or oversights? Whether your answer is yes or no:

    ▷ Is this part of their training?

    ▷ Is it part of your company's culture?

▶ Do your employees have the tools and information they need to prompt customers to avoid an error? (Can your employees see it coming? Do you have a customer data system that can reliably recall individual customer transactions and preferences, and make them available at all customer contact points?)

▶ If your business were a person, would your customers trust it to return a misplaced $5 bill?

▶ Relative to your immediate competitors, do you think customers find your company's trustability to be higher, about the same, or lower? Why?

▶ Is there anything about your relationship with a customer that would upset or displease a customer, if he knew it?

▶ Are there things about the way you charge for services or handle problems that you keep secret in order to avoid customer complaints?

▶ Do customers know what they actually pay your company for the services you render or the products you sell? (The question here is not whether you formally "disclose" this information, but whether customers actually *know*.)

▶ If one of your salespeople could make a sale by taking advantage of a customer's lack of knowledge, would he do so? For example, suppose an employee knows that a service contract or extended warranty agreement is not actually appropriate for a customer, but the employee still gets a commission for selling it. If you knew about this behavior on an employee's part, what would you do?

▶ Does your firm treat customers the way you insist that they treat you? When a customer makes a mistake in dealing with you—ordering the wrong item, for instance, and having to return it for a different one— you may ask the customer to pay a "restocking" fee, in addition to bearing the cost of the return. But if you were accidentally to ship a customer the wrong item, would you provide any kind of compensation to the customer, other than simply bearing the cost of the return?

▶ How do you define your company's "doing the right thing"? Is it more likely to mean:

> ▷ Doing what's best for the company's bottom line?

> ▷ Doing what's right for customers (and possibly the employees and the community)?

> ▷ Doing what's best for both?

▶ If "doing the right thing" for a customer meant incurring an expense, would your company still do it? For example, Amazon reminds you that you already have a book you're trying to order and saves you from paying them again for the same book. Who sets that policy and how is it evaluated?

▶ Do you use customer data and analytics to develop a sharper picture of what each customer needs from you, or are your analytics systems geared entirely toward assessing your customers' profitability, relative value, and likelihood of spending or not spending in the future? Stated another way, what examples can you name of how your customer analytics system has been used to improve the different customer experiences that your different customers have with your firm?

▶ Does your business have empathy for customers? How is this demonstrated? Would your customers agree? (Hint: If your customers don't seem to have empathy for your business, then most likely they don't feel empathy from you.)

▶ Do your employees trust one another and work well together? Does your company ever admit errors to customers, or confess any kind of vulnerability? If it does, how does it make up for the mistake with customers? And if you admit mistakes, how do customers react?

[3]

TRUSTABILITY: CAPITALIST TOOL

No one would remember the Good Samaritan if he'd only had good intentions. He had money, too.

MARGARET THATCHER

Okay, enough with the unicorns and fairy dust. The clash between trustability and a company's own short-term financial interest is real. It is a serious and continuing obstacle to be overcome, and we don't want to minimize it. Urging companies simply to "do the right thing" isn't likely to change how management sees the world. The profit motive does that. So in this chapter we're going to demonstrate why trustability is actually a tool for generating the kind of profits that ought to be beloved by any good capitalist.

[**Why Your CFO Will Learn to Love Trustability**]

We're lucky that trustability is a very big tool, because the profitability issue is a very big nut to crack. The U.S. retail banking industry generated some $32 billion in bank fees in 2006 alone, according to a GAO report, which means about half of all the industry's income comes from fees! And the FDIC says fee income at banks has soared 44 percent in the past ten years. Not all the fees that banks levy against customers are untrustable. But no one believes that customers have begun to violate good banking customer practices 44 percent more than they used to!

Banking may be an extreme case, but large and attractive profits can also be generated from unsuspecting or misinformed customers in the mobile phone industry, retailing, credit cards, and most other categories as well. Billions of dollars are at stake just in the "breakage" of prepaid and gift cards. Businesses have a lot of profits at risk when it comes to treating customers fairly. It shouldn't be a surprise to anyone that becoming a genuinely trustable enterprise may look to be a very costly undertaking for many businesses.

This doesn't mean they won't attempt it, however. *Regardless of the expense*, trustability will inevitably develop in commerce. Even if it were to cost billions of dollars in real money, trustability is still going to become a dominant characteristic of business competition, because the rise in expectations with respect to trust and trustworthiness is being fueled by the steady, irresistible drumbeat of technological progress. The world *will* become ever more interactive and transparent, and competitive pressure *will* compel companies to adjust their business models to be more trustable.

But when we examine it closely, trustability is in fact financially attractive for a business, even though in many situations it may cost money up front in the form of forgone profits or newly incurred expenses, as many business improvements do. When Amazon reminds you that you already bought the book you're about to order, the company is giving up an immediate profit—a profit you were more than willing to give the company, before you noticed you'd already bought that book before. If current-period earnings were the only criterion by which Amazon evaluated its financial performance, it would never do anything so "stupid" or "irrational" as refusing to make a profit from a willing (if forgetful) customer. But the fact is that what Amazon actually gains in this transaction is far more financially valuable to the firm, including your loyalty and continued patronage, and the increased likelihood that you'll recommend Amazon to friends and colleagues.

The clue to understanding why trustability can be financially attractive to a firm is recognizing that many of its economic benefits don't come immediately, but over time, as returning customers buy more and as a company's solid reputation continues to generate more new business.

Quantifying these benefits—including the value of increased customer loyalty, referrals, and additional sales—requires a robust customer analytics capability, as well as a financial perspective that fairly balances short-term and long-term results.

[Short-Termism: Don't Worry About the Long Term, IBGYBG]

Unfortunately, however, at the heart of most companies' untrustable behavior is a nearly manic obsession with short-term financial results and total disregard for longer-term financial implications. Short-termism generates many dysfunctional and even self-destructive business practices, as profit-oriented companies dismiss the long-term consequences of their actions in order to generate current-period profits—profits that feed the bonus pool, pump the stock price, and meet analysts' expectations. Short-termism stinks of unadulterated self-interest and directly conflicts with trustability, but it is still easily the most pervasive and destructive business problem on the planet today.

But don't take our word for it. Do your own survey. Ask any ten senior business executives at ten different companies if they think their business often makes mistakes because it focuses too narrowly on short-term financial results or costs. And don't be surprised if your survey returns a *unanimous* guilty verdict. As business people, we all know deep in our guts that we should do what's right for our company in the long term, but at most businesses the pressure to make the current numbers— to show concrete financial results, *right now*—is just too overwhelming. In one survey of 401 chief financial officers (CFOs) of large, publicly traded companies in the United States, for example, 78 percent of them confessed that they would be willing to give up actual "economic value" if it was necessary to hit the quarterly numbers.

Short-termism like this emphasizes the "selfish" aspect of free-market competition, without allowing room for the empathetic, nonselfish side of every person's nature. Elinor Ostrom, the first woman to win the Nobel Prize in Economics (2009), has suggested that "when we assume people are basically selfish, we design economic systems that reward selfish people. Obviously there's no longer any question that a free-market system is much more efficient and fair than any state-controlled system could ever be, but the "greed is good" philosophy that animates so many is testimony to the fact that it offers its biggest rewards to the most selfish people.

The truth is, however, that short-termism only reigns supreme at most businesses because *the financial metrics we apply to business are not economically true measures of success.* They never have been, and they haven't substantially changed since being introduced at the beginning of the Industrial Age. The way most businesses "do the numbers" to document their financial performance focuses entirely on the past—that is, on the most recent financial period. Most companies' financial reports to shareholders include absolutely no consideration of the way the most recent performance has either helped or harmed a firm's prospects for generating future profits, leaving this detail to the stock market analysts and others to figure out. Yes, a good business will track customer satisfaction or maybe NPS or customer lifetime values,* and as Orkun Oguz, Managing Director, North America, Peppers & Rogers Group, says, this allows the company to "gauge the impact of customer experience on business outcomes." Ultimately, though, these figures *should* have more effect on how earnings are calculated. Unfortunately, today earnings from the most recent financial period are the Supreme Performance Metric, the KPI† to beat all other KPIs.

Managers sometimes take comfort in the sophistication and precision of their short-term financial metrics, ignoring the long-term effects simply because they can't be as precisely defined. But this is like the classic joke about the man who lost his car keys late one night and is now look-

---

*Net Promoter Score® (NPS), developed by Satmetrix Systems, Inc., Bain & Co., and Fred Reichheld, is a popular measure of the difference between customer satisfaction and dissatisfaction based on a customer's willingness to recommend a product, company, or brand to others.
†KPI = Key Performance Indicator.

ing for them near a street corner, even though he lost them half a block away, closer to where his car was parked. When a police officer asked the obvious question—why?—the man glanced up at the street lamp illuminating the corner and said, "Because the light's better here."

The simple fact about business metrics: If you aren't measuring the right things to begin with, you're not going to get better results by measuring them more accurately.

> When your headlights aren't on, the best rearview mirror available isn't likely to improve your driving.

Nowhere was this no-headlights philosophy more in evidence than during the run-up to the 2008 Great Financial Crisis, a global disaster brought about by rampant, overconfident short-termism. Short-term metrics and incentives, when they are applied to businesses based on current-period financials, almost inevitably end up promoting the interests of commission seekers, bonus-earning senior managers, and short-term investors. Usually this is directly counter to the legitimate interests of a company's shareholders, not to mention its customers, employees, partners, and other stakeholders.

In his book *Saving Capitalism from Short-Termism,* Alfred Rappaport argues persuasively that the inordinate focus on short-term results by corporations is due to the fact that business managers, fund managers, and others have personal interests that are in direct conflict with the interests of the organizations they are paid to manage or represent. A professor at Northwestern's Kellogg Graduate School of Management, Rappaport calls this "agency capitalism," which he contrasts with "entrepreneurial capitalism," the kind of business structure that characterized most companies in the early twentieth century. It used to be that businesses were managed by their principal owners, rather than by professional managers paid to serve as agents for the shareholder-owners. As hired employees, a company's professional managers are paid salaries and incentives that rarely align well with the best interests of the shareholders or owners of a company. You can hardly blame a manager for trying to maximize his bonus, even though in doing so he might sometimes risk his shareholders' capital.

Moreover, the conflict between the interests of professional managers and shareholders is exacerbated by the fact that most shareholders themselves are now also represented by agents, in the form of fund managers. In just the twenty years from 1986 to 2006, for instance, the proportion of shares directly owned by individual investors, as opposed to institutions and managed funds, declined by more than half, from 56 percent to 27 percent. And, according to Rappaport, forty-one of the fifty largest financial funds are themselves owned and operated by even larger financial conglomerates. So not only have company managers become agents, but even the shareholders themselves are now agents.

In effect, the kind of agency capitalism that Rappaport says now characterizes the Western world's economy involves managers managing other people's companies, which are owned by other people's money being managed by others. In this environment, even though everyone is *supposed* to be acting in the interest of someone else (their principals), we shouldn't be too surprised that the actual result is an orgy of self-interested wealth transfer, as company managers and fund managers alike respond quite rationally to their own self-serving economic incentives.

No matter its origins, short-termism terribly distorts a company's view of the economic reality of its situation. "IBGYBG" is a text-messaging acronym, like LOL or OMG, frequently used during the run-up to the 2008 financial crisis, and it perfectly captures the rationale of "agency capitalism." Individual bankers earned irresistibly attractive bonus and commission checks for packaging mortgages that were less and less sound into securities to be sold to investors who were less and less discerning. If you aren't from the investment banking industry yourself, you may not be aware that a high proportion of the individual traders and bankers involved in this death spiral knew (or strongly suspected) that the increasingly hectic traffic in mortgage-backed securities was based on a precarious idea, and likely to implode sooner or later.

In addition, because the investment banks orchestrating these deals had largely transitioned themselves from private partnerships to public companies during the 1990s, the bankers now doing deals were gambling their shareholders' money, rather than their own capital. Even if shareholders lost in the long term, these bankers' bonus payments and commissions would not have to be returned.* One account of the run-up to the crisis tells the story of two private investors who each made a killing by betting *against* housing prices and mortgage bonds. They bet against the trend because they were highly skeptical about the deals being done, and in January 2007 their skepticism was confirmed at a convention of investment bankers in Las Vegas. At one point the investors approached a banker from Bear Stearns and asked him what was likely to happen to these securities in seven years or so. Weren't they almost inherently doomed, in the long term? The banker's answer: "Seven years? I don't care about seven years. I just need it to last for another two."

IBGYBG was shorthand for a phrase passed between individual bankers to allay pangs of conscience. When two bankers putting together a securities deal or a trade stopped to think more carefully about it, one might worry about the deal's long-term consequences, in which case the other might console him with the advice that you can't worry about the long term, because in the long term IBGYBG—"I'll be gone, you'll be gone."

Somebody else will have to pay the price. Later.

---

*In the business of financial trading, being trustworthy in the eyes of the other party clearly has some benefits, in terms of being able to act swiftly and efficiently. However, proactively acting in the interest of the other party is never likely to be the norm because the two parties to a trade have directly antithetical interests. Concealing information and trying to get an edge over the other party to a trade are integral to each participant's success, and this situation is unlikely ever to change, as long as there is a trading industry—in financial instruments, commodities, or anything else. It is highly unlikely, therefore, that genuine trustability—in the form of proactively protecting the interests of the other side of a trade—will ever become the norm. But proactively protecting the interests of your own investors or shareholders—the people whose money you are responsible for—is likely to be more and more expected.

[Taking the Long-Term View]

Today's most successful firms focus on the long-term value of their customers, and the importance of maintaining their trust and confidence, despite the fact that sometimes the actual economic value can be difficult to quantify. In his portrait of one such forward-thinking firm, *Googled: The End of the World as We Know It*, Ken Auletta tells the story of how its founders approached their IPO (initial public offering):

> *. . . Google's two 31-year-old founders were driving the company with a clarity of purpose that would be stunning if they were twice their age. Their core mantra, which was echoed again and again in their IPO letter, was that "we believe that our user focus is the foundation of our success to date. We also believe that this focus is critical for the creation of long-term value. We do not intend to compromise our user focus for short-term economic gain."*

And Google has shown again and again that it remains focused on earning the trust of its users by acting in their best interests, no matter what the short-term attractiveness might be for doing otherwise. The company never accepts money for a search result or a higher search ranking, for instance. And rather than trying to "capture" users and keep them on the Web site, Google's philosophy is driven by the goal of setting its users free as soon as possible, so they can quickly navigate to any of the search results shown. On search results pages the ads are ranked primarily in terms of the amount of clicks they generated from users. The more clicks, the more relevant or attractive an ad is to users, and so the more prominently it is displayed. No amount of money (short-term benefit) can generate a higher-than-justified prominence for an ad (long-term erosion of trust).

And in *The Facebook Effect: The Inside Story of the Company That Is Connecting the World*, author David Kirkpatrick repeatedly makes reference to the fact that the company's founder is not consumed with making money in the present, but with creating lasting value:

They all knew Zuckerberg only approved projects that fit into his long-range plan for Facebook. "Mark is very focused on the long run," says one participant in the meetings. "He doesn't want to waste resources on anything unless it contributes to the long run . . ." While Zuckerberg had been forced by circumstances to accept advertising, he did so only so he could pay the bills. Whenever anyone asked about his priorities, he was unequivocal—growth and continued improvement in the customer experience were more important than monetization.

To forward-thinking online companies like Google and Facebook (not to mention Amazon, Apple, Zappos, and other successes), it is the customer relationship that links long-term consequences with short-term actions. These companies are following a course of action that is intuitively obvious to them even if it might be difficult to quantify mathematically. Don't forget: Jeff Bezos was monomaniacally focused on Amazon.com's ultimate success even though the company lost money for twenty-eight consecutive quarters after it was formed.

We're not saying that Google and Facebook and Amazon are perfect. Like all innovative firms—even those with the best of intentions—they've made mistakes. But it's interesting that they are managed by *owners*, not just *agents*. That is, when we talk about the long-term vision of Sergey Brin, Larry Page, Jeff Bezos, the late Steve Jobs, or Mark Zuckerberg, we are discussing the visions of the company founders—people who maintained a very substantial personal ownership stake in their own companies. Many analysts think that online companies are better able to see the direct link between customer experience and shareholder value because they have a more direct connection with their customers, with less interference from channel partners and more efficient customer interactions. But while the nature of the online business model is undoubtedly an advantage, we can't overlook the fact that online companies are also more likely to be managed by their actual owners, simply because they are newer, and as a result they are less subject to the short-termism of agency capitalism. (One implication for this line of reasoning is that as technological change and innovation continue to accelerate, as we'll show in chapter 5, we may see more frequent examples of successful entrepreneurial capitalism, while companies under the direction of agent-managers fall victim to creative destruction even more rapidly.)

Regardless of how it happens, a trustable company has to be managed with the discipline and foresight to focus on creating long-term value by earning the trust and confidence of customers rather than going for the instant gratification of a temporary sales bump. Being able to delay gratification in order to achieve a more important objective is a key factor in anyone's emotional maturity. It's one of the key markers used to assess how "grown up" a child is. So in that sense, a trustable company could be thought of as more "emotionally mature" than a nontrustable company, which would be more "immature." Psychopaths operate at a very low level of emotional maturity.

[Customer Relationships: A Link to Long-Term Value]

When it comes to understanding how trustability creates financial value for a business, there are basically two approaches to the issue—a simple, philosophical approach, and a quantitative, analytical approach. The simple approach is to state your company's value proposition as a straightforward quid pro quo:

1. You want to create the most possible *value* from each customer.

2. On the whole, a customer is likely to create the most value *for* you at about the point he gets the most value *from* you.

3. The customer gets the most value from you when he can *trust* you to act in his own interest.

Therefore, to maximize the value your customers create for your business, you need to earn and keep their trust—that is, to act in their interest and to be seen doing so.

The quid pro quo model for justifying trustability is a commonsense approach that can be usefully employed by any business, not just high-end, billion-dollar online firms. Simply choose whatever action is most likely to generate a customer's trust.

A homebuilder we know has applied this model very profitably. When you build a home for sale to someone else, some states require you to guarantee the structure for some period of time (usually twelve months or more). During this warranty period the builder is required to fix all structural flaws or defects at its own expense. Now homebuilding is a business that has very few repeat customers, but this particular homebuilder generates about twice as many referrals of new customers as his competitors do simply by acting in his current customers' best interest. When a home warranty period has thirty days remaining until expiration, the builder contacts the homeowner and reminds him or her. Then he suggests that he can send a team over to examine the house for any defects, in order to ensure that they are repaired within the warranty period.

The reason a quid pro quo like this works is not that it generates current-period earnings, because it doesn't. In this case, it clearly costs the homebuilder something to fix defects that his customers might otherwise have forgotten to ask about until after the deadline, when they'd have to pay to make corrections on their own. But the quid pro quo generates immense long-term value. Customers have memories. Whether you remember them or not, *they* remember *you*. So when you treat a customer well today—say, by reminding him that his warranty is almost up or by preventing him from inadvertently paying too much—the customer will remember this in the future, and will likely change his future behavior as a result, perhaps buying more from you himself or referring friends and acquaintances to you.

It is your relationship with an individual customer, in other words, that provides the "missing link" between your company's short-term, current-period earnings and its long-term, ongoing value as a business enterprise. Apply this philosophy to enough customers and you'll be able to overcome the temptation of short-termism.

But how much can you really afford to spend *today* in order to create a good experience for the customer, based on her expected future change in behavior? This is a question we have to answer with numbers. If the first approach to the question of how trustability creates financial value is a philosophical approach, the second is a quantitative, analytical approach. Here's how to think about it:

Every business executive knows that customers are financial assets.

> Each customer is like a tiny bundle of future cash flow with a memory.

And, as is the case with any other financial asset, every customer has a certain value, based on the cash flow he can be expected to produce for the business over his lifetime.

The usual term for this customer asset value is *lifetime value* (LTV). And while no one can ever know with certainty how much cash flow any particular customer will generate in the future, increasingly sophisticated analytical tools do allow businesses today to model their current customers' likely future behaviors statistically, based on what previous customers have done—that is, similar customers in similar situations. It will never be completely accurate, of course, because no matter how good the analysis is, predicting the future is impossible. But as data become richer and analytical tools become more capable, this kind of modeling has become more and more practical for a variety of businesses.

The inputs for calculating any customer's LTV include, among other things, her loyalty to the brand (or her probable longevity as a customer), her willingness to buy additional products or services from the company, the positive or negative recommendations she makes to her friends, and the cost of serving her. And even though the results of statistical modeling are imprecise, they are still useful enough that you would be hard-pressed today to find any senior business executive anywhere who hasn't at least thought about these facts:

- All customers have lifetime values;

- Customer lifetime values are different, meaning that some customers are more valuable than others; and

- Customers not only spend money today (current earnings for the company), but their experience today will likely increase or decrease their lifetime values (future earnings).

It is the third point that we should pause to reflect on for a minute. When a customer changes her future behavior based on the good or bad experience she has with you today, or based on her good or bad feelings about your business today, her lifetime value will go up or down. This increase or decrease in LTV represents economic value that is being created or destroyed by the customer's experience, *today*. So every day, with every customer experience your company delivers, customers are creating and destroying both current value (costs and profits) and long-term value (changes in their lifetime values).

Suppose you have a very valuable customer, for instance, who calls you to complain about something, and for some reason you don't handle her complaint very well, with the result that at the end of the call she hangs the phone up in disgust. She no longer trusts you. There can be little doubt that her LTV declined as a result of the call. The amount of this LTV decline can be thought of as the shareholder value destroyed by this unsuccessfully handled complaint. You won't realize the actual cash effect of this event until sometime in the future, when the customer doesn't return to buy more things, and maybe some of her friends do a little less business as well. But the value destruction occurred today, with the phone call. The question to ask is whether the cost saved by not handling the customer's complaint better was more or less than the decline in her lifetime value. And while the statistical modeling can be complex, in the end this is a straightforward calculation.

If you could add up all the lifetime values of all your customers, including those you have now and all the customers you will ever have in the future, the result would be something we call "customer equity," and it represents the real economic value of your business as a going concern. So for the manager of a company, this means there are two different ways to create genuine economic value for shareholders:

1. You can generate current-period earnings (short-term value), and

2. You can add to your customer equity (long-term value).

Every dollar added to customer equity by a good customer experience is a dollar added to a firm's shareholder value. Economically, after we apply a discount rate to account for the time value of money, this dollar is equivalent to a dollar of current earnings—it is a dollar of value generated now, although the cash effect won't be felt until some later point. And the link between today's customer experience and tomorrow's cash effect is the *individual customer relationship*.*

Ideally, you would want to take actions today that feed *both* current earnings *and* customer equity, as when you sell something to a customer and the sales process itself inspires more confidence or trust in the customer's mind, increasing the likelihood that the customer will come back to buy again. In their study published in *MIT Sloan Management Review,* V. Kumar and Denish Shah's research concluded that "certain marketing techniques can influence a company's stock market valuation—if the techniques increase customer lifetime value." However, even when you forgo some current earnings it may be the case that customer equity is increased by an amount that will more than offset this loss, and using

---

*Serious readers are encouraged to turn to *Return on Customer: Creating Maximum Value from Your Scarcest Resource* (Currency/Doubleday, 2005), by Don Peppers and Martha Rogers, Ph.D., for a comprehensive discussion of the statistical, mathematical, and practical issues involving calculation of up-or-down changes in individual customer lifetime values. As an operating business creating value for shareholders, customer equity is virtually the same as a company's economic value, because the economic value of any business is the discounted net present value of all future cash flow yet to be generated by the business.

today's metrics and methodologies, this increase in customer equity is documentable. Sometimes it's even acknowledged by stock market analysts. In 2006, for instance, an analyst for American Technology Research, Shaw Wu, said of Apple's first-quarter slump, "We are not too bothered" by the dip, because, "from our checks, Apple's sales representatives have been instructed to not push PowerPC Macs on customers who want to wait for Intel versions. In this day and age where making numbers is important, *we believe Apple is in a rare group of companies willing to sacrifice its near-term revenue opportunity for greater long-term success by developing customer trust.*" (Italics ours.)

Earning the trust of customers often does require an upfront investment like this—forgoing the profit on a customer mistake, for instance, or reminding a customer that the warranty is almost up and almost certainly incurring some immediate costs in the process. But these kinds of "investments," done prudently and carefully, can almost always return many times their cost in terms of increased customer equity. The increase in your company's customer equity is the financial benefit you will get from earning and keeping the trust of your customers.

In a nutshell, two different kinds of current-period business success are on every company's menu, and it's critical to know the recipe for both:

- Good current profitability, while generating more customer trust and customer equity (have your cake and eat it too); or

- Good current profitability, while eroding customer trust and customer equity (use your cake up so there's nothing left).*

---

*Look at it this way: If your stockbroker came to you at the end of the year and summarized your dividends and interest payments for the year, but refused to tell you whether the underlying value of your stocks had gone up or down, you'd fire that stockbroker because it would be impossible to make investment decisions based only on knowledge of current cash flow. And yet, companies that operate only on current-quarter earnings reports without *also demanding to know whether underlying customer equity is going up or down* are basically making the same mistake. See our discussion of these issues in Don Peppers and Martha Rogers, Ph.D., *Rules to Break and Laws to Follow* (John Wiley & Sons, 2008), pp. 80–84.

Who will *your* customers flock to when their choices include companies that embrace trustability in their charter and do not include an obsession with short-term numbers? And how will your short-term success compare with the long-term value created by companies capable of balancing the short term with the long term?

John Stumpf, the CEO of Wells Fargo & Company, describes the period when he entered banking thirty-five years ago as being like the classic Frank Capra movie *It's a Wonderful Life*. Since then, Stumpf notes, trust has declined sharply as many institutions have become "practically anti-customer" and institutions are focused on how to rebuild customer intimacy and trust. For B2B and B2C, he says, trust is the basic element of any healthy relationship. He notes that Wells Fargo is a huge organization; it does business with one in three Americans. A customer with Wells Fargo now averages six products and contacts the bank eighty times a month, including ATM, mobile, and online touches. Stumpf says,

> *We owe our team members a full customer view so they help each client get the most from their relationship with us. Our hardest work should be behind the scenes; we should become intuitive about how to help each client. We have to balance our long- and short-term goals; for example, we had to spend a lot on our operating system but that allows us to see each client completely and individually. It's not a customer's job to become profitable to us; it's our job to get the roadblocks to customer profitability out of the way. For a customer to trust us, we have to take the customer's perspective and also get the details right. Even if we do it right 99.9 percent of the time, if we're down for that one customer, then for that customer, we're down 100 percent of the time.*

And something more to consider: The competition for customer goodwill is already heating up. In the past, your for-profit company has been competing against a bunch of other companies hell-bent (like you) on making their own short-term numbers. But in the future, more and more productive activity is going to take place based on social goals in addition to economic ones. Cooperatives and nonprofits have always existed, of course, but two trends are driving more and more economic activity in this direction. First, as the cost of interaction plummets, volunteer and not-for-profit activity gets easier and easier to organize, and second, people in developed countries simply *want* to give back, to contribute to others, and to make a difference. Whether it's consumers texting on their mobile phones to contribute $3 at a time to aid a disaster recovery effort, or software engineers volunteering some of their spare time to write code, your next "competitor" might just be an organization more interested in the welfare of your customers than you are. Ask Microsoft what it's like to compete with Linux, the free computer operating software created and updated entirely by volunteers, for instance. In our next chapter we'll consider both the threat and the opportunity represented by "social production" like this.

[Trusters and Distrusters]

We can already hear the whining. Is it really financially smart to treat each customer the way the customer wants to be treated? What if the customer just wants the product for free? What if the customer doesn't want to pay anything at all, or wants to try everything out without charge, or wants to be able to return every item even if it's been damaged? Surely there must be some *limit* to a firm's willingness to proactively protect the interest of its customers. There is, and being profitable by being trustable doesn't require that we behave as though every customer is "good" every time.

Protecting the interest of a customer should not mean you have to give up your own economic interest or subject your employees to needless abuse. Some people just don't deserve to be trusted—customers as well as companies. And even though psychopaths and borderline personalities are rare, they do exist.

Research will demonstrate that earning the trust of customers almost always has substantial financial benefits. One way to snap a picture of this process is to focus on the different behaviors and attitudes of customers who say they trust a firm and customers who say they don't, and to identify those actions of a company most likely to enhance or diminish a customer's perception of trustability. In 2011 our company, Peppers & Rogers Group, fielded a research survey to develop some top-line insights with respect to how customer trust affects the mobile phone category. The study involved more than 2,400 respondents, each of whom was a U.S. resident and a customer at one of the five major U.S. mobile operators: AT&T, Sprint, T-Mobile, U.S. Cellular, or Verizon. We began by asking each respondent how much they thought their mobile services provider could be trusted. Some rated their carriers fairly high on trust, others fairly low, and others in between, and we divided our respondents into three groups of roughly equal size: the trusters, the distrusters, and the neutrals. (The distrusters were actually the largest group, but not by much.)

What we found were very significant differences on a variety of issues that add up to a great deal of money for a business. Trusters were much more likely than distrusters to say that they would buy more things from their carriers without hesitation, including new data services, additional lines, and upgraded phones. Trusters also said they would be more likely to remain as customers for a longer period, citing a strong sense of emotional loyalty to their mobile carriers. In addition, far more trusters than distrusters said they felt no need to search for alternatives because of a delightful customer experience, and would recommend their carrier to others and defend it from criticism.

This research effort was spearheaded by Marc Ruggiano, partner, and by Tom Lacki, Ph.D., research director, both at Peppers & Rogers Group, who pointed out a few additional findings from the research. First, the single most important statement distinguishing trusters from distrusters was "My mobile services provider focuses on doing the right thing for its customers." Even though competence matters, in other words, the primary determinant of customer trust, at least in this study, was the customer's interpretation of the vendor's intent. Second, several of the attributes that consumers associate with being trustworthy are actually "free" to the mobile carrier. Being "warmly greeted" by a call center representative, for instance, would require virtually no investment to implement. And third, participants said they would be willing to pay about $11 more per month, on average, for a mobile carrier consistently demonstrating a higher level of trustability.

And finally, the study points out, the research demonstrates that with the right analytics it may actually be possible to know which of a firm's customers trust it and which do not. In other words, a company should be able to identify individual trusters, distrusters, and neutrals, giving it the ability to treat different customers differently, and greatly improving the efficiency with which a company can implement policies designed to promote trust.

The overall conclusion of our research is that although the financial benefits of earning the trust of customers may or may not show up in current-period results, there can be little doubt that trustworthiness and its higher standard, trustability, have the potential to return significant benefits over the long term. More research will follow, and you can check updates and studies in additional industries at www.trustability.com. (The health care industry will be examined next.)

[There's No Such Thing as One-Way Reciprocity]

Good intentions are based on the principle of reciprocity, and there's no such thing as one-way reciprocity. I treat you the way I think you'd want to be treated, assuming that you're treating me in basically the same way. If I conclude that you're abusing my own good intentions, then I have every right to watch out more carefully for myself. If I'm a business manager, I have a duty to my other customers, my employees, and my shareholders to do so.

Customers are all different. Most customers (like most people) are good, but some are bad, and some will change their spots on a moment's notice. Fortunately for businesses, computer technology has made it possible to analyze and track customer differences in some detail, and as the world becomes ever more transparent it's likely we'll learn more and more about how to identify and deal with untrustable customers. Trustability, in fact, may soon become a routine measure of customer value, just as credit risk, transactional performance, and social influence are today.

In ordinary life, empathy is almost always returned in kind, and every business would be wise to keep this principle in mind. Most customers will feel good toward vendors who seem to feel good toward them. Numerous studies have shown, for instance, that the single biggest predictor of medical malpractice complaints is not the technical quality of a doctor's care but the doctor's bedside manner. Caring, empathetic doctors don't get sued so often, because patients simply won't sue medical professionals they consider to be friends, regardless of the merits of the case. But whenever doctors (or companies) fail to connect with people, or when they fail to inspire empathy, or to relate to others with a human face, then lawsuits result more frequently.

Reciprocity and empathy have a great deal to do with customer loyalty. When managers consider the issue of customer loyalty, they usually focus on its financial benefits. But there are two ways we can talk about loyalty: *behavioral loyalty* is demonstrated by a customer's repeat buying, and *attitudinal loyalty* occurs when a customer has a liking for a brand or company. Obviously, attitudinal loyalty usually leads to behavioral loyalty, but not all behavioral loyalty results from a loyal attitude. For instance, if you're a frequent flyer living in a major city you will almost certainly be "loyal" to whatever airline uses that city as its primary hub, even though you may not have a favorable feeling toward it. Or you might be loyal to your retail bank because you think it would just be too much trouble to switch, or because you think all banks are going to be equally disappointing anyway.

Attitudinal loyalty, on the other hand, is usually driven by a customer's emotions, and emotions can be extremely powerful motivators. An emotionally loyal customer may go out of her way to deal with a particular brand, based on a generally favorable feeling about the brand that might be hard even for her to put into words.

Ken Tuchman is founder and CEO of TeleTech, one of the largest global providers of transformational customer experience strategy, and technology and business process outsourcing solutions, based in Englewood, Colorado, serving large business clients. One thing Tuchman knows a great deal about is the nature of customer loyalty, because customer loyalty has been the primary metric of his company's success since its founding in 1982. In Tuchman's view,

> *There is absolutely no question that emotional loyalty is different from pure behavioral loyalty. And while behavioral loyalty obviously pays the bills, the right way for any company to get there is to create a desire in the mind of a customer to do business with it. Companies like Apple, USAA, and Costco—these are companies that "get it" in their bones. These are the kinds of companies that customers trust to do the right thing.*

Companies that reach out empathetically to their customers (or to other stakeholders) will usually see the same kinds of empathetic behaviors coming back to them. This will often be reflected in less fraud, fewer service problems, more customer loyalty, and better word-of-mouth recommendations. But sometimes it can be even more dramatic, because reciprocity is a very powerful concept.

Remember our story about USAA, the banking and direct-writing insurance firm whose customers returned their refund checks? USAA built its reputation for trustability over several decades, based largely on a call-center model of direct interaction with customers. (Importantly, the firm also placed a strong emphasis on improving the efficiency and accuracy of its services, focusing not just on "good intentions" but on "competence" as well.) USAA is a company we've cited many times as an example of trustability. The company's mantra is to "treat the customer the way you'd want to be treated," and Forrester has ranked USAA higher than any other financial services firm in North America when it comes to "customer advocacy," or "the perception by customers that a firm does what's best for them, not just what's best for its own bottom line." Forrester calls it "customer advocacy," but this is just another way to say "reciprocity."

As technology continues to improve our ability to interact with others, it is likely to promote wider and deeper empathy among businesses, customers, and employees, with more and more companies choosing to imitate USAA.

For instance, while most companies forbid customers to post reviews and comments directly on their Web sites, Amazon trusts its customers enough to allow them to post uncensored customer reviews of any merchandise they sell. Building enough financial success through mutual trust, they were able to make an otherwise nonsensical offering—unlimited two-day shipping for a yearly flat fee. Is this working? In 1996, executives from Barnes & Noble offered Jeff Bezos a chance to sell Amazon to B&N before B&N started selling books online and creamed him with their better-known brand. As we know, Bezos declined, and in retrospect it appears to have been a good decision on his part. By October 2011, B&N's market cap had dropped to $750 million, while Amazon's market cap was more than a hundred times greater, at $105 billion.

Or consider Zappos, the online shoe merchant. Realizing its customers would have to trust their company to order shoes without trying them on first, Zappos trusted its customers first by offering free shipping both ways and no-questions-asked returns. Zappos sold its first pair of shoes in 1999 and sold to Amazon for $1.2 billion in 2009.

Reciprocity in Action: The world's largest credit union with $44 billion in assets and 3.6 million members, Navy Federal Credit Union in Vienna, Virginia, announced in April 2011 a contingency plan for supporting its members in the case of a possible government shutdown. Their major initiatives included covering the April 15 payroll for active military members who have direct deposit of their pay at Navy Federal, expedited approvals for lines of credit, and 0 percent fee balance transfer for credit cards. Members who were concerned about loan payments were invited to call or visit a branch. Navy Federal president and CEO Cutler Dawson said, "For over seventy-five years, Navy Federal has been there to serve its members' financial needs. If a government shutdown does occur, we want [our members] to know that their credit union has programs in place to help them in this time of uncertainty."

Will their members—or their children—ever bank anywhere else?

Recent advertising from Nationwide Insurance makes the point that they are owned by their members, "not by Wall Street," and therefore they can do what's best for members. The short term is certainly seductive, but reciprocity generates truly immense long-term benefits. So the right question to ask now is:

How will you compete against companies that balance making a profit with building long-term business value?

[Trustability and Self-Interest: A Paradox]

The fact that earning your customers' trust has economic benefits for your business sets up an interesting philosophical conundrum: if you "do the right thing" for customers because it benefits your business economically, aren't you really just being *self*-oriented? Let's put it this way: If trustability requires that your "intent" is to act in another's interest, but your real purpose is to further your own economic interest, then doesn't that set up a conflict of interest?

An inquisitive sixth grader might ask it this way of her Sunday school teacher: If you get to Heaven by being good, then aren't you just being good so you can get to Heaven? In Sunday school this dilemma is easily resolved, because God can see into everyone's heart. But here on Earth none of us can actually know what's going through any other person's mind. We can only judge others' intent by observing their actions.

On the other hand, we all know there's a difference between being genuinely concerned with the interests of customers and merely appearing to be. Some companies want to be *seen* as trustworthy even though their deepest motives are entirely selfish and usually have to do with making the short-term numbers. They may look good at first, but before long the cracks begin to reveal that they are willing to bend their stated values to achieve their own economic goals, even at the customer's expense. (Theoretically, if the behavior of a company portrayed constant reciprocity even though the secret wishes of its top decision makers were entirely selfish, we suppose the company could, technically, still be considered "trustable," but we don't think most business managers are good enough actors to pull it off.)

Which brings us right back to our argument about the nature of "good intentions." Trust is as trust does. It doesn't matter at all to a customer whether his interests are being proactively looked after on account of the benevolence of a company's management or on account of their desire to benefit their own shareholders. Either way the customer gets better served. It is the firm's actions the customer can see, not what's in the company's heart.

However, motive *does* make a difference *within the firm*. That is, in order to have a company that seriously tries to earn its customers' trust, there must be some unifying message or sense of mission that drives employee behavior at all levels to do this, in the thousand decisions they make every day. This is a tall order, because no business rule or line of software code will ever be sufficient to ensure that employees treat customers right. Your employees have to *want* to do that. To have this kind of an organization you have to focus carefully on the corporate culture, and on the "unwritten rules" that govern how your employees approach their jobs.

In reality, the issues of intent and action are probably destined to become just as entangled and inseparable for a business as they are for a person. From the standpoint of human psychology, research shows that behavior often leads intent. One surefire way to cheer yourself up, for instance, is simply to force yourself to smile. Physically. *Make* your face form into a smile, *keep* it there for a while, and soon you'll actually feel your mood lifting. It's just a part of human nature: not only does intention lead to action, but action leads to intention.

And it's highly likely that something analogous would happen in a company as well. If the financially directed mandate is to treat the customer the way you'd like to be treated if you were that customer, simply because this policy best promotes the financial interest of the company, then pretty soon these self-oriented mercenary intentions will likely be supplanted by genuinely good intentions. The mission of the firm will become: Earn the trust of customers. That's what would be in the firm's "heart," if it had one. Or maybe we'll come to a point where we are innovative enough, competitive enough, and smart enough to figure out how our interests and our customers' interests are aligned. We'll succeed when our customer succeeds, and our customer will succeed when we do.

But there's more to it than this. If we're right, and if good intentions really can be grafted into an organization simply by pursuing the self-interested goal of creating shareholder value, then even "psychopathic" companies may yet find salvation. So as a citizen, consumer, employee, and voter, you should sleep a lot better knowing that companies won't choose to be trustable just because it's the right thing to do, but because they won't last long in a competitive marketplace if they don't.

Which would put a new light on the adage that "greed is good." As long as it's an educated greed that's aligned with the best interests of our customers, it really is.

TRUSTABILITY
TEST

Think about how you'd answer these questions based on how things work at your company, institution, or government agency. Talk about your answers with your colleagues. Visit www.trustability.com to see how other visitors' responses compare with your own for these and other questions.

▶ How important is it for your business to make each quarter's sales and earnings numbers?

    ▷ Probably more important than almost any other legal outcome

    ▷ Very important, but not more important than anything

▷ Important, but we balance customer satisfaction or other metrics as well

▷ Equally important to long-term value building and growth in customer equity

▶ Assuming your company can track your customers' actual behavioral loyalty, can you also estimate the degree to which different customers are attitudinally loyal?

▶ Which of the following topics are relevant to *most* internal business discussions about "customer loyalty" within your firm (choose all that apply)?

▷ Your points or frequency marketing program

▷ Repeat purchases from a customer

▷ Avoiding churn, or winning back customers who have left

▷ Gaining a greater and greater share of a customer's business over time

▷ Keeping a customer even if there's a problem

▷ Getting a customer to say good things about your brand or business, and/or recommend it to friends

▷ Higher customer satisfaction

▷ Less customer dissatisfaction

▷ "Customer-centricity"

▷ "Retention"

▶ What portion of your company's customers are "captive," in the sense of remaining loyal because of convenience, or geography, or a contract or "plan" agreement, but not on account of their positive attitude or preference?

▶ Do any customer engagement metrics (such as customer satisfaction or Net Promoter Score) figure into business unit planning, employee rewards, or business unit performance?

▶ Does your company's analytics system quantify the financial benefits of customer retention? Of Net Promoter Score or lifetime value metrics or other customer-satisfaction measures? Do you track customer referrals and calculate their financial benefits?

▶ Does your company model customer lifetime values, or have some other analytically capable means of evaluating the financial asset values of customers? Can your analytics systems measure customer profitability on an individual or segment basis?

> ▷ Does your firm have the analytical capability to predict *changes* in individual customer lifetime values based on current interactions and events?

> ▷ Do any customer-asset metrics (such as actual and potential value, changes in lifetime value, or Return on Customer) figure into business unit planning, employee rewards, or business unit performance?

▶ Do salespeople, executives, or others in your firm receive incentives for short-term performance that might prompt them to ignore or minimize long-term issues?

▶ If your stock is publicly traded, does your company make earnings forecasts to analysts? If so, do you think this has ever affected your willingness to "do the right thing"?

▶ Would your customer analytics system be able to track the financial effect of:

> ▷ Higher or lower average customer satisfaction scores within a group or segment of current customers?

▷ Different customer acquisition offers, in terms not just of acquisition rates, but of retention, cross-sell, and service costs of newly acquired customers?

▷ A poorly handled (or well-handled) complaint from a particular customer?

▷ A salesperson at your firm who alerted a particular customer about a refund the customer didn't know about?

▷ Revenue generated by a particular customer referred to you by another customer?

▶ Have you calculated your firm's approximate customer equity (see page 72)? Would it be possible to do so with your current analytics capabilities? Have you ever had a serious discussion about trying to do so? Would it be possible for you to update such a calculation regularly, or in real time?

[4]

SHARING: NOT JUST FOR
SUNDAY SCHOOL

Have you ever used Wikipedia? Firefox? Skype? These are just a few of the thousands of examples of "social production," in which products and services become available through the voluntarily shared efforts of unpaid, individual contributors, working collaboratively with little or no top-down direction.

- Millions of individuals now generate their own content and upload it to the network for others to read or view on a wide array of hosting Web sites, from Yahoo! and YouTube to Flickr and Facebook. (London's Science Museum surveyed three thousand people to ask what they could not live without. Facebook came in ahead of flushing toilets and fresh vegetables.) Peer-to-peer networks such as Skype and BitTorrent eliminate the need for hosting servers altogether. And nearly a million new blog posts are uploaded daily to the more than 130 million blogs around the world tracked by Technorati.

- Wikipedia, a poster-child example of social production, offers more than nine million articles in 250 languages and is today one of the world's most used references. It was created and is maintained entirely by unpaid contributors—nearly 300,000 of them altogether.

■ The Mozilla family of Web applications, including the Firefox browser, is "open source" software, free for anyone to use, and maintained by a small army of volunteers who continually update and improve it. Apache software, another open-source application, is used by about 70 percent of corporate Web servers, including those for many high-traffic commercial sites. And large companies like Google, CNN, and Amazon power their Web sites with the GNU/Linux operating system, which is also open-source and free.

■ "Crowd service" is augmenting traditional self-service for many firms, especially when they sell more complex products or services. Go to the customer service section of Verizon's Web site and ask a question about installing a home network or programming a high-definition television, for example, and the answer may come from some other customer—a completely unpaid volunteer. Other companies, including Best Buy, Linksys, Cisco, HP, Nintendo, AT&T, and iRobot (makers of the Roomba robotic vacuum cleaner) also facilitate crowd service on their own customer service Web sites, and for some a majority of service inquiries are answered by other customers, rather than by company employees.

■ The fastest, most powerful supercomputer in the world is Folding@home, a network of hundreds of thousands of volunteered PC processors and PlayStation 3 game consoles working together to help scientists do the high-intensity calculations necessary to analyze protein folding and complex molecular dynamics. Other examples of volunteered computer power include SETI@home (the "Search for Extraterrestrial Intelligence"), Einstein@Home (to detect gravitational waves), the Malaria Control Project (Malariacontrol.net), and Climateprediction.net.

[Value Creation: Invented by Somebody,
Owned by Nobody, Valuable to Everybody]

"Social production" like this is an entirely new way to create economic value that has only become practical on such a large scale with the advent of cost-efficient interactive technologies. The fuel for commercial production is money, but the fuel for social production is trust. People volunteer, they collaborate, and they *share* their own time and energy with others, not in return for some market payment, but for the personal satisfaction of creating and sharing, or enjoying the goodwill of others, or simply feeling more connected.

During the political debate between left and right that dominated economic discussion throughout the twentieth century—with the right advocating more free-market solutions and the left advocating more government regulation—social production was never considered. The very idea of it would have seemed preposterous, like proposing to boost GDP with a series of barn raisings. But now that the technology is available, unpaid volunteers are in fact creating billions of dollars' worth of time savings, entertainment, instruction, new information, and knowledge, through a wider and wider variety of social production enterprises.

This is what your customers do in their spare time.

And social production can often prove far superior to commercial production. Presumably, billion-dollar firms like Google and Amazon don't power their Web servers with open-source software because it's free, but because it's good. According to SourceForge.net, a kind of registration site for open-source software projects, there are now more than 260,000 such projects involving more than two million registered users, all of whom, more or less, are volunteer software coders.

Clay Shirky suggests that one of the main reasons for the dramatic upswing in social production is that new technologies enable us (that is, the human race) to pool our collective free time and creative energies (what he calls our "cognitive surplus"). Shirky estimates that, globally, our collective free time amounts to about a trillion hours each year, so even a minuscule portion of it, if properly organized, could generate immense productivity and actual value. He estimates that Wikipedia's creation to date, for example, may have consumed around 100 million hours of collective effort from the 300,000 volunteer contributors who have been involved in it—or roughly 0.01 percent of our annual collective free time. And there are literally thousands of other examples of online social production that are creating great value today, accomplishing tasks that range from proofreading digitized books or compiling a database of recipes to mapping the surface of Mars or maintaining a comprehensive directory of Web sites. In June 2011, for instance, it took online readers just hours to annotate an unsigned album of World War II snapshots, including identification of the photographer.

There are many reasons why people spend time documenting their opinions for others they have no connection with, or improving software they have no commercial interest in. Empathy is a good catchall category for giving vent to your urge to help others. But there are additional motivations at work, too, many of them more akin to pure self-interest. It takes time and effort to share an opinion, so why do it at all? Because we *enjoy* sharing our perspectives or ideas, that's why. Some of us feel fulfilled by offering helpful advice, and some of us get a thrill from influencing others' opinions. If you're a revolutionary protester in the Middle East, China, or Myanmar, you want the world to know what you're going through.

In addition to a satisfying sense of accomplishment, you can earn the respect of others, you can validate your own importance and significance, and you can improve your personal status. One reason often given by computer programmers for volunteering their efforts to an open-source project, for instance, is simply "control over my own work"—something more difficult to obtain from working at the direction of an employer. The choice between plodding along with the status quo or feeling good helping others and making things happen is a no-brainer.

It's obvious that social production is entirely different from for-profit production or government-mandated activity, but frequently it can still be harnessed directly to serve the interests of for-profit companies or governments. In his book *Remix: Making Art and Commerce Thrive in the Hybrid Economy*, Lawrence Lessig maintains that the *dominant* form of organizational design in the future is likely to be some kind of hybrid that combines for-profit or government-mandated action with social, volunteered action. Lessig says one example is Red Hat, a software service and consulting firm that earns a profit by helping its clients get the most out of their GNU/Linux software. Even though any user can dig into the source code for GNU/Linux and tinker with it, there's no support system if help is required,* which is the gap Red Hat sought to fill. Red Hat has been very successful, and is now owned by IBM. In fact, even though IBM holds more software patents than any other company in the world, it earns more money from servicing the unpatented, open-source Linux operating system (through Red Hat) than from all of its software patents combined. And Red Hat has spawned a whole industry composed of firms that now compete with it to do the same thing—that is, to provide professional services to help maintain GNU/Linux.

Social networks, being social, usually spring up spontaneously to meet any of a wide variety of objectives shared by network members, but many such networks also have significant implications for companies operating in the commercial economy. Lostpedia, a Web site dedicated to tracking the comings and goings and inside stories of the multiyear ABC-TV series *Lost*, has been maintained entirely by the volunteer efforts of hundreds of fans who collectively authored roughly seven thousand articles. With more than two million registered users, Lostpedia is just one of hundreds of different fan sites for this series, which is filled with the kind of mysteries and incomplete stories designed to intrigue viewers and keep them engaged. ABC, of course, has a definite interest in the success of Lostpedia and other such networks, because they drive profit-making viewership. And Lostpedia itself operates on a Wikia platform, a service

---

*Many large firms with mission-critical computer systems (like a phone company, say) use Linux because if their servers go down they can drill down into the system themselves and fix the problem immediately. If they use a commercial operating system they can't do this because vendors keep their code a secret to protect their patents, so the client company has to wait for the vendor to deploy resources to fix the problem. As a result many large firms with mission-critical computer systems consider open-source software a necessity.

launched by Jimmy Wales, founder of Wikipedia. While Wikipedia may not be a profit-making venture, Wikia most definitely is.

In addition to benefiting from the spontaneous networks created by people, companies can also make money by using social production to supplement their own for-profit activities. The "crowd service" volunteers who help other customers clearly benefit the bottom line of the organization sponsoring the service, reducing the cost of handling inquiries and improving the satisfaction of customers whose inquiries are handled. SolarWinds, a network management software provider, built a user community of 25,000 network administrators who help one another with their problems through crowd service, enabling the company to handle the service inquiries and problems of their 85,000 customers with just two full-time customer service employees of their own.

And sometimes social production can make the difference between success and failure for a profit-making firm. Case in point: eBay. Pierre Omidyar's going-in assumption when he founded eBay was that "people are basically good," but within weeks his venture was on track to become a complete failure as a result of rampant fraud and cheating. Rather than hire the staff required to check credentials and vet contributors from some central office, however (an extremely costly, likely unfeasible task), Omidyar decided to enlist his own customers, who cheerfully chipped in. For free. By incorporating a voluntary ratings system that allowed buyers to evaluate the trustworthiness of sellers on an objective basis, eBay became successful. Without the volunteered "social" part of the eBay business model the company would have failed, but now it is a publicly traded enterprise generating more than $2 billion of annual profit for its shareholders, not to mention the tens of thousands of small and large businesses that rely on eBay to generate their own revenues. eBay succeeded because the company figured out how to get its own users to create a system that made it possible for total strangers to trust one another—and it works, nearly all the time.

Craigslist, founded by Craig Newmark in 1995, began as a completely free community Web site for San Francisco, where people could post free ads offering everything from home rentals and jobs to vintage clothing.

It has now expanded to some seven hundred U.S. cities. While almost all craigslist ads remain free, the site has imposed fees for apartment rentals in New York and for job listings in seventeen cities. These fees are estimated to total about $20 million a year, paying the cost of maintaining the rest of the site. The fact is, craigslist could turn a much greater profit by charging more for its listings and perhaps taking advertising, but Newmark has said publicly that "we're not out to make lots of money." So even though craigslist is run, technically, as a privately held, for-profit company, it has been obvious to everyone from the beginning that the firm operates primarily within the sharing economy. Lessig points out that when Hurricane Katrina pulverized New Orleans, it was to craigslist that most residents turned for information, posting notices of missing relatives and friends, and letting others know where to find temporary shelter, even before the public service PeopleFinder site was put up.

Nor should it be a surprise that most social production initiatives are not launched by big businesses or governments in order to accomplish complex tasks (like supercomputing), but by ordinary citizens accomplishing ordinary tasks. Some social production initiatives grow large, like Folding@home and Wikipedia, but more often they stay small. In Lahore, Pakistan, for example, some teenagers mobilized via Facebook to pick up trash around the city—a task apparently beyond the capability of a corrupt and listless city government. And in Oakland, California, in the wake of a racially charged court verdict, several citizens relied on Twitter and Ushahidi, an open-source disaster-mapping platform from Kenya, to minimize violent rioting, saving lives as they alerted police and tracked events in real time, scooping the media on most stories by twenty to thirty minutes. Elsewhere around the world, people increasingly turn to the network in order to mobilize their efforts—to find bone marrow donors for a leukemia victim in Israel, or to collect money and organize gifts for their friends, or to expose and publicize a dictatorial regime's heavy-handed policies in the Middle East.

And companies themselves can use social media tools to stimulate the same kind of self-organization, which is often the most efficient way to handle complex, interconnected, or geographically dispersed processes.

DemandTec, for instance, is a company in the business of collecting, analyzing, and deploying product and customer data within the retail category. Its customers include research and marketing firms, retailers, and consumer manufacturing companies, and it serves these users not just with its own products and services but via the contributions of dozens of partner companies in various disciplines, from analytics to technology implementation to software. Billing itself as a "collaborative optimization network," in 2011 DemandTec launched an internal "enterprise social media" platform to facilitate its employees and all its various business partners and customers working together, including tools that allow different users to "follow" one another, form discussion groups, post comments, generate and track status updates, tweet out inquiries, and so forth.

[You Can't Trust Everybody]

Okay, so which is it? Are people naturally empathetic and "basically good" or not? We've already established that nonpsychopathic people have a natural empathy for others—but didn't Omidyar's experience with cheating and fraud on eBay just prove this wrong?

No, actually eBay's success is a perfect demonstration of the importance of empathy and social awareness, when it is used to hold bad behavior in check. Think about it: if people weren't social—if they didn't have empathy for others—why would they bother to write reviews at all?

The fact that most of us have empathy for others most of the time doesn't mean that everyone is good all the time. People aren't binary. Every normal person's personality is driven by a complex mix of empathy and self-interest, and this mix varies substantially by individual, because people are all different. Some are more naturally empathetic and caring, and more alert to the sensitivities of other people, while others are more naturally consumed by a self-interested desire to compete, achieve, or triumph over others. To a certain extent there is a male-female, Mars-Venus distinction to the way empathy plays out in human beings, but at best this is no more than a gross generalization, because individual personalities are highly diverse even among demographically identical people.

And people change their dispositions all the time—based on their mood, or the context of the situation, or their physical location, or the people they are associating with at the time. Circumstances change the balance between empathy and self-interest, even for individual personalities. Being able to feel others' pain unconsciously is one of the most important building blocks of empathy, but for all of us it's easier to feel another's pain when they are close. The more distant we are from a person (physically, emotionally, or socially), the easier it is to ignore that person's feelings. It may be the case that only a minority of U.S. infantrymen fired their weapons directly at enemy soldiers during World War II, for instance, but virtually 100 percent of B-17 bombardiers released their bombs from thousands of feet in the air, killing dozens or hundreds of people at a time, some of them even innocent civilians.

In eBay's case, a little transparency in the form of customer reviews makes a big difference, because this e-commerce business uses the empathy of reviewers to hold in check the otherwise dominant self-interest of sellers. While there are many people willing to cheat others—especially anonymous and faceless others—if people weren't "basically good," there would be no honest reviews at all, and Omidyar's venture would have failed even after he appealed to his customers for help!

Sometimes, however, when there is no adequate check and balance in a social system, or when a group of people get together with little conscience or scruples, we see examples of social production that don't create value, but destroy it. The same social networking platforms and interactive technology that made rebellion so potent throughout the Middle East during the Arab Spring of 2011 also made it possible for ad hoc gangs of hooligans and thieves to assemble spontaneously and run amok in England during the summer, and for gangs of impoverished youths to come together for the purpose of committing racist violence in the United States.

Flash mobs are a modern phenomenon organized through social platforms. Twenty-eight million people have viewed the YouTube video of hundreds of people weirdly "freezing" motionless for five minutes at Grand Central Station in New York, before dispersing as if nothing had happened. And 10 million have watched a dance tribute to the memory of Michael Jackson, spontaneously organized on a Stockholm city square. Now imagine dozens of people flooding into a retail store all at once and milling around, before suddenly each grabs hundreds of dollars of merchandise simultaneously, and leaves. Some commentators have said that participants in such gang criminality actually relish seeing themselves in the security camera tapes that inevitably find their way onto television news broadcasts and YouTube.

As with eBay, Wikipedia, or Folding@home, criminal undertakings like these are successful because people are social by nature. Think about it: Gang violence that has been organized online is just another example of social production. Social media technology makes all social actions—even criminal ones—easier to organize and coordinate. But this kind of activity also illustrates the evil we are all capable of, whenever our empathy for others extends only as far as our gang, our tribe, or our race or ethnic group.

In the final analysis, simple empathy will carry a society only so far. To maintain order, something else is called for, and this something else can be applied formally through some kind of legal or political system, or it can be applied informally through social mechanisms. Either way, the basic human motivation for enforcement and punishment is still driven by empathy. Because we really do feel the pain we see others experiencing, most of us have a sincere, emotionally compelling urge to punish injustice or unfairness whenever we encounter it, even when it is not directed toward us personally. The pleasure generated by meting out vengeance to a wrongdoer is something we can all relate to, and this biological phenomenon itself is important for maintaining social order.

[Trust, Punishment, and the "Monkey Mind"]

▪ *A man born without arms entered a bank in Florida and tried unsuccessfully to cash his wife's check. He was refused because, although he could provide two forms of identification, he couldn't provide a thumbprint. The story circulated on the Internet and in mass media.*

- *When a customer's DVD, recently and legally purchased from an electronics store, did not work, the manufacturer told him to return it to the retailer. The retailer told the customer to return it to the manufacturer. The customer spent $20 and ninety minutes on the DVD and still didn't have anything to watch, vowing to pirate content in the future. He's in his twenties and recommended the same to all his friends on Facebook.*

- *Our friends were given a $100 gift certificate for their wedding. Right after the ceremony, they moved to Costa Rica, where they worked on assignment for their company for the next eighteen months. When they got home, they took the gift certificate to the store to use it, but discovered that it had expired after twelve months. Turns out companies offering gift and rebate cards make a big profit from the 10 to 20 percent of cards that regularly go unredeemed, forgotten, or lost. Our friends vowed never to buy another one, from anybody.*

- *In Canada, a young boy accompanied by his mother entered a bank to start his first savings account. After he waited in line with his jar of carefully saved change, the lady behind the counter wouldn't open the account, since the coins had not been counted and wrapped before the little boy came to the bank branch. He was so upset that his father, the CFO of a major business, transferred the company's business to a different bank that welcomed the little boy's loose coins. The story was told at the next international banking association meeting, where it quickly passed into the blogosphere.*

- *Four men in Belgium, completely fed up with the lousy customer service and impenetrable call center of a large telecom provider, decided to protest. They set up a call center of their own in a large shipping container, and had the container delivered to the telecom company's main office, thereby blocking the entrance. When the company security guard called the phone number on the side of the container, he was subjected to the same kinds of impenetrable phone trees and unhelpful call handling the company's customers have to endure.*

The pranksters managed to drag out a simple phone call requesting them to move the container to a three-hour telephone "service" ordeal, in their attempt to simulate the company's own treatment of customers. The story has become a hilarious YouTube vignette.

This list could go on for pages. In fact, we bet you already have your own stories to add to this list, which you can do at www.trustability.com.

Dan Ariely, Duke University's respected behavioral economist, suggests that "revenge, even at personal expense, plays a deep role in the social order of both primates and people." He describes an experiment involving two chimpanzees placed in neighboring cages, with a single table of food just outside the cages but still within each chimp's reach. The food table is wheeled, and either chimp can reach out to pull it closer to its own cage (and therefore farther from the other's). However, a "revenge rope" leading out from each cage is rigged so that if either chimp pulls it the table will collapse and spill all the food onto the floor, out of reach of both of them. Use of the rope is carefully demonstrated to the chimps, so they each know that it destroys any possibility of either of them reaching the food. Researchers have found that if both chimps share the food, all goes well in this experiment. But if either chimp rolls the table too close to its own cage and the other can no longer reach it, then that other chimp will sometimes explode in a rage and yank the rope, collapsing the table for both of them.

> . . . among people who design software for group use, human social instincts are sometimes jokingly referred to as "the monkey mind."
> *CLAY SHIRKY*, HERE COMES EVERYBODY

Empathy and the urge to punish injustice are not the only ingredients in our complex social natures. Our need to maintain a workable social structure is also addressed by a number of other, not so admirable human motives. One social scientist noted that in purely evolutionary terms even jealousy and envy could serve an important purpose in helping our social species to survive and prosper, "motivating achievement, serving the conscience of self and other, and alerting us to inequities that, if fueled, can lead to escalated violence."

But empathy's role should not be underestimated, and its connection to the enforcement of socially accepted norms is critical. As human beings, almost all of us are hardwired to expect empathy, to the point that we get upset or angry when we see others not showing it. It may not sound polite to say this in public, but taking revenge on people who violate your trust (or the trust extended to them by others) is actually a good way to improve society's overall functioning. When any member of a group can punish any other member who behaves unfairly, the result is more trustworthiness in the system, with a fairer and more just social environment for everyone.

We're not advocating that you seek out opportunities to take revenge on people whose behavior upsets you, because exacting your own personal revenge can be a crime all by itself. Unlike chimps, we humans use civil and criminal legal processes to avenge wrongdoing. Most people shy away from openly acknowledging that a prison sentence is an act of revenge, preferring to suggest the more politically correct term "rehabilitation." Sometimes we dress our motives up in terms such as justice for the victim, or perhaps getting violent offenders off the streets.

But make no mistake: Punishment is the primary social good delivered by our criminal justice system. Rehabilitation is secondary. A guilty party will be sent to prison for punishment whether or not rehabilitation is likely to be successful or even attempted. And the preponderance of studies shows clearly that, while not perfect, deterrence is still generally effective. Thus, punishing injustice is *socially* beneficial because at least to some extent it deters unjust and unfair behavior by individuals. This is why sociologists say that punishing others for injustices done is a "prosocial" behavior—because it promotes stronger, more trusting social ties.

Trust and trustworthiness will increase over time not because *every* company and individual will always be trustworthy, but because technology empowers punishers more and more to keep untrustworthy behavior in check. Punishment makes our social world go 'round, and serves as the ultimate enforcer of trustworthiness, whether it's twenty-five to life for murder or a low review for a lousy product. Punishment keeps psychopathic capitalism in check, so:

> The easier it gets for customers to seek revenge, the more trustworthy businesses will *have* to be, for their own survival.

[Death by Tweet]

However we frame the issue, punishing unfair behavior is an essential part of being social. And there's a reason for the phrase "sweet revenge." Don't you feel a little tingle of satisfaction yourself when you learn about a heartless or cruel criminal getting a tough sentence? Behavior that is too selfish or "not fair" is the opposite of trustworthiness. Our human urge, our emotional impulse based on all our social biases, is to punish it. To seek revenge or payback of some kind even if it costs us something. To upset the food cart.

Nor is trustworthiness purely an animal instinct. At least in humans, having empathy for others and getting upset at injustice are also learned cultural traits, and the degree to which these traits are reinforced by culture is directly related to the type and importance of interactions within the culture. Studies show that the desire to punish injustice varies from society to society, with the citizens of more highly developed and interconnected economic cultures having a much higher sensitivity to injustice than members of less advanced cultures.

Online technologies, of course, allow us to avenge wrongdoing in a highly social, highly interconnected way. Revenge has never been easier or more satisfying, and it can be far more long-lasting and punitive. Reminder: once an opinion about you hits the Internet, you may as well count it as immediate, ubiquitous, and *permanent*. As one advertising executive said, "You can't un-Google yourself."

Or, in a more picturesque image relayed by one influential blogger:

> Dude, you can't take something off the Internet . . . that's like trying to take pee out of a swimming pool.

We've all been entertained by the creativity and effort of victims exacting revenge by YouTube on companies and brands that have wronged them, and as word-of-mouth communication among consumers continues to accelerate, you can expect that the punishment imposed for poor service or a less-than-acceptable product will arrive ever more swiftly.

Case in point: Sacha Baron Cohen's 2009 movie, *Bruno*. Even though a lot of people usually like Cohen's movies, *Bruno* was different. Released to theaters in the United States on Friday, July 9, 2009, this movie was apparently *so* tasteless, *so* over-the-top, and *so* overbearing in its self-conscious need to violate every possible taboo that people walked out of it in large numbers on that very first night. And that's not all. As they walked out, they were using their smart phones to text and tweet their friends, advising them not to bother seeing it. Stay away. The result: *Bruno*'s box office receipts on Saturday were down by an astounding and unprecedented 40 percent from Friday's. John Horn, movie critic and journalist for the *Los Angeles Times*, speaking on NPR's *All Things Considered*, suggested the movie was so bad that it was pretty much immediately killed by negative word of mouth. Before Twitter and Facebook and other status-updating social media platforms, he said, word of mouth on a movie just didn't get passed around so fast. According to Horn, "even if they had a turkey, [studios] used to get two weeks of business before the stink really caught up to the film. Now they have 12 hours."

[Cooperators, Free Riders, and Punishers]

According to Nicholas A. Christakis and James H. Fowler, authors of *Connected: The Surprising Power of Our Social Networks and How They Shape Our Lives*, Wikipedia works well because over time a social community of interested contributors develops to participate in fashioning the most authoritative entry for each topic. The majority of these participants are what Christakis and Fowler call "cooperators." They are the people who do most of the work that lies behind Wikipedia's success as a reference tool. By contributing new thinking, expertise, writing, and editing, cooperators help others to jointly produce and refine articles in their subject area of expertise. But in addition, the Wikipedia crowd includes a number of "free riders"—people who, in the authors' words, "want to use the credibility of the information established by others for their own purposes." A free rider might highjack a particular Wikipedia entry to publicize himself, or to advance a biased perspective on some politically charged or controversial issue, or perhaps to paint a favorable view of his own company.

If contributors and free riders were the only types of Wikipedia participants, then a single free rider could easily sabotage or undermine any collective action that other Wikipedia members undertake, regardless of their larger numbers, although the collective action of others would slowly and constantly provide course correction. (You can test this. Read a Wikipedia entry about even a noncontroversial person in the news. Wait thirty days, and read it again. It will be a different article. Wikipedia, like all socially produced projects, is a living organism, ebbing and flowing based on free riders and legitimate contributors.)

So what accounts for Wikipedia's success? Why hasn't it cratered as a result of the self-serving sabotage of free riders? Free riders are held in check and Wikipedia is sustained as a viable example of genuine social production because there are literally thousands of "punishers" patrolling various Wikipedia entries. These folks may or may not have contributed their own material at some point, but they take umbrage at the offenses committed by the free riders. Punishers take it upon themselves to control the damage done by free riders, by reversing inappropriate, biased, or inadequately supported entries, by posting chastising notes on the personal "talk" pages of individual free riders, and even (in collaboration with other contributors) by preventing some egregious offenders from making further contributions.

Wikipedia's punishers are like a human being's white blood cells, seeking out dangerous germs and eliminating them. Punishing a free rider on Wikipedia (or punishing another critic whose point of view isn't trustworthy) requires time and effort. But people get upset when they see injustice, so they do take the time and they do make the effort. What makes Wikipedia stable, as a social *system,* is the balance among creating, sharing, and punishing.

It's important, however, to maintain the right balance in a system, and sometimes the feedback loops have to be adjusted in order to ensure continued viability. We mentioned before how eBay only became viable because of the reviews volunteered by users. But as the company flourished and users became accustomed to shopping for sellers with the best reputations, the sellers themselves began trying to game the system. More and more, some sellers would rate their buyers high even *before* the sale transaction actually occurred. This action on a seller's part was specifically designed to influence the buyer's rating of the seller, and apparently it was having an effect. As a result, in early 2008 eBay changed its system so that sellers would be allowed to give positive ratings *only* to actual buyers. eBay's action was designed to keep its system in balance—to keep it trustworthy.

When companies engage in untrustable behavior, punishers can also become active within the company itself. Employees are human beings, and the vast majority of them don't want to be seen as untrustable any more than you or I do.

Verizon Wireless used to sell many of its smart phones with buttons that could easily result in connecting to the Internet unintentionally, often resulting in a data charge of as much as $2 per instance. After an FCC investigation, the company installed a "landing page" for users accessing the Internet—so if you push a button by mistake you can cancel the transaction before incurring a fee. Even with this change, however, many users continued to find mysterious data charges on their phone bills. If someone "never" uses the Internet from their mobile phone because of the cost, for instance, then why would they incur these charges, except by mistake?

According to *The New York Times,* the company was apparently charging customers for their mistakes intentionally, in full knowledge that the charges were erroneous. This, at least, was the allegation leveled by one of Verizon's own customer service reps, in a communication with one of the newspaper's reporters. Verizon's phones have a feature that allows users to block accidental Internet access altogether, but according to this employee the company had instructed its reps *not* to inform customers about this feature unless they specifically asked about it! And the company went to some effort to ensure that refunds were only grudgingly given, if at all, covering a maximum of a single month of erroneous charges.

Now think about this for a bit, because the truth of the matter is, even if all these allegations are 100 percent true, Verizon did nothing illegal or even technically "untrustworthy." It isn't cheating a customer to charge them what you say you're going to charge them when they themselves use their very own fingers to press a button that makes it happen. It isn't technically a violation of trust simply to refrain from telling a customer how to avoid making mistakes with your product. So why was this employee so upset? Because *even though the company wasn't proactively deceiving customers, it wasn't proactively respecting their interests either*. Verizon was trustworthy, in the old-fashioned sense, but not *trustable*, the way companies have to be in the age of transparency. No "Extreme Trust" here.

As people become more and more efficiently interconnected they will inevitably become more social, so the "pro-social" motivations that drive us, including empathy, reciprocity, and avenging injustice when we see it, will rise steadily in importance in all our dealings—not just with other people, but with the companies and brands we buy from as well. We may never know exactly what motivated this particular customer service rep to blow the whistle on Verizon, but it's a safe bet there are employees at virtually every untrustable company in business today who also don't like having to come to work with the goal of tricking customers out of their money. And as technology continues to drive us closer together socially, they will like it less and less.

David Kirkpatrick argued in a 2011 *Forbes* cover story that every company in business today has become vulnerable to the judgments and actions of its customers and employees, who are now able to mobilize themselves using social networks. According to Kirkpatrick, "companies and leaders will have to show authenticity, fairness, transparency and good faith. If they don't, customers and employees may come to distrust them, to potentially disastrous effect."

The role that trust plays in our everyday, routine interactions with others is an important driver for the "sharing economy" and social production. But trust's role directly conflicts with the role that self-interest plays in the market economy. In the next chapter we'll discuss how and when to apply the principles of empathy, sharing, and trust, versus the principles of self-interest and monetary incentives.

TRUSTABILITY
TEST

Think about how you'd answer these questions based on how things work at your company, institution, or government agency. Talk about your answers with your colleagues. Visit www.trustability.com to see how other visitors' responses compare with your own for these and other questions.

▶ Do your employees know of untrustable behaviors and policies at your company?

　▷ Have you ever asked them?

　▷ What would they do if they did know?

▶ Has your business ever been the victim of customer revenge for perceived bad service or untrustworthy behavior?

　▷ If so, did your company actually do what the customer accused you of (even if the customer's story was not scrupulously accurate)?

　▷ How did your company handle the accusation?

▶ If not—if your company has been unfairly victimized by some bad press or a false story—did any of your own customers come to your defense?

▶ Do you facilitate your customers' connecting with and helping one another to use your products or get the most benefit out of your products (i.e., crowd service)? If you don't, do you know whether and to what extent your customers connect with and help one another on their own?

▶ Have any of your customers formed a user group or another, similar organization?

▶ Are there any social production initiatives that are displacing commercial activities or profits in your industry or business category? If so, what do you think is the primary motive for people participating in these initiatives?

▶ If there are social production initiatives in your category, do you

▷ Ignore them?

▷ Discourage them?

▷ Compete with them?

▷ Participate in them?

▶ Do any social production initiatives supplement or improve business activities and profits in your industry or category?

▶ Do your employees, suppliers, and distribution partners collaborate, using social media tools, in order to operate more efficiently and serve customers better?

[5]

TRUST AND THE E-SOCIAL ETHOS

"It's up to you."

In October 2007, the alternative rock group Radiohead, which *Time* magazine called "the most interesting and innovative band in rock" at the time, announced that it would release its seventh album, *In Rainbows,* with an interesting and unprecedented offer. Rather than using a record label to produce a slick CD, they planned to launch their fifteen-song album in an online, downloadable format from their own Web site. But in addition, the group said they would specify no price for the album, allowing each buyer to make his or her own decision about how much their music was worth. As *Time* described it, when *In Rainbows* is dropped into the checkout basket on Radiohead's Web site,

> . . . *a question mark pops up where the price would normally be. Click it, and the prompt "It's Up To You" appears. Click again and it refreshes with the words "It's Really Up To You"—and really, it is. It's the first major album whose price is determined by what individual consumers want to pay for it. And it's perfectly acceptable to pay nothing at all.*

One commentator suggested that Radiohead's message to its fans was that even though they know that anyone can easily steal the music with an illegal download, "if you really like us, give us whatever you feel is right. *We trust that you will do the right thing.*"

[The e-Social Ethos]

In addition to reciprocity, empathy, and the desire to avenge injustice, our social interactions are subject to a whole set of customs and "unwritten rules" that have developed over untold generations of people conversing with each other. When you discuss something with a friend, colleague, loved one, or stranger you adhere to these customs even without thinking. Don't interrupt. Listen first, show an interest. Respond to what others are saying.

But there are subtler principles as well. Suppose, for instance, a good friend were to ask your help in getting a job at the company where another friend of yours is a vice president. All he really wants is an introduction. He's your friend, and he would certainly do the same for you. But what if, in asking for this favor, your friend also offered you $100 to make the introduction? Or $500? Wouldn't you be totally put off by this? Maybe he's not really your friend after all, you might think, because this certainly isn't how friends deal with friends.

This conflict represents one of the most important differences between how we interact in a commercial setting versus in a social setting. The commercial economy is characterized by people freely exchanging money with other people. You buy from me, I sell to you, and if we do it right we both consider ourselves better off. Nor does this seem out of line to any of us. We all expect to pay for the things we want. When you pay the grocer $6 for a twelve-pack of Diet Coke, you don't begrudge him the money. You expect to pay. You wouldn't even consider asking the grocer to give you the soda for free. And if the grocer asked you for a favor—say, stopping in to help restock the shelves some evening—you would be just as baffled as if a friend offered you money for making an introduction or doing a favor, or demanded money for spending time with you.

With the rise of modern, free-market capitalism, these two domains of human activity—social and commercial—became quite distinct and separate, but technology seems to be smashing them together. Social production, for instance, combines features of both domains, being fueled by social interaction, trust, and sharing, but generating real economic value as well. Whether the sharing involves someone's free time, honest opinion, computer coding, editing and curating, or computation cycles on their computer hard drive, the end result is genuine economic value, worth real money.

Over time, the e-social "ethos" that comes to govern our online interactions will develop as a set of purely informal and unwritten customs, much like the customs that have already developed to govern our offline social interactions. A number of organizations have already sprung up to help fashion the standards and customs by which a social sharing economy would function more smoothly. Creative Commons, for instance, is a nonprofit organization that aims to "increase the amount of creativity (cultural, educational, and scientific content) in 'the commons'—the body of work that is available to the public for free and legal sharing, use, repurposing, and remixing." The Creative Commons organization has produced several different licenses for intellectual property that are similar to patents and copyrights but different in important ways. While a copyright or patent imposes an absolute "all rights reserved" restriction on someone else's use of an idea or original material, Creative Commons' various "CC" licenses, now recognized in all major legal jurisdictions, can be applied to original work *in lieu of* a copyright, whether the work involves a software application, book, movie, photograph, song, or anything else original. (For instance, the "Attribution Share Alike" CC license allows others to use and modify your work provided they credit you and allow others to use *their* updates or revisions on the same terms. This is the type of license most commonly applied to protect open-source software. If you create a new patch or write new code for an application, and you make it freely available to others, you don't want someone then to incorporate your software into their own update and claim it as a restricted product.)

Regardless of the legal and regulatory protections or mandates eventually enacted, however, it is clear that *trust* will be a dominant guiding principle in the e-social ethos, because maintaining trust is essential for the smooth functioning of the overall system. An ethos that rewards and encourages trust—and punishes untrustworthy behavior—is inevitable, because it will always succeed more efficiently than one that doesn't.

As a result, the importance of trust and trustworthiness is continuing to increase as interactive technologies continue to improve. Over the last several years, as more and more people have become familiar with and participated in various social production activities by uploading, collaborating, and volunteering, we have already come to rely more on sharing and trust. And while the task of policing trustworthiness used to be in the hands of just a few offline organizations—the Better Business Bureau, *Consumer Reports*, the FDA, the newspapers—already this task is being performed more efficiently online, and everybody participates. People share their opinions, and they punish unfairness, socially. We are more trustworthy, and we trust more.

Given the quirky combination of sharing and value creation that characterizes social production, it should be no surprise that the whole idea has often perplexed and confounded corporate executives and others more accustomed to evaluating the worth of a business in terms of its ability to generate a profit by selling things to willing buyers. To Steve Ballmer, CEO of Microsoft, open-source software once seemed "communist." And to Robert McHenry, a former editor for *Encyclopaedia Britannica*, Wikipedia was more like a public restroom than an encyclopedia.

[How Friends Treat Friends]

The unfamiliar workings of the e-social ethos can easily trip a business up when it tries to deal with social media simply as a new channel for marketing or to generate positive word of mouth, because most marketing and business tactics that make sense in the commercial domain just don't apply in the social domain. Marketing is a vital part of the commercial economy, a setting characterized by people freely exchanging money with other people. But most people use social media to interact for the same reasons they attend parties or participate in casual conversations with friends—not for a financial benefit or to accomplish some task, but for the enjoyment and fulfillment they get from connecting with others, or for the gossip, insight, and inside information they acquire. Mixing up these two domains can lead to real problems, because social influence can't be *bought* any more than friendship can. You can buy advertising exposure with media dollars, you can buy better customer insight with data and analytics, and you can buy Facebook "likes" with sufficient discounts or giveaways. But you can't *buy* word-of-mouth recommendations or social influence. That's just not how friends treat friends.

In September 2006, a blog appeared entitled *Wal-Marting Across America*. It featured two intrepid RV owners, known only as Jim and Laura, who were driving from Walmart to Walmart across the United States, visiting stores along their way, and interviewing a whole stream of ever-upbeat Walmart employees. Other bloggers, however, suspected that Jim and Laura were fictitious, not real people driving their motor home around from store to store. And soon enough it was revealed that the two bloggers were actually paid contract writers for Walmart, hired by Edelman, the company's PR firm, to create a series of glowing articles. This ignited a firestorm of protest from others in the blogosphere, with people lashing out at both Walmart and Edelman. Walmart's initiative perfectly illustrates the single biggest error most companies commit when they try to operate in the social media space: rather than respecting the e-social ethos, they think they can treat social media just like any other marketing "channel," in this case using it to create a kind of advertising message. ("I'm not a motor-home owner, but I play one on TV.")

To the PR agency's credit, CEO Richard Edelman jumped immediately into the fray, personally and vigorously, with multiple online apologies and mea culpas, answering most of the angry inbound e-mails and social media postings himself. He knew that in an age when anyone at all can comment publicly, "no comment" has become a confession all by itself. It's no longer possible simply to run from mistakes, or to hunker down and wait for the furor to subside. Once the pee gets into the pool, the only possible remedy is adding more and more water.

What Walmart learned was that even though the social domain can serve as a marketing channel, the social ethos still has to be respected. You can advertise to viewers using a fictional story to entertain them on television, but you don't lie to your friends and call it "advertising."

In the social domain, very few of us would change our point of view or announce it to others in exchange for compensation, and most of us would consider it insulting to be offered money to do so. Crass commercialism is simply out of place in such social interactions. You can't buy your friends the way you buy your groceries, and you can't buy your social media exposure the way you buy your advertising.

Disney figured this out almost the moment they started dabbling in social media. At one industry conference on social media two Euro Disney executives related that their firm had discovered it needed to use completely different rules for selling in the "marketing space" to consumers who had enlisted for one of the company's e-mail newsletters, as compared with selling in the "social space" to consumers who had friended one of Disney's many characters on Facebook. While offering cross-sell deals and other promotions to e-mail newsletter subscribers was fine, they found that if they tried to make such offers to Facebook friends, a large number of them took offense. It wasn't just that the response was lower. The response was *negative*, because marketing offers, when made in the social space, can actually generate ill will. Forget ROI. Marketing in the social space can be worse than no marketing at all.

Lawrence Lessig tells an interesting story about sitting next to a young man on a cross-country flight who had a binder chock full of DVDs, most of which were pirated copies of commercially released movies. As a lawyer with a substantial interest in the field of intellectual property, Lessig was of course highly conflicted about this. He admired the man's collecting expertise on one hand, but he was also acutely aware that "[i]n building his collection, he had violated a billion rights." Eventually, he says, with time on his hands and noticing that one of the DVDs was a film he'd never gotten around to seeing himself, he asked the man, whose name turned out to be Josh, whether he could rent it for, say, $5? But, Lessig relates, this only generated

> . . . *a look of utter disappointment on his face. Suffice it to say that I had found the single most profound insult to hurl at Josh. "What the fuck?" he spat back at me. "You think I do this for money? I'm happy to lend you one of these. But I don't take money for this."*

By offering money to Josh, Lessig had violated the e-social ethos, and this had aroused Josh's complete disgust. "Of all the possible terms of exchange within a sharing economy," Lessig says, "the single term that isn't appropriate is money."

Sensibilities do matter, and the social and commercial domains are colliding more and more. While offering to "rent" one of his pirated DVDs might have offended Josh's sensibilities, it isn't hard these days to find borderline cases, where the boundaries really have blurred. You might be offended (or just baffled) if your grocery were to ask your help stocking shelves, but what about when JetBlue or Southwest Airlines asks passengers to be sure to clear out their seat-back pockets, as a courtesy to the next passenger? Most people accept this suggestion at face value—but what if it were United Airlines, say, asking the same thing from its first-class passengers?

A few weeks after Radiohead released its online-only, pay-what-you-want music, a comScore survey estimated that the *In Rainbows* album had seen perhaps 1.2 million downloads, with roughly 60 percent of those downloading it choosing to pay nothing at all, while the remaining 40 percent paid an average of roughly $6 each, generating perhaps $2 million in digital income. And as Radiohead's Thom Yorke told *Wired* magazine:

> *In terms of digital income, we've made more money out of this record than out of all the other Radiohead albums put together, forever—in terms of anything on the Net. And that's nuts. It's partly due to the fact that EMI [the band's former record label whose contract had*

expired] wasn't giving us any money for digital sales. All the contracts signed in a certain era have none of that stuff.

Radiohead's 2007 experiment was soon imitated by other performers and groups, and praised as an attempt to deal with the true dynamics of online technology in the music world. Online music and entertainment was Josh's world—the hacker world of illegal downloads, remixing, and sharing in the social domain. And even though hackers may not respect money, property rights, and many of the other mechanisms that make the commercial domain so successful, they still have a strong sense of *trustability*.

Offering money or compensation is as inappropriate in the social domain as creating a faux blog post is. But if you ask for volunteers, as Radiohead did (and as Josh demanded), then in the right circumstances you might be able to shift gears entirely, transitioning a business proposition into a friend-to-friend interaction—an interaction based on trust and sharing, rather than on money and self-interest. Doing it any other way will call your own intentions into question, undermining your trustability in the eyes of others.

We're not saying you can never launch a pure marketing initiative that uses a social media platform like a "channel." Many companies do this, and they can get good results from it, but it's not a *social* strategy, and it shouldn't be portrayed as one. Most brands' Facebook fan pages, for instance, serve primarily as vehicles for disseminating discounts, coupons, and other goodies to their customers (in contrast to Disney's fan pages where people friend various cartoon characters). There's nothing at all wrong with a brand using Facebook or Twitter or other social platforms to disseminate rebates or incentives, or to publicize sales, but *selling* is not *friending*. Selling is a *marketing* objective, not a social objective, and the consumers who become "fans" of a commercial brand fully understand this. Boosting the number of Facebook "likes" or Twitter users who follow your brand bears little similarity to generating the kind of goodwill or positive reputation that comes from having genuinely social relationships with customers—relationships that are based on friendship and trust.

To borrow yet another analogy, we all know the importance of "networking" when it comes to advancing our own careers, but only a psychopath would consider friends to be valuable *only* in financial terms. Companies that use social media for marketing purposes are usually doing the equivalent of sound professional networking—they are procuring contacts and increasing familiarity in order to improve their chances with customers and prospects. But they probably aren't producing many supportive, trusting, or long-lasting relationships, and they shouldn't kid themselves. In the online world, no one posts a legitimate opinion or product review in return for money, or for a product discount. If you read a flattering reference to yourself on Facebook or Twitter you might share it with your own friends, but you wouldn't even think about sending the author money. That's just not what friends do.

Traditionally, bloggers who take money in return for their posts have been condemned as sell-outs or hacks, because taking money for a positive blog post is a violation of the e-social ethos. The online social space is for friends to associate with friends, and you don't have to be a hard-core "netizen" to know that it's just wrong to take money for introducing a good friend to a commercial product or service. You either do it because you think your friend will benefit, or you don't. Taking money demeans your integrity and corrupts the ethos. It's just not trustable behavior.

There has always been an important role for sharing and generosity within business life, but it hasn't always been recognized just how important. The ever-insightful Seth Godin has argued that nothing is more critical to your own personal career than giving gifts—contributing value, for free, in order to help others. He's not talking about buying presents for coworkers, but about doing "emotional labor" for someone else's benefit—a new idea freely shared, perhaps, or even a compliment to a coworker.

First, you benefit from the making and the giving. The act of the gift is in itself a reward. And second, you benefit from the response of those around you. When you develop the habit of contributing this

gift, your coworkers become more open, your boss becomes more flex-
ible, and your customers become more loyal. The essence of any gift,
including the gift of emotional labor, is that you don't do it for a
tangible, guaranteed reward. If you do, it's no longer a gift; it's a
job. The hybrid economy we're living in today is blending the idea of
capitalism ("do your job and I won't fire you") and the gift economy
("wow, this is amazing").

In a sharing economy such as the e-social domain, giving gifts is the
primary mechanism for creating value, with participants eschewing the
use of money altogether. Money is too crass and commercial for social
interactions based on sharing. So while transactions in the commercial
economy function more smoothly with some level of sharing and trust,
transactions in the sharing economy *only* function *because* of trust. I share
with you, and I expect you to share with me—but it's not a quid pro quo
exchange, metered at the till in terms of dollars and cents. It's an unstated
ethos, a culture of sharing, based not on a contract but on mutual trust.

[This Blog Post Brought to You By . . .]

On the other hand, it's not just good friends who might read your blog
post or view your video, and as the social domain and commercial domain have continued to blur together, a growing business in "sponsored"
social commentary has developed, with some beauty bloggers on You-
Tube earning upwards of a thousand dollars a month by promoting cos-
metics products, for instance. And one survey estimated the volume of
money now being spent by companies to buy online social commentary
is approaching $50 million annually. This kind of marketing was helped
along by a set of guidelines introduced by the Federal Trade Commission
in 2009 requiring sponsored blog, video, and other social content to con-
form to the rules of other sponsored advertising.

After its *Wal-Marting Across America* fiasco, Walmart has been
careful to navigate the social domain more authentically, and one of the

most interesting programs it launched has been a sponsored-blog program, Walmart Moms. More than twenty different women bloggers have been recruited into the program. Their blogs, with names like "Domestic Diva," "Chic Shopper Chick," or "Green Your Décor," continue to be operated by each individual woman, independently, but occasionally they may feature Walmart products or special deals. Any time they do, however, Walmart's sponsorship is fully disclosed. On the "Walmart Moms" home page, the store advises:

> *Participation in the Walmart Moms program is voluntary. Participants in the program are required to clearly disclose their relationship with Walmart as well as any compensation received, including travel opportunities, expenses, or products. In the event that products are received for review, participants may keep or dispose of product at their discretion.*

In 2011 Tesco, the UK-based retailing chain, bought BzzAgent, a U.S.-based word-of-mouth marketing firm. BzzAgent's business has recruited some 800,000 volunteers who signed up to receive occasional product samples, mostly from consumer packaged goods companies. They are encouraged to blog or tweet or otherwise publicize their impressions of these products in social media channels, although no monetary compensation is provided. With this acquisition Tesco, widely known for its sophisticated use of customer data (Tesco already owns dunnhumby, the customer data analytics firm), will gain access to a large amount of interesting social network data, regardless of whether the firm ever uses BzzAgent to promote its own products.

[The Kenneth Cole Affair]

It isn't hard to trespass across the boundary that separates the commercial domain from the social domain. Even experienced social media users can trip themselves up occasionally.

The revolt in Egypt against the thirty-year rule of Hosni Mubarak was largely organized and coordinated through some of the rebels' Facebook pages. People around the world followed developments on the ground in real time through Twitter and Facebook updates being posted by thousands of demonstrators armed only with pent-up rage and mobile phones. Their tweets included hashtags like #Egypt and #Cairo so they could be tracked and followed by millions of online spectators around the world.

On February 3, 2011, the Twitter feed from Egypt included such heartrending entries as "3 dead, 1500 injured as clashes continue in #Cairo #egypt" and "at least 3 rights activists & lawyers arrested from human rights NGOs offices in #Cairo by military police from 1hr. #Egypt."

Then, in the middle of this revolutionary drama being played out before the eyes of the world, clothing and accessories designer Kenneth Cole tweeted out the following message: "Millions are in uproar in #Cairo. Rumor is they heard our new spring collection is now available online at http://bit.ly/KCairo –KC."

Cole's tweet was in such bad taste that it ignited an immediate firestorm of online outrage. "WTF is wrong with you, @KennethCole?" read a typical tweet, which was retweeted more than a hundred times and read or exposed to more than a million users, all by itself. "@KennethCole Totally poor taste. People are dying in the streets and you want to advertise your fashions? #boycottKennethCole" read another.

Needless to say, within just a few hours Cole apologized for having posted the tweet (apparently he personally authored both the tweet and the apology), but it only took minutes before a parody of Cole's insensitivity went up on Twitter, as someone opened the fake @kennethcolepr account, someone else started a #kennethcoletweets hashtag, and followers began competing to upload the most tastelessly funny tweets. Early entries included such jewels as "Hey Zsa Zsa—You can still wear one new KC pump" and "Need an undershirt? Layer with one of our tanks! Don't be a Tiananmen Square."

[Trustability and Social Production]

But even though money and other commercial inducements aren't appropriate for social interactions, you can still have a positive effect in the e-social domain as long as you respect the ethos and concentrate on the *noneconomic* things that people value—the social things. While you may be able to buy the "sponsorship" of a blog post, as soon as you do you've redefined the post as a commercial, rather than a friend's objective opinion. And no matter how hard you try, you can't buy a friend's good opinion. You can influence it, on the other hand, by speaking to your friend's own needs or interests—by helping your friend.

So let's think of what actually motivates an influential blogger or Twitter user—someone whose opinions matter to thousands of followers. Yes, most key influencers would be offended if you offered to compensate them for a favorable post, but they are still human beings, and like all the rest of us they still have ambitions. They want to be noticed and to increase their own influence. They want to write better, more original and authoritative posts. And there are a number of noneconomic services or benefits you can provide to key social media influencers that will help them achieve some of these ambitions. If you're a student of employee motivation, what we're talking about here is focusing not on "extrinsic" benefits, such as compensation and perks, but on "intrinsic" benefits, such as appreciation, encouragement, camaraderie, and fulfillment.

And before delving into the intrinsic benefits that influencers will find most appealing (see sidebar), a quick word of caution: Be sure you understand your influencers' own perspectives. The overwhelming majority of social influencers do not consider themselves to be experts on any particular business category, company, or brand per se. Rather, they think of themselves as having an authoritative point of view with respect to some particular issue or problem of concern to them and their followers. It might be a business issue or a health issue or a relationship issue—but it's unlikely that they will think of their own central mission in terms of rating or evaluating the products and services offered by you or your competitors. Their central mission is to be of value to their friends and followers—those who depend on their opinion and thinking. Talking favorably or unfavorably about your brand or product has to be seen in this context—as a service they are performing for the benefit of their own network of friends.

INFLUENCING THE INFLUENCERS

The intrinsic benefits social media mavens value most can be categorized in terms of acknowledgment, recognition, information, and access. You can remember these benefits easily if you remember the mnemonic word "ARIA," as in the solo sung by your favorite opera star.

ACKNOWLEDGMENT: Simply identifying influential bloggers or social media influencers and acknowledging them with your own message will go a long way toward having a positive influence. If you haven't yet assigned people in your organization the task of identifying those tweeters and bloggers with the most credibility and influence in your particular category, then it's time to do so. When you identify someone important, reach out to her, and do it genuinely. Post a comment on her blog, retweet a smart update, e-mail her with a thoughtful (but non-self-serving) suggestion. Acknowledge her existence, and by implication her significance, by letting her know that *you* know she exists, and that *you* are paying attention.

RECOGNITION: Bloggers, product reviewers, and others who become expert in your business's category want to be recognized as such. Recognition is a key motivator for all of us, but it's even more crucial in the social media world, where monetary compensation is completely inappropriate. So be sure to recognize a key blogger by forwarding the link to his or her Web site on to others. You might even consider mentioning very authoritative bloggers in your own press communications, providing not only recognition to the blogger but additional sources for whatever reporters or other commentators follow your firm. If you have a crowd service system that relies on some knowledgeable customers handling the complicated inquiries of other customers, be sure to recognize the most expert contributors or the most prolific participants with special badges, emblems, or status designations. Everyone wants to be Platinum in something.

INFORMATION: Information is power. Think about it. More than anything else, *information* is exactly what influential bloggers want to provide their readers, and what Twitterers want to provide their tweeps. Key influencers want the inside dope, the straight skinny. So when you identify social media influencers in your category, be sure to provide them with all the information you can reasonably manage. Don't provide truly confidential or commercially sensitive information, unless you think it might do more good for you if it were to become widely known (assuming, of course, that it's not illegal or unethical to release it). But even without violating anyone's confidence or divulging the kind of "inside" information that might get a public company in trouble, you can almost certainly provide a key influencer with a more useful perspective and insight about your business or your category, including the problems you face, the threats to your business you are trying to avoid, and the opportunities you see.

ACCESS: Just as useful as providing insightful information is letting an influencer make direct contact with the author of the insight, or the operating person at your business who is most connected to the information. Talk about getting the straight scoop. Probably nothing will pay bigger dividends in terms of social media influence than simply allowing the influencers themselves to have access to some of your own people, your own experts and authorities. Providing this access is, all by itself, a form of acknowledgment and recognition also. Not everyone gets this kind of access, because you can't take the time for everyone. But you should definitely take the time for someone who has an important enough following in social media.

Influencing your influencers, if you do it right, will help empower customers to share their ideas and thoughts with other customers, to help other customers solve their problems, and to simply participate more in the social world that surrounds every set of commercial transactions. In addition to the benefits you will realize in terms of being seen as more trustable, this kind of customer-oriented activity is almost certainly going to generate additional revenue and business as well. eBay, for instance, created customer support forums for its customers so buyers and sellers could exchange tips and suggestions, but it later found that customers who were active users of the support forums were generating 50 percent more revenue for the firm!

When people get together and exchange ideas, they do much more than simply critique the honesty of a vendor or the experience they have when they buy from someone. This sharing of information is only a part of a much broader, more robust effort—a social effort—to solve some commonly perceived problem, or to meet some commonly felt need. People have always turned to one another for help in solving problems, whether it was prehistoric hunters cooperating to run down big game, or Wikipedia contributors curating a new entry. But the technology of cooperation has never been so efficient, so robust, and so capable as it now is. So as cooperation accelerates, the speed of problem solving increases too. We experience it as "innovation."

[Innovation Thrives Where Trustability Rules]

The importance of trust in fueling economic growth and progress is often overlooked, but trust plays a critical role in interaction between people, and interaction is what generates technological innovation in the first place. Interaction between people is how the spark of human creativity gets applied. Every "new" idea you have, personally, is based on some combination of previous concepts in your own mind, even if you combined these concepts subconsciously. All our technologies, our highly advanced tools, our intricate and diverse culture—the entirety of human civilization, in fact—have only been developed through social interactions, and social interactions depend on trust.

This point was made brilliantly by the economist Leonard Read in a 1950s essay about the making of an ordinary wooden pencil. As simple as a pencil is, he says, *"not a single person on the face of this earth"* knows how to make it! Why? Just consider the task of harvesting the wood for making the pencil, using saws and axes, ropes and other gear. Of course, you'd first have to mine and smelt the ore to make these tools, raise and prepare the food to feed the lumberjacks, clear the land for a road to the mill, and even pour the concrete for the hydroelectric dam to provide power. You'd also have to travel to Sri Lanka to mine the graphite for the pencil's core, mixing it with ammonium hydroxide and sulfonated tallow. Then you'd have to cut the graphite mixture to size and bake it at 2,000 degrees Fahrenheit before treating it with a hot mixture of candelilla wax, paraffin, and hydrogenated natural fats. All this is before you start on the eraser.

Read's argument is not just that no single person could ever *do* all these things, but that no single person even *knows how* to do all these things. No one. (Quick: Have you ever heard of candelilla wax or sulfonated tallow? Could you recognize graphite when it is in the ground, before it's mined?)

But if no one knows how pencils are made, then how do they appear in stores? The same way beehives appear in fields or ant colonies spring up on the ground. Pencils emerge from the collective actions of many different people doing different things, just as a beehive emerges from the collective actions of thousands of individual bees. No single bee "knows how" to make a hive, any more than any single human being knows how to make a pencil. Pencils *emerge* from our collective intelligence along with virtually every other technological tool or artifact any of us ever use in our daily lives.

As far back as 1922, the American sociologist William Ogburn pointed out that every innovation inherently draws from some combination of previous innovations, suggesting that the pace of technological change resembles a compound interest curve, because "the more there is to invent with, the greater will be the number of inventions." More picturesquely, the English writer Matt Ridley has observed that innovation occurs when ideas get together to "have sex" with each other.

Because new technologies, from stone tools to pencils to silicon microchips, are *socially* developed as much as they are intellectually developed, the general rate of human economic progress depends not just on the inventory of previously known ideas, as Ogburn pointed out, but also on the intelligence and number of creative minds that can be deployed, the speed and efficiency of interaction among them, and the level of trust and mutual respect they share.

Over the years, businesses everywhere have usually worked hard to maintain the "secrets" of their innovative ideas, assisted by a legal regime of patent and copyright protections designed to penalize usurpers. But because of the role that interaction plays in the innovating process, businesses operating in today's hyperconnected world find themselves in a kind of quandary. A business can elect either to:

1. earn a greater profit by keeping an innovation secret and maintaining (even for a short time) an edge over the competition, or

2. *share* its innovation with other firms or entities, losing its momentary competitive edge with respect to that product, but generating additional innovations faster.

The second option, called "free revealing," has become more and more attractive to businesses as new ideas have become more complex and intricately connected. Facebook announced in early 2011 that it would voluntarily reveal to everyone, including its own competitors, the formerly proprietary technical details of its highly efficient server installation just built in Prineville, Oregon. According to *The Wall Street Journal*, Facebook's servers have 38 percent more energy efficiency and operate some 24 percent more cost-efficiently than previous server designs, and the decision on Facebook's part "comes as power and energy consumption have emerged as key hurdles for many high-tech companies." But CEO Mark Zuckerberg maintains that by releasing such things as specifications for its battery backup system and even building design details, the company could facilitate collaboration in the overall data and IT industry, suggesting that "By sharing this, we will make it more efficient for this ecosystem to grow."

Similar reasons lie behind the 2011 decision by LexisNexis Risk Solutions, a part of Reed Elsevier, to freely reveal the software code for its high-performance computing cluster technology platform called HPCC Systems, which is now available as a dual-license, open-source big data processing platform. Other companies, including the firm's own competitors, now have access and can tinker with this highly sophisticated technology. However, the idea of granting competitors free access to such a valuable software tool doesn't bother the firm's management. According to James Peck, LexisNexis Risk Solutions CEO, "We've been doing this quietly for years for our customers with great success. We are now excited to present it to the community to spur greater adoption [and] further the development of the platform for the benefit of our customers and the community."

"Free revealing," of course, is at the very heart of social production—the free and unencumbered sharing of innovative ideas to generate some collective good. Social production is orchestrated by a community of individuals who come together for their own reasons, often to solve a problem or create some kind of valuable service, but usually not related to making a profit per se, and (as we said before) making a profit would actually be regarded as a violation of the e-social ethos that unites many such social enterprises.

However, when companies like Facebook or LexisNexis choose to share their formerly proprietary or competitively sensitive innovations through free revealing, they are in fact increasing the trust others have in them. By declaring themselves to be socially aware participants in a community, they can harness many of the benefits of social production themselves. And they're engaging with the community entirely through the mechanism of trust, in the same way other members of the community engage: You help me, I help you, and we don't try to "keep score" using a cash register.

In the end, no one really knows how things will sort out as the commercial economy is smashed together with the e-social ethos. But with all this power in the hands of regular folks, interconnected, we do need to ask ourselves: What happens to the power that has been wielded by heads of state and heads of companies? Heads of state met the Internet in the Arab Spring. Heads of companies are the subject of our next chapter.

TRUSTABILITY
TEST

Think about how you'd answer these questions based on how things work at your company, institution, or government agency. Talk about your answers with your colleagues. Visit www.trustability.com to see how other visitors' responses compare with your own for these and other questions.

▶ Has your company ever considered the possible benefits of making any of your intellectual property—including patents, copyrights, and proprietary information—more generally available to outsiders?

▶ Has your firm ever considered "free revealing" any aspect of the company's proprietary or confidential business processes or technologies?

    ▷ If it were to consider doing so, who at your firm would likely advocate in favor of it, who would be against it, and who would have the final decision?

▶ Are your company's lawyers familiar with the several different kinds of "Creative Commons" licenses governing the use and reuse of intellectual property?

▶ To the extent that your company sells or benefits from "content" (e.g., entertainment, music, news, or information rendered in print, audio, or video form), how easy is it for people to copy or pass it along to others? Is this an issue that would be dealt with by sales and marketing staff, customer service, legal staff, or someone else?

▶ In its marketing programs, does your company treat social media more as a channel for reaching customers and talking to them or as a mechanism for talking with customers and discussing issues?

▶ Do you have a social media policy that encourages, limits, or prohibits employees from participating, as employees? What other company social media policies have you reviewed, if any, in setting up your own?

▶ Does your company monitor Twitter, Facebook, and other social media platforms for mention of your company, your competitors, and your business category?

▷ What is the protocol when your company, your products, or your brands are mentioned?

▶ Have you identified the high-influence commentators in your business category—the people who blog and critique your brand, your business, and your competitors' brands? Do you reach out to them? How?

[6]

CONTROL IS NOT AN OPTION

Knock knock.

Who's there?

Control freak. And now YOU say "Control freak who?"

If a psychopath is someone who can't *be* trusted, then what do you call someone who can't *trust*? Control freak. Psychopaths and control freaks are flip sides of the same disorder. *Nobody* can trust a psychopath, and control freaks can't trust *anybody*. But e-social technologies raise the general standard of trustworthiness for all of us, no matter which side of the interaction we're on. Trustability is an incoming tide lifting all boats. It happens a little unevenly, perhaps, generating a few bumps and collisions here and there, but this incoming tide is driven by Moore's law, and no man can resist Moore's law.

Extending trust to others is a particularly scary idea for executives and managers, stirring up nightmares of cheating, disengaged employees and litigious customers. You can't take the "manage" out of "manager" without creating a feeling of insecurity. But inevitably, the power equation governing commercial transactions will be upended by this incoming tide. As transparency increases and customers know more and more, every advantage a business used to have as a result of one-sided information flow will evaporate. Companies can no longer control the knowledge that gets "out there."

In this chapter, we're going to suggest that business success in the transparent, trustable future is likely to depend just as much on extending trust to others as on being trustable yourself.

[The Illusion of Control]

Within the cacophony of hormones and emotions buffeting your brain whenever you think you're making a calculated judgment is a strong urge to remain "in control" at all times. Everyone feels this need. It's a survival instinct, and it can't be denied. If you aren't in control of yourself you aren't "you." Face it: "out of control" is not the way we want people to think of us.

As thinking creatures, we interpret the events we observe in a cause-and-effect way. Whenever we see something happen, our instinctive reaction is to search for the cause, and this is one way we satisfy our need to be in control—to understand the "why" behind our environment. Our natural thinking method involves recognizing patterns, and over the eons our ability to detect patterns has yielded distinct survival benefits. Imagine one of our Neolithic ancestors, hearing loud noises in the underbrush, which could indicate an approaching predator. Sometimes (perhaps the majority of times) these loud noises are actually caused by friendly animals or by the wind, but an ancestor who ducks at *all* noises probably will live to produce more offspring than one who occasionally fails to detect a genuine predator. In evolutionary terms, seeing a pattern when there really isn't one (a false positive) is more advantageous than not seeing a pattern when there really is one (a false negative).

An important role for superstitions, in fact, is to supply causes for otherwise inexplicable happenings. Ghosts, Friday the 13th, black cats, mental telepathy, miracles, numerology, tarot cards, or alien abductions can all be rallied to "explain" coincidences or incomprehensible events, and these explanations almost always defy scientific or logical reasoning. Even atheists have superstitions. In one 2002 survey of UK residents, while more than a third professed no belief in God, a majority still believed that "psychics have real powers."

In the 1970s a man won the Spanish lottery with a ticket he'd specifically chosen for its ending number of 48. Very proud of his "strategy" for winning, he explained: "I dreamed of the number 7 for seven straight nights, and 7 times 7 is 48."

As irrational or even preposterous as superstitious beliefs can be, they serve an important psychological purpose. Even the rituals we employ to deal with superstitions give us some comfort that we are in control, and this *illusion of control* is like a placebo that serves as "an immensely powerful mechanism to immunize against harm."

According to Steven Pinker, "People assume that the world has a causal texture—that its events can be explained by the world's very nature, rather than being just one damn thing after another. They also assume that things are laid out in space and time." Because this is the way our mind catalogues memories, this is not just how we see and remember the world, it's how we *predict* the world will be. It's how we form our beliefs.

But the world is inherently, marvelously, *not* predictable, and our talent for pattern recognition, despite its evolutionary advantages, can easily undermine our rationality and taint the way we interpret things. For one thing, human beings have something psychologists call a "self-serving bias," which blinds us to our own faults and thereby keeps us sane and functional. We assume that our successes are caused by our own superb capabilities, while we search for or make up external reasons for our failures, rather than confronting ourselves with the truth of our inadequacies. When people make decisions we agree with, they seem completely rational, while we often characterize decisions we disagree with as illogical or—well—"emotional," which is sometimes code for "crazy."

We adopt these views unconsciously and they protect our mental health, because the world is far too complex and irrational for any single mind to comprehend fully, but we must remain confident enough to continue functioning. Ironically, there is one group of people known to be much more accurate in their perceptions of themselves, in terms of their own limitations and flaws. In the words of one psychiatric researcher, "Their self-perceptions are more balanced, they assign responsibility for success and failure more even-handedly, and their predictions for the future are more realistic. These people are living testimony to the dangers of self-knowledge. They are the clinically depressed." (So yes, a supremely rational human being—one who is completely objective in his self-evaluation *and* motivated entirely by self-interest—would be a clinically depressed psychopath.)

The problem is, when we combine a self-serving bias with the illusion of control, what we get are people who are confident that their own efforts can bring about positive results, even though in many situations this feeling is incorrect and leads to bad decisions. One social experiment, for instance, asked Wall Street traders to try to "control" a flashing light that was actually random. As reported by Cordelia Fine,

> *Interestingly, the statistics showed that the more arrogant the trader was about his influence on the computer task, the less he earned on the trading floor. According to the researchers' analyses, traders with a high score on the illusion of control scale earned about $100,000 per annum less than traders with only an average score.*

Because we believe we're in control even when we aren't, most managers believe the effects they generate through their own actions are greater than they really are.

> Almost 90 percent of chief marketing officers believe that customers trust their own company's brand as much as or more than they trust competitors' brands!

But just because *we* believe our brand is trustworthy doesn't mean our customers do. Not that we don't try to convince ourselves. Another human thinking flaw is "hindsight bias," which is our tendency to see events in retrospect as more predictable than they actually were (related to seeing everything in cause-and-effect terms). As one wag suggested, "Any event, once it has occurred, can be made to appear inevitable by a competent historian." Hindsight bias obstructs our ability to evaluate an executive's performance or to fairly critique any management strategy or practice. And nowhere is it more on display than when we provide praise and awards to companies, stock pickers, and others for past accomplishments. Management gurus tend to heap praise on companies that have already performed well, when what gurus ought to do (if they are really gurus) is *predict* which companies are likely to do well in the future. And be proven right.

Or consider the praise heaped on Bill Miller's Legg Mason Capital Management Value Trust fund, which outperformed the Standard & Poor's 500 index fifteen years in a row, from 1991 through 2005. A *Wall Street Journal* story suggested that the odds of any fund manager beating the S&P fifteen years in a row were about 250,000 to 1 (like getting heads on fifteen consecutive coin tosses). Morningstar named Miller "Fund Manager of the Decade," and *Money* called him "The Greatest Money Manager of the 1990's." But this is just hindsight bias, aided and abetted by a poor intuitive grasp of statistics. In actuality, out of roughly one thousand fund managers tracked over a forty-year period, the probability that *purely by chance* at least one of them would beat the S&P every year over some fifteen-year period is about 75 percent. Had Miller been celebrated at the beginning of the 1990s for what was about to happen, then it would have been justified, but *after* it happened, it was just another bogus cause-and-effect story. And sure enough, immediately following the celebrations, the Value Trust fund fell from grace. Regression to the mean is a powerful attractor.

One of the principal benefits of truly enjoying the trust of customers is that executives will be able to deal more rationally and purposefully with those random fluctuations in every company's financial fortunes that would otherwise tend to throw a management team off its game. Trust is a *long-term* quality, conferring *long-term* financial benefits. When you focus on earning and keeping the trust of customers you are inherently focusing more on long-term value creation, so you will be less likely to fall victim to the same self-serving, retrospectively obvious biases that afflict all short-term management decisions. People are human. *You* are human. But this doesn't mean you shouldn't at least be aware of your own human weaknesses.

[Credit Cards, Biases, and Trustability]

Over the years, companies and salespeople have learned how to employ human biases to achieve their own goals, and the results usually involve exploiting customers. In his groundbreaking 1984 classic *Influence: The Psychology of Persuasion,* Robert Cialdini categorized six different psychological methods that salespeople use to persuade customers to part with their money. Exploiting customers' emotions and biases is easier in a less transparent world because the flow of information favors the company, not the customer.

But as the world becomes increasingly more transparent, trustable companies will be careful to watch out for their customers' genuine self-interest, rather than simply exploiting their emotional needs. A company that is proactively trustworthy will find ways to use customers' natural biases to work *for* them—to improve their lives or better solve their problems.

Consider how credit card companies operate. It's well known that one of the secrets to every credit card's success is the natural bias we credit card users all have toward short-term, instant gratification, as opposed to the long-term, steady accumulation of savings. As we saw in chapter 3, it was partly our inherent bias toward short-termism that led to the financial crisis of 2008. Credit card companies* make money largely by catering to this bias. Two MIT professors, for instance, once conducted an auction

---

*By "credit card companies" we mean not just banks and financial institutions, but also all the stores and other companies that issue credit cards for their own customers.

of Boston Celtics tickets as a social experiment, telling half the participants that they had to pay with cash, and the other half that they had to pay with credit cards. After averaging the bids for the two groups, they found that the average credit card bid was *twice as high* as the average cash bid!

Obviously, it's in no customer's interest to fall victim to irrational short-term thinking, although the traditional credit card business model is based on the fact that many customers will. In fact, the *least* profitable type of credit card customer to have is one who pays her bill off every month and never incurs a late fee, which is why, as we said in chapter 1, credit card companies refer to such customers as "deadbeats."

But if a credit card company were actually trustable, how would it operate? What would a proactively trustworthy credit card be like? For one thing, rather than encouraging spending and borrowing, a trustable credit card would counsel its customers to spend wisely and use the card prudently. (Think of the utility company urging you to turn off the lights or adjust the thermostat when you leave the house, for instance.) It would provide incentives for customers to pay off their balances, perhaps reducing the interest rate applied when a balance is reduced. Such a company would be careful not to earn too much of its profit from late fees, which would indicate a flaw in the business model; in fact, it might provide extra incentives for on-time payments.

Imagine being offered a credit card by a highly trustable issuer. Rather than exploiting your instant-gratification bias, such a trustable credit card might even use this bias to craft an incentive to promote more long-term saving. For instance, it could offer you a savings account fed by an extra charge applied each month to your bill, so that the more you spend in the present, the more you save for the future. What if, for every dollar you charged on your card, five cents went into a savings account (or you could specify some other amount)?

To help you rein in your own spendthrift ways a trustable credit card company might ask you to set a monthly spending budget, and then text you during the month to keep you apprised as you "use it up." If you get to the middle of the month and you've already spent more than your planned budget allows, at least you'd know.

To operate in this way, a credit card company would have to make some changes to its business model. There is a lot of short-term profit to be made by encouraging consumers to borrow and spend, regardless of their own interests, so a trustable credit card issuer wanting to remain in business must figure out how to make money from more customer-friendly activities. Discover's Motiva Card, for instance, allocates some of its "cash back" rewards program to an incentive for simply paying each month's bill on time.

As far as we know, there are today no fully trustable credit card companies like the one we've just described. We predict there will be, sooner or later, because rising levels of transparency make it virtually inevitable that some credit card company somewhere *will* find a way to turn trustability into a competitive advantage. And once that happens, other credit card issuers will have to figure out how to offer a similar level of proactive trustworthiness—of *trustability*.

[Social Relationships, Cocktail Parties, and Systems]

While the illusion of control and all our other natural biases already make it tricky to manage social relationships, things are about to get even dicier as people become more efficiently interconnected. Connections between people create feedback loops. Feedback loops create complex systems. And complex systems aren't predictable.

We've heard experts use a cocktail party as an analogy for the e-social phenomenon, and it's not a bad place to start. At a cocktail party some guests are more active than others, initiating many of the conversations while others congregate around them, and still others—the majority—mostly just watch and listen. Good conversations at a party are free-wheeling and spontaneous, going in different directions depending on the varied interests and energies of the participants and interventions of the host or hostess, if there is one. And even though someone might not talk much at a party, it doesn't mean they didn't enjoy it.

People interacting with other people constitute a "complex system" of individual participants. Whether it's a party or an online social network, a complex system is more than the sum of its parts, with behavior driven by both positive and negative feedback loops, and the overall result is often difficult or impossible to predict. When a school of fish turns in unison, or when an economy's numbers cycle up or down—these are the things we observe a system doing, but it is virtually impossible to know how quickly or sharply such turns will happen. *The Wall Street Journal* once reviewed its own surveys of top economists' predictions since 1982, for instance, and found that the average "expert" correctly predicted the *direction* of interest rates (forget the magnitude) just 22 percent of the time, which is considerably less accurate than a coin toss!

The problem with trying to *manage* a system (such as, for example, a social network) is that the feedback loops keeping it stable and resilient over time will behave according to their own invisible logic. Think about a spinning top, for instance. This is a system under all sorts of hidden influences, including angular momentum and inertia, and these influences interact with one another in a variety of counterintuitive ways. Every grade-school science student knows that if you push on the upper part of a spinning top it will move sideways, rather than in the direction you push it, because of the way these forces operate on the overall system. Like pushing on a spinning top, efforts to direct a system's behavior are prone to failure, because the system's own feedback loops generate unintended consequences.

Negative feedback loops put a damper on things. Your thermostat turns the furnace off in the winter once the room temperature has climbed to a certain level. Other examples of negative feedback include many of the unintended consequences of policy actions. We might try to reduce the supply of illegal drugs by raising the penalty for selling them, but raising the penalty increases their price on the street, which makes drug dealing more attractive. Or we could add more lanes to a highway to relieve congestion, but this means that houses built along that highway will be more attractive to own, so construction on more new houses will start as soon as the lane additions are planned. In a social network, when someone posts a biased or inaccurate article on Wikipedia, someone else is likely to make a correction in it or delete it altogether.

Positive feedback loops drive a system's behavior in the other way, re-inforcing outcomes rather than confounding them. In the real estate market, because a house is valuable it qualifies for a higher mortgage, but because it qualifies for a higher mortgage, it becomes still more valuable. Or in social networks, positive feedback creates a cascading effect so that when someone's opinions are well thought of, others rate them highly, they become even more well thought of, and others rate them highly again. In stock market bubbles, higher stock prices beget even higher stock prices.

The interaction between negative and positive feedback loops in a complex system can easily make the system's overall behavior virtually unpredictable. A system might generate a steady and predictable rate of activity, or it could be characterized by moderate oscillations up and down, or even wild and unpredictable swings back and forth and every which way. Outcomes like this defy our human intuition. A spinning top shouldn't move sideways to our push—should it? Effects must have causes, so we look for the reasons behind a system's up or down movement. How many times have you heard, for instance, that some daily fluctuation in the stock market could be "explained" by a newly released economic report or a particular company's profit announcement? But simulation studies have conclusively demonstrated that sometimes a stock market will go up and down in cycles without any outside influence at all! Its systemic behavior is to oscillate. This doesn't mean economic news doesn't affect a market's behavior, of course, but even without any news at all it will still oscillate, because that's just what a stock market does, in the same way that heavy traffic will speed up and slow down on the interstate even when there are no accidents or other obvious blockages.

Although we might accept the fundamental inevitability of a system's erratic behavior, we still look for patterns in its oscillations. We're human beings, so that's what we do, look for patterns. And indeed, relying on modern computer simulations of complex systems, it isn't all that difficult to find such patterns, involving power laws, recursive growth, fractals, Feigenbaum's constant, and the Fibonacci series. Finding such patterns, however, is not the same as making useful predictions with regard to a system's future behavior. In her book *Thinking in Systems*, Donella Meadows warned:

> *People who are raised in the industrial world and who get enthused about systems thinking are likely to make a terrible mistake. They are likely to assume that here, in systems analysis, in interconnection and complication, in the power of the computer, here at last, is the key to prediction and control. This mistake is likely because* the mind-set of the industrial world assumes that there is a key to prediction and control.

Managers assume there is a key to prediction and control because in many of the "manageable" situations they encounter, there is. Engineers solve problems with mathematical certainty, while financial analysts calculate values, tabulate costs, and predict sales trends with a reasonable amount of confidence. And whenever we are dealing with groups of isolated, individual customers—members of a statistical population whose past behaviors and transactions have been tracked and analyzed—it is quite possible to make decently usable predictions about trends and probabilities. It isn't hard to infer from certain usage patterns that a particular type of grocery customer prefers premium brands, while a different type prefers generic brands. Nor is it difficult to predict that increasing the ad budget by *a* will generate *b* more impressions, or that boosting a discount by *x* will increase sales by *y*, or that because of his usage pattern a certain mobile phone customer is 75 percent more likely to defect in the next three months than other customers.

So when we are confronted with an economic cycle or a pattern of sentiment in a social network, we want to take it apart, look at the individual components of the system, and try to figure it out. In 2007, researchers for *The Wall Street Journal* analyzed 25,000 user contributions at six large sharing-and-collaboration Web sites. What they found in each network was that a very small number of participants commanded extremely high levels of influence. Of Netscape's million-plus users, for instance, 13 percent of the postings rated "most popular" came from a single one. And of the 900,000 users of Digg, a third of the contributions rated highly enough to make it to the home page came from just 30. The newspaper's researchers decided to track down one of Reddit's most widely read users, a blogger named Adam Fuhrer, in order to figure out why his opinions on software and legal issues had been so widely praised by other users. What they found was that Adam was twelve years old, and lived with his parents in Toronto.

Now here's the thing: if you were to come to us and ask us to find the next Adam Fuhrer—*that's a completely impossible task.* That would be like asking us to predict whether it will rain in Dubuque on May 12 next year, or at what instant a school of fish will turn in unison. Such problems are "uncomputable"—meaning not just that they can't be solved with the computer power available, but that they can *never* be solved even with all the computing power in the universe.

On the other hand, we can say with a fair degree of confidence that there *will* be another Adam Fuhrer, just as there *will* be a few highly influential participants in every other social network, and it *will* rain in Dubuque sooner or later, and sooner or later a school of fish will turn. That much is predictable.

This is difficult for many managers to accept. Traditional business, after all, is a *discipline;* it's not a social conversation. And the discipline of marketing, specifically, is a manageable thing. It could never reasonably be compared to a cocktail party, or to a freewheeling discussion among many different participants. Because social interactions are *social,* involving each participant's awareness of and reaction to the actions of other participants, the feedback loops themselves subvert most efforts to impose control, or to manage the system.

Statistical data from a population of independent customers can be used to generate decent predictions, *but the more those customers interact with one another,* the less predictable their behavior is likely to be. Like drips from a slowly leaking faucet, or thunderclouds gathering on the horizon, cascades of opinion and sentiment in a social group are certain to occur from time to time, but their timing and magnitude are impossible to predict.

It is in the nature of electronically transmitted word-of-mouth opinions that the system's feedback loops are prone to generating very significant, very rapid, and completely unpredictable waves of sentiment— oscillations that can't be foreseen, and that can spring to life in days, or even hours. In an interconnected complex system, once the feedback loops kick in, the whole system can be off to the races in an instant. Or not. But the implication is that if you don't pay attention to what is being said about your company, your brand, or your product on a more or less continual, real-time basis, then you will always be at the mercy of the e-social system's e-capriciousness.

Late in 2008 the Motrin brand of painkiller (owned by a division of Johnson & Johnson) launched an ad campaign showing mothers with their babies in slings, and suggesting that the sling was something like a fashion accessory. Toting a baby can be hard work, but the sling "totally makes me look like an official mom" is the way one ad put it. The ads were launched on September 30, and ran for weeks before some mothers began to take offense at what they regarded as an insult. Babies aren't fashion accessories, and motherhood shouldn't be trivialized. Perhaps because many of the offended mothers were using Twitter's microblogging service rather than Facebook or some other vehicle (Twitter being a relatively new service at the time), once negative sentiment reached some critical mass it boiled over quite suddenly, all on one November weekend. As social media commentators Darren Barefoot and Julie Szabo tell the story:

> *All hell broke loose on Friday night, after marketing departments had gone home for the weekend. Oh, what a Monday was in store for them! On the Web, 48 hours is an eternity, and by Sunday night, news of the Motrin ad was everywhere, along with plenty of speculation about whether Motrin would respond, apologize, or even set up a crisis blog. So much damage was done in just two days that not only did Motrin take down the video and pull the print ad, but also the company begged forgiveness from the army of mommy bloggers calling for its head.*

In the end, the company posted an official apology on its Web site from the marketing vice president, and this apology spread nearly as quickly as the original controversy had flared up. (Barefoot and Szabo helpfully suggest, however, that Motrin's online apology would have spread even more rapidly had it been rendered in text on the Web site rather than as a graphic, which made it more difficult for bloggers and online media to pass it along to others. Nice tip here from the social media culture to the rest of us!)

[Staples Sees a Good Program Die, Defeated (Mostly) by Chance]

Random, unpredictable fluctuations in the blogosphere can trip up even the best efforts of managers to generate value with customer referrals or word-of-mouth marketing. It's one thing to host honest customer reviews on your own Web site, but it's another thing entirely to encourage customers to recommend your product to others, no matter how good your product is. Even the best, most carefully constructed word-of-mouth marketing programs can be difficult to implement, because cascades of opinion, critical or not, can appear suddenly and unpredictably.

The office-supplies retail chain Staples launched a word-of-mouth initiative called "Speak Easy" a few years ago. Speak Easy was designed to encourage the company's most valuable customers to spread the word among their colleagues and associates about the benefits of various Staples products. Staples used the shopping records from its loyalty card program to identify its most frequent, high-spending customers and invite them to join Speak Easy, and then each month the firm would send a package of free product samples to those who had signed up. Included in each customer's shipment was a write-up of talking points touting the benefits of various products, and Staples hoped that these benefits would find their way into whatever conversation about a product a program member might occasionally have with others.

That was as intrusive as it was, however, and there was no follow-up by the company to see whether any recommendations were ever made.

Other than the free samples themselves, Staples gave no additional compensation or benefit to program members, nor did it attempt to track whether customers actually recommended the products or not. So on the surface, in other words, Staples seemed to have designed a very customer-friendly program. From a privacy and sharing standpoint, at least, the company did nothing wrong. There were no commercial incentives, there was no violation of the sharing ethos, and no unseemly spying on customers.

Despite this careful, trust-based architecture, however, the Speak Easy program soon became the subject of controversy on a number of customer blog sites and in the press, with one newspaper article labeling it "a stealth—some would say sneaky—marketing program." And sure enough, interest fell and Speak Easy was soon canceled.

In retrospect, however, it could just as easily have gone the other way. Other companies had launched word-of-mouth programs with less care, and with no outcry, and the cascade of opinion that felled Speak Easy seemed capricious. So what could Staples have done differently to increase its chance of success with Speak Easy? Actually, quite a lot. Stay tuned, and we'll come back to this story before the end of the chapter.

[Unarmed, Nestlé Fights a Battle of Wits with Greenpeace]

Like a bad habit, the *urge to control* continues to plague many companies' efforts to participate in the increasingly robust network of e-social connections now available. Things seemed to be going smoothly for Nestlé and its Facebook fan page right up to early 2010, when a Greenpeace initiative turned Nestlé's own fans' conversation against the company. In a campaign to get Nestlé to stop using palm oil in its products, contending that it was damaging the environment, Greenpeace used Facebook to organize support. They rebranded the Nestlé Kit Kat bar with a faux "Killer" bar logo, and posted a video on YouTube disparaging Nestlé's practices.

The first reaction on the part of Nestlé's public relations and marketing staff was to try to *control* this unruly and threatening discussion. The company contacted YouTube to have the video taken down on the grounds that the made-up logo violated Nestlé's trademark, but of course the video had already been widely circulated on the 'net, and people could still find it easily on other sites like Vimeo. (The pee, so to speak, was already in the swimming pool.)

For Nestlé, it all went predictably downhill from there. Some of the company's Facebook fans began posting comments promoting the Greenpeace video and urging others to get onboard the campaign to pressure Nestlé to stop harvesting palm oil. Other fans designed their own unflattering modifications to Nestlé's logo. The hapless control freaks at Nestlé tried to stifle the discussion with an escalating series of actions that, in retrospect, appear naïve and petty. They deleted some critical comments posted by customers on their Facebook fan page (like maybe people wouldn't notice?) and they even began pointing out spelling and grammar errors in some of their critics' messages. This of course only stirred the embers of the smoldering Greenpeace issue into a roaring inferno, converting what might once have been a customer-engagement opportunity into a five-alarm PR disaster.

As the inferno blazed higher, it made the leap into mainstream media as well, and Nestlé's resistance to Greenpeace's demand was soon overwhelmed by public pressure. Within days, the company announced it would no longer use palm oil. But from Nestlé's actions it was obvious that the marketing types—or at least the folks in charge of the social media effort—failed to realize until late in the episode that *control was not an option*.

> You can't solve a social media problem by throwing lawyers at it.

If you create a Facebook fan page to showcase your brand and to generate discussion among your most valuable and involved customers, then your first impulse as a manager is to *control* the operation to ensure everything is displayed just right, in the same way you would handle an ad campaign or a press release. In the end, Nestlé's mistake with its Facebook fan page was similar to Walmart's with its blog. Brands and marketing messages have always originated with the marketer, and a conscientious marketer has always made it her business to ensure that the brand is well taken care of. After all, that's why we call it brand "management."

But as Randall Rothenberg, former advertising columnist for *The New York Times* and current president of the Interactive Advertising Bureau trade group, has said, "Conversations cannot be controlled. They can only be joined." If you want to engage customers in interactive conversation, you simply can't monopolize the discussion. It would no longer be a discussion; it would be a "speech." And you certainly can't resort to brute force. Imagine trying to settle a disagreement at a cocktail party by having your lawyers eject the other person from the premises!

Nestlé's story will now achieve immortality on the 'net, haunting the company forever, and we hope business school professors will use it as a case study in how *not* to deal with the new power of consumers. (Unfortunately, it's one of many such case studies now available.) But could Nestlé have obtained a better outcome by doing things differently? Stay tuned . . .

[Facebook Learns the Hard Way]

Facebook, of course, is the five-hundred-pound gorilla of social media. Some 35 percent of the entire U.S. population logs on to Facebook, as do more than 30 percent of the populations of sixteen other countries. More than half a billion users around the world spend an average of an *hour every day* on Facebook. As mighty as it has become, however, even Facebook had to learn how to let go of the urge to try to control the conversation, and it took several attempts before they figured it out. In a series of events from 2006 to 2009, Facebook found it simply could not "control" its own business. Instead, that control belonged with the users themselves.

In 2006 Facebook introduced its "News Feed" feature to the 9.4 million users it had accumulated by then. Up to that time, members wanting to find out how their friends were doing had to visit each friend's individual profile, one at a time, and simply eyeball it for any changes— did their relationship status change? Did they go to an event without telling me? Do we have a new friend in common I didn't know about before? So the Facebook team created News Feed to push relevant updates out to friends. Using a sophisticated set of algorithms to decide which status changes would be most interesting or relevant to which friends, News Feed was designed to take the pain out of the process of having to click through profile after profile just to keep up.

When the company launched the service, however, the overwhelming majority of users objected to it immediately. The very first message posted, in fact, was "Turn this shit OFF!" and only 1 percent of user messages were positive. As negative sentiment continued to build, users organized themselves into about five hundred different Facebook groups with angry names like "THIS NEW FACEBOOK SET-UP SUCKS!!!," "Chuck Norris come save us from the Facebook news feed!," and "news feed is a chump dick wuss douchebag asshole prick cheater bitch." In just seventy-two hours, the biggest anti–News Feed group, "Students Against Facebook news feed," had grown to 750,000 members, and altogether some 10 percent of the company's entire member base chose to join one or more of these groups. (It was deeply ironic, of course, that all these user groups were able to find out about each other and mobilize themselves by using Facebook's News Feed!)

The company's first reaction was to attempt to quell objections and *control* the situation. About twenty-four hours after News Feed had launched, CEO Mark Zuckerberg described News Feed's benefits in a blog post headlined "Calm Down. Breathe. We Hear You." Trying to reason with the mob, he said everything in News Feed was already available to a member's friends anyway; it was all information people used to have to spend time digging out. But the protest grew, spilling into other media, and two days later Zuckerberg was more or less forced to post another blog entry, this time acceding to the crowd's demands: "We did a bad job of explaining what the new features were and an even worse job of giving you control of them . . . We didn't build in the proper privacy controls right away. This was a big mistake on our part, and I'm sorry for it." It was only when Zuckerberg apologized and *gave up control* to his members that the disturbance died down. News Feed was withdrawn and re-launched later, with upgraded privacy controls.

In late 2007, Facebook made a similar mistake, this time with its Beacon advertising product. By now Facebook had grown to almost 60 million users, but 68,000 of them (just 0.1 percent of the total) joined a group protesting the new product, and after three weeks Facebook again had to withdraw the service, incorporating a few of its features in Facebook Connect when it was launched later. And in early 2009 another firestorm erupted when Facebook's legal department introduced a seemingly innocuous redesign of the "terms of service" on its site. In three days, a group calling itself "People Against the New Terms of Service" had accumulated 100,000 members. This time, however, Zuckerberg immediately announced that Facebook would revert to the old terms of service, then invited members to join a newly formed group to have a discussion on what the revised terms of service ought to say, promising a member vote to approve the new rules. This, of course, immediately ended the controversy.

[What Could Companies Learn from Facebook's Experience?]

Facebook has spent the last several years learning important lessons about how to survive and prosper in the e-social environment. The crowd always wins, so work with the crowd, not against it. Apologize for mistakes. Be honest. Sentiment can build suddenly, so be flexible and respond immediately.

These lessons could benefit any business now trying to stick its toes into the e-social realm, whether grappling with a social-media-fueled PR problem, trying to stimulate word-of-mouth references, or simply trying to improve its brand reputation among customers.

What Could Staples Have Done Differently? Let's revisit the Staples Speak Easy customer word-of-mouth program. Once the program itself became public, there was no way for Staples to have derailed the negative press coverage. A few early descriptions of the program in blogs and in some of the mainstream media developed their own cascading effects in the e-social conversation about the program, and *this was entirely out of Staples' control.* However, knowing what we know now about how social media systems are prone to these cascades of opinion and complicated feedback loops, could the company have done anything differently *before* it launched the program, in order to increase the chances that the program would succeed?

First, recognize that success for such a program will only come if the company has the good wishes and support of its very best customers. In fact, a word-of-mouth program's success really depends on Staples' best customers taking ownership of it. So rather than interviews or focus groups with a few high-value customers to assess their likely interest in the program as it was envisioned by Staples, the company should have actively recruited a cadre of customers to *design and create* the actual program.

A customer-designed Speak Easy might or might not have had an architecture similar to the program actually launched, but it would have had one critical feature the actual program lacked: shared parentage. If

Staples really wanted to invest in interactive dialogues with customers—if it really wanted to *join* and *participate* in the conversation rather than *control* the conversation—then it should have asked its own customers to help it figure out what to do, and then should have done it. If this had been the company's path, then when the first negative blog posts or news articles appeared, it might have been Staples' customers themselves who defended the program, because they would have been the ones who created it in the first place.

But it's not enough to get just any high-value customers involved. The customers taking ownership of the program would have had to have been well connected and influential in the beginning, already enjoying the respect of other customers. They should have been customers with networks of friends or colleagues connected to other networks. The company might have recruited a few active small-business bloggers, for instance, and maybe a few other opinion leaders to help them set up the program. (And to influence these influencers, Staples could have followed the "ARIA" principles outlined in chapter 5.)

Importantly, however, the reason high-influence customers have influence isn't because they make product recommendations, but because other customers see them to be helpful, and they aren't going to team up willingly with any company that doesn't help them continue in this role. So before Staples could have recruited any high-influence customers, it would have had to prove itself worthy, by demonstrating its *trustability*. High-influence customers can't be expected to rely on Staples as a resource for their friends and followers unless the company helps them continue to solve problems and meet needs, and this means the company has to act in the interests of its customers. For a word-of-mouth program to succeed, these high-influence customers must *want* the company to prosper because that would be a benefit to their own constituents.

So the question is, did Staples have enough trustability? Sadly, no. Don't get us wrong. Staples' stores are clean, its prices are fair, and its service is good enough, but the company offers very little to customers other than an assortment of retail products, priced and arranged, commodity-like, in convenient rows. The truth is, no one would really mourn Staples' departure from this world as long as Office Depot or OfficeMax or some other competitor remained to fill the void.

So the question is, what could Staples have done to build up its trustability in advance? Well, lots of things, actually. As a well-known retailer of office supplies it could easily have leveraged its reputation to offer services, assistance, advice, and business counsel to customers. What if, *prior* to trying to launch the word-of-mouth campaign, Staples had offered services on its Web site to help business owners and business product buyers better meet their needs? For instance, its site could have offered:

- Customer reviews and ratings of all the various products Staples carries, with the company playing a role as curator and authenticator.

- Different discussion groups for small businesses, for large enterprise office managers, government organizations, and nonprofits—so that Staples' different types of customers could find and communicate with others who have similar problems and needs.

- Advice and tips on how to manage your inventory of office products and supplies, from paper and envelopes to desk chairs, pens, laptops, and printer cartridges. Some of this advice should be from other customers, so the company should reach out to solicit comments.

- Office supply inventory management tools and other applications designed to reduce costs.

- Ways to set up auto-replenishment or other enhanced delivery options, such as proactive reminders of exactly which ink cartridges will be needed, and when.

The point is that if Staples had developed a reputation as a trustable firm genuinely trying to *help* its retail customers, rather than simply selling to them, then not only would high-influence customers have been easy to recruit, but many of them would have *wanted* Staples to succeed, because the company had so much to offer in terms of helping business owners, office managers, and other professionals.

What Could Nestlé Have Done Differently? Nestlé's whole Kit Kat brouhaha took place on the company's own Facebook *fan page*, for heaven's sake—an online space specifically designed for the brand's best and most loyal customers. Gee, isn't it puzzling why a few more of these customers didn't come to the company's defense?

First, of course, we should recognize that the Greenpeace assault was an unpredictable event. Greenpeace just happened to pick Nestlé for this particular issue, but there are many other firms out there guilty (in Greenpeace's opinion anyway) of egregious antienvironment policies. Certainly there are a lot of companies that use palm oil. It could have been any company, but in this case it was Nestlé.

Nevertheless, once the crowd was mobilized, Nestlé should have recognized that the argument was almost certainly lost, at least on the PR front. This doesn't mean the crowd was right; it just means the crowd was more powerful, and sooner or later it would likely prevail. So rather than trying to "control" the discussion to avert this nearly inevitable outcome, what if Nestlé had reached out to the ones most invested in the movement? Since the argument was lost anyway, there would have been little downside for Nestlé if it had announced a temporary moratorium on palm oil use, for instance. Coupled with an appropriate corporate acknowledgment and apology, this action might have been seen as a peace offering, taking much of the wind out of the other side's sails. (An immediate moratorium without an apology, on the other hand, might have been taken as a sign of weakness and an invitation to further activism. We'll talk more about the power of apologizing and showing your vulnerability in chapter 7.)

This might have quelled the uproar at least long enough for Nestlé to have begun engaging its actively interested customers in a dialogue to consider more carefully both the science and the economics behind the issue. When Facebook allowed its own users to rewrite and then vote on the company's terms of service, the new policy still met virtually all the requirements Facebook had started with. Nestlé's situation would have been a bit different, because the issues involved in the use of palm oil probably involve complex technical and engineering details that might have been more difficult for many people to grasp than the more straight-forward requirements surrounding Facebook's legal exposure, but just making the effort to have a rational discussion would have been benefi-cial. And who knows what a crowd of "fans" might have come up with, anyway? It's possible someone would have proposed something quite novel or useful—but of course Nestlé will never find out now.

Rather than deleting comments it considered too critical, Nestlé could have actively engaged in the conversation. It didn't have to be con-trite or servile or defensive—just authentic. It could have earned credi-bility by publicizing the most useful or thoughtful posts, on both sides of the argument, perhaps even engaging one or two of its adversary cus-tomers to help curate a more objective, and less strident, discussion.

The problem with all this, of course, is almost identical to the prob-lem that Staples had. Did Nestlé actually enjoy enough *trustability* with its customers to be taken seriously if it were to try to initiate such dia-logues? And again, the answer is no.

In order for Nestlé to have had any traction at all in this e-social con-versation, it would have had to establish its trustability with customers in advance. Every participant in the discussion, of course, would have known full well that Nestlé's own business interests were at stake. No one would have trusted what the company said unless it had a reputation for trustability. But it didn't.

We're not suggesting that Nestlé is a bad company. Far from it. Nestlé is a highly regarded brand, a brand with a great "reputation." But the company just hasn't invested much time or effort in improving its trust-ability among consumers. Likability, yes—quality, yes—familiarity, of course—popularity even. But authenticity? Transparency? Trustability? No. A brand can be *good*, in the old-school sense of brand equity and top-of-mind recall, but this doesn't necessarily mean it is *trustable*.

So what kinds of things could Nestlé have done to build its trustabil-ity in advance of this controversy? It would have boiled down to getting on the customer's side of the product, rather than on the company's side. What are the needs that customers are meeting with Nestlé's products? And how can Nestlé do a better job engaging with customers as they try to meet these needs? Of course, the Greenpeace controversy was all about chocolate, but Nestlé's brands include a wide variety of other things as well, including pet products, baby food, ice cream, and even weight management services. It may not be office supply inventories and business problem solving, but there's still a lot to work with. So what if Nestlé's consumer Web site had included:

- Diet guidelines that objectively compare Nestlé's chocolate products to other brands, in terms of calorie and fat content.

- Encouragement to parents and children to make chocolate the sweet treat part of a nutritional diet, along the lines of "Drink responsibly."

- Recipes, cooking guides, and how-to pages, with customer contributions incentivized.

- Chocolate stories and videos, with contests for the most creative or entertaining.

- Taste tests and recipe contests: try out different formulas of Nestlé with and without palm oil, live—in real time—for example, to show the progress that Nestlé is making toward a healthier and more responsible—and still delicious—chocolate.

- Social responsibility discussion groups, emphasizing environmental issues in advance.

Coordinating any kind of "quick response" at a company as large and complex as Nestlé is extremely difficult. Imagine just making the decision to eliminate the use of palm oil, for instance; it would certainly be as complicated as making a pencil. And one of the biggest learnings for many companies, when they begin a "listening" program to monitor problems involving their brand on Twitter, Facebook, and other social media platforms, is that just trying to identify who within a large corporation has actual responsibility for a problem can often be mind-numbingly difficult.

For example, in 2008 Frank Eliason helped launch the widely celebrated Comcast Cares program, an initiative designed to allow the giant cable company to identify customer problems and complaints by monitoring Twitter and other social media and microblogging sites. By scanning constantly for mentions of the Comcast name (and other, related monikers), Eliason and his team were able to pick up budding complaints, usually before they were called in to the contact center or escalated into more serious issues. Although responding quickly and honestly to complainers went a long way toward defusing bad situations, Frank told us that his team seemed to spend the majority of its time (90 percent, he estimated) just trying to determine who, within the broader Comcast network of companies, operating units, and subsidiaries, was actually "in charge" of whatever process had given rise to each customer problem identified.

Regardless of the difficulty, however, it's important to make decisions of this kind quickly, when necessary, if you want to be able to show a genuinely "human face" to customers. If you act slowly you'll look like a bureaucracy or—worse—a psychopath. So unless you want every such crisis escalated immediately to the CEO suite, we suggest you might want to consider running the same kinds of "fire drills" for social media problems that many companies already run for other PR-type problems. As one commentator suggested:

> *A major area where social media crises differ from "real world" crises (although one often begets the other now), is that most companies have not yet identified their communication protocols. If something unfortunate happens to your brand in social media, who in your company is in charge of identifying the problem? Who do they call? Who needs to be alerted? The same way most companies have call lists and alert procedures determined for offline crises, you must develop similar processes for social media.*

If Nestlé had worked in advance to improve its trustability with customers, and then run just a few fire drills in advance of the Greenpeace assault to prepare for the possibility of such events, the company might have been able to come out of the crisis with its brand reputation intact.

[How Employee Autonomy Builds Trustability]

"Division of labor," as an economic concept, generates benefits by allowing a business or other organization to break complex tasks down into steps that can be carried out by different people, or automated by machine. When making a pencil, some people cut the wood while others mine the graphite. Carried to its logical extreme, however, division of labor has a dark side as well. Frederick Taylor's landmark theory of "scientific management" was famous for its controversial contention that the best laborer would be a tireless and unthinking automaton—someone who never questions orders, only follows them. And Henry Ford once complained, "Why is it when I need a pair of hands, I have to get the whole man as well?"

Enter Stage Left: Karl Marx. Marxist theory is based on the idea that specialized, repetitive work is inherently alienating to people. It separates workers not just from the completed products they are assembling, but from themselves and from their essence as human beings as well. Today, rather than alienated, we would say such workers are "actively disengaged."* They might be listening to their iPods but they aren't tuned in to their employers.

When technology is used more thoughtfully, on the other hand, it allows us to reintegrate the mechanical tasks assigned to individual peo-

---

*"Employee engagement" is one of those fashionable management terms that can have a range of exact meanings, but Hay Group defines it as "a result achieved by stimulating employees' enthusiasm for their work and directing it toward organizational success." This definition is from "Beyond Employee Engagement: Motivating and Enabling Individual and Team Performance," a presentation by Mark Royal, Senior Consultant, Hay Group Insight, and Tom Agnew, Senior Consultant, Hay Group Insight, delivered as a Webinar, October 25, 2006.

ple, engaging them in their work and improving their enthusiasm and output simultaneously. When a customer service representative is allowed to handle a complaint as a "case" to be tracked from first call to final resolution, for instance, or when a line engineer at an automobile assembly plant suggests a better way to handle a technical support process—these are both examples of how labor is being reintegrated. Information technology and electronic connections are the tools that make this possible, but managers also have to be willing to let go of the control they used to exercise on the factory floor.

Charlene Li suggests that one powerful way to generate a more engaging "culture of sharing" at a firm is to grant customers and other key stakeholders access to your data. For many marketers, schooled in the principle that information is king, the idea of allowing outsiders to gain access to corporate information is not an option that would ever be seriously considered. But according to Li, nearly every company has, somewhere within it, "a rich warehouse of data that could be of interest and benefit to customers and partners." (Of course we're not talking here about trade secrets, or the formula for eleven herbs and spices, or privacy-protected information about individual customers or employees, or special customer insights gleaned from learning relationships.)

Li relates how Best Buy, for instance, put its data on nearly a million current and former products online for the benefit of software developers, employees, and customers, who may want to "build a better Best Buy" for their own constituencies, whether customers, other employees, or distributors. New Web sites like Camelbuy.com and Milo.com soon sprang up, using Best Buy inventory data to provide price drop alerts or to track product availability across different retail outlets. But one benefit the company hadn't even anticipated from this new policy was that employees themselves soon volunteered their time to use the data in helping customers with their problems. A Florida worker, for instance, used just a bit of basic programming knowledge to build a tool (i.e., an "app") for making recommendations for home theater configurations.

What's important about this story is that no one at Best Buy, and no one in the Best Buy ecosystem, was instructed, guided, pushed, cajoled, or rewarded in any way for making use of the newly available inventory and product specifications data. Instead, Best Buy's management figured their product information would prove useful in a variety of settings, most of which would be beneficial to the company, and they simply trusted that others would figure out ways to create more value for their customers if they were given access to it. Many companies are now finding they can use interactive tools, along with a willingness to relinquish a bit of control, to create a culture of sharing among their own stakeholders—engaging them as members of more collaborative, empathetic, trusting groups that collectively serve the interests of the business quite well.

Giving up control can generate benefits in terms of employee motivation as well. Universally, humans crave autonomy—they want to be the ones in charge of their own lives, their own work, their own destinies. The American Psychological Association considers autonomy (i.e., "the level of control individuals feel over their surroundings") to be one of the four principal elements of a person's overall psychological well-being and happiness in life, along with relatedness, competence, and self-esteem. Autonomy has been linked to overall well-being in studies around the world, from the United States to Korea, Bangladesh, Turkey, Russia, and elsewhere. Elderly patients given control over their nursing home environments have been found to have just half the mortality rate after eighteen months of other elderly patients given little or no control. And research on students has shown that a sense of autonomy "promotes greater conceptual understanding, better grades, enhanced persistence at school and in sporting activities, higher productivity, less burnout, and greater levels of psychological well-being."

Autonomy in the workplace is an extremely strong intrinsic performance motivator, especially for heuristic tasks, which might range from devising a new software application to solving an unusual customer service problem. A Cornell University study of more than three hundred small businesses found that those offering the highest levels of employee autonomy grew at four times the rate of the more control-oriented firms, and had only a third as much employee turnover. Autonomy leads employees to take responsibility and concentrate on developing "mastery" in their area of expertise. In one study of eleven thousand U.S. scientists and engineers, the desire for mastery was found to be the single best predictor of productivity. Even controlling for the amount of effort involved, scientists more concerned with pursuing mastery filed a significantly higher number of patents, as opposed to those who were primarily motivated by money. And autonomy is undoubtedly one of the principal attractions for contributors to open-source software and other social production enterprises. Software pioneers Andy Hunt and Dave Thomas make the point that autonomy creates a greater sense of ownership and responsibility on any software project, allowing people to pursue mastery and improve their craftsmanship, rather than simply abdicating responsibility because the "boss" assigned the project.

There's the rub. When the "boss" assigns the project, employees can abdicate responsibility. If you want your employees to be truly engaged in their work, you have to be prepared to give up some control. To trust them to do what's right. Giving up control, in the end, is all about trusting others, and helping them trust *you*.

Autonomy among employees is also a prerequisite for self-organization, and more and more firms are finding that when their employees and partners can self-organize, using collaborative and social networking technologies, they have a huge competitive advantage over top-down bureaucratic management structures, in terms of resilience, innovation, and speed of action. Don Tapscott and Anthony Williams, in their book *Wikinomics*, note that ubiquitous electronic connectivity has made the very nature of work "more cognitively complex, more team-based and collaborative, more dependent on social skills, more time pressured, more reliant on technological competence, more mobile, and less dependent on geography." Because of this, firms all over the world have begun decentralizing their decision making and relying more and more on individual initiative and responsibility.

And in *Drive,* Daniel Pink suggests that the ultimate kind of organized but autonomous working environment is something called "ROWE," or the results-only work environment. Pink maintains that

ROWE is the "antithesis of the billable hour," which is obviously an extremely controlling work measurement tool. Interestingly, according to Pink, the very first large company to adopt the ROWE model was Best Buy, at least in its corporate offices (although not yet in its stores.)

Providing autonomy, expecting workers to organize their own problem-solving efforts, and relying on them to initiate their own pursuit of subject-matter mastery can all be thought of as important elements in an employee culture based on trust. Your workers almost always want to do the right thing for your business and for your customers, so in most cases you just need to get the roadblocks out of their way. If you take the right approach to this, it will mean deemphasizing monetary compensation, and concentrating more and more on the intrinsic motivators that are far more persuasive for most folks who no longer punch a clock. Not that money doesn't matter, but for all the reasons we've given already—our biases, our needs, our internal motivations— money is much less a determining factor than most managers assume. Unless, of course, they hire clinically depressed psychopaths, in which case money will be the only thing that ever matters.

Zappos, a firm that has become legendary for its high customer service as well as its avid use of Twitter to keep in touch with customers, has a novel approach to hiring. New employees are trained and indoctrinated for a two-week period, and then each is offered $2,000 simply to quit the firm. CEO Tony Hsieh figures that anyone willing to take the money instead of staying for a career at the company isn't properly motivated or engaged in the business in the first place. If you think a couple thousand dollars now is better than a long-term career at Zappos, in other words, then you probably won't be good at helping the company build the long-term value of customers, so good riddance.

Providing more autonomy and control to workers requires managers to break their own addiction to controlling things, and the withdrawal symptoms can be frightening, no matter what Karl Marx said. According to Charlene Li, who spoke to hundreds of business managers in preparing to write her book *Open Leadership,*

Business leaders are terrified about the power of social technologies, but they are also intrigued and excited about the opportunities. . . . A few have actually taken steps to embrace social technologies and are doing well, while many began the journey enthusiastically only to fail. There is neither typical rhyme nor reason in these successes or failures—the size of the company, industry, or even prior experience with social technologies did not dictate the outcome. Instead, my research shows that the biggest indicator of success has been an open mindset—the ability of leaders to let go of control at the right time, in the right place, and in the right amount.

In other words, let go of control in a controlled way. But isn't that dangerous? Doesn't that introduce significant risks to the organizational mission? That depends on how your overall system functions. Just because you don't control things doesn't mean things aren't being controlled, or that chaos is inevitable.

[Dealing with Unpredictability: Embrace the "Chaos of Community"]

For companies operating in the midst of the e-social revolution, the ineffectiveness of management control has already become extremely clear. Tara Hunt's advice: "Embracing the chaos of community means letting go of the need to plan everything and the fantasy that you can control any given situation . . . You need to be hyperaware of your surroundings and be able to tap into opportunities as they arise and that you never could have predicted."

The e-social system, driven by its feedback loops and cascades of sentiments, is chaotic by definition and will resist any effort on your part to control or manage it. It is beyond the control of any manager, no matter how sophisticated the manager's data, analytics, and other tools might be. And everything is complicated by the way our interactions play upon our natural biases and prejudices, being the social creatures that we are.

This is the emotional landscape Raj Sisodia, Jag Sheth, and David B. Wolfe are referencing when he argues that the purely "rational" economic calculations thought to drive good business decisions are neither purely rational nor good business. Instead, he suggests, the most successful companies in the future will be those driven not just by economic calculation but by empathy, passion, and the very human urge simply to do good: "The consciousness that has ruled business enterprise over the past two centuries is rooted in classical notions that reason is superior to emotions in the affairs of people . . . [T]his has been a mistake." Not only are we entering a highly interconnected age likely to be characterized by more and more random fluctuations and complex-system oscillations, but our brains are not equipped to deal with such randomized events in a rational way. We prefer control and order. We crave it. When necessary, we lie to ourselves to preserve it.

This randomness now characterizes business issues more than ever before, and nowhere is it more threatening, or more visible and confounding, than in the arena of e-social interactions—among customers, among employees, and between them and the companies they deal with. So is there *any* strategy a clear-eyed person could adopt to avoid being sucked into this unreasoning, uncontrollable, chaotic vortex? Yes, actually, there are a number of things you can do.

Six Strategies to Succeed amid Rising Chaos

1. Use analytic techniques that don't require high accuracy.
Simple statistical models are often more reliable for dealing with highly complex situations than more detailed models. This is especially good advice for the marketing professional, who may be used to seeing awareness and preference data with three decimal places. The problem in dealing with social networks and other complex systems is that a sophisticated model is more likely to fit past data well but fail to predict the future, while a more basic model is less likely to fit past data, but more likely to be able to anticipate possible future scenar-

ios. *Consumer research using a multivariant trade-off analysis may predict demand for your product quite accurately, but then over one weekend the mommy bloggers suddenly take offense. . . .*

2. **Prepare for multiple outcomes.**
Rather than trying to make the one right guess as to what will most likely happen, make multiple guesses. Place many small bets on a variety of options. This is the way any truly innovative process works, and innovation is a good analogy for prediction. Don't bet the farm on the Edsel, in other words, without also having a Mustang or Thunderbird in your portfolio.

3. **Find and rely on the predictable elements of the situation.**
You may not be able to predict who the next Adam Fuhrer will be for any particular social network, but you know there will be one. You can pretty much count on the fact that there <u>will</u> be a few participants with extremely high influence, and there <u>will</u> be cascades of sentiment, sometimes sudden. In the same way, you may not know how long it will be before technology makes it possible for a specific customer to find out you tricked him into paying more than necessary, but you can pretty much count on the fact that sooner or later technology <u>will</u> make it possible. Just because you don't know which particular day it's going to rain, in other words, doesn't mean you should sell the umbrella.

4. **Focus your evaluation of initiatives on the inputs, not just the outputs.**
Randomness will confound even the best efforts to produce results. But when you assess a project or initiative's effectiveness, one of the things you're most interested in evaluating is the quality of the decision to undertake it. So don't rely solely on the actual outcome of the project (bad <u>or</u> good), but take into account the quality of the <u>process</u> that went into its planning and execution. A bad leader can sometimes get elected despite the evidence, but as long as the election was fair, you shouldn't throw out the democratic process.

5. **Remain agile, and strive to respond quickly.**
There's no substitute for awareness, listening, and detecting events as soon as they happen. Focus on "sense and respond" as an organization, and empower your people to act quickly and decisively. Have a social media <u>policy</u> that is strong on principle but general enough to be flexible, remembering that actual results can vary. And stage a social media fire drill every so often.

6. **Cultivate your reputation for trustability.**
In the end, you have to be prepared for failure, success, and everything in between. <u>But if others find you trustable, then you'll never be on your own.</u> As long as your focus is always on <u>doing the right thing,</u> then your customers, your employees, and your other stakeholders will all have an interest in seeing your company weather whatever unpredictable storm might come your way. We could call it <u>trust-proofing.</u>

Sometimes, the only logical course of action is simply to do the right thing and hope for the best. You can't control what people are going to say, but you *can* control what your company does. If you are trustable day after day, you will build a base of true customer advocates over time. Then when one person out there whines about something or tries to make trouble, your best customers are more likely to drown out that negative voice.

An interesting development noticed almost immediately at Comcast, once the Comcast Cares program had been up and running for a few months, was that many of its customers took a personal interest in the well-being of Frank and the other members of the Comcast Cares staff. In back-and-forth Twitter conversations, customers would ask about personal issues and learned the names of the staff. Just a few months into the program, for instance, Frank said, "Originally when I started to do this, I used the Comcast symbol instead of my picture . . . Then I listened to some customer feedback, and one was: 'Where's your picture?'

Now when they think Comcast, they think Frank . . . It gives a face to Comcast."

Putting on a human face is what inspires empathy, and empathy is not something that can simply be deployed or managed. It springs from one human being to another. In Comcast's case, the staff at Comcast Cares soon noticed that if they missed a complaint or problem, the company's customers themselves would sometimes chip in to help complaining Twitter users.

These kinds of customers are advocates, and once customers become advocates, you become partners. In his blog post for *Harvard Business Review*, Matthew Rhoden, former partner at Peppers & Rogers Group, suggested that a customer advocate:

- *supports your company by defending it in a bad moment, and looking for additional ways to buy from you;*
- *actively promotes the company or its products in social media and provides unsolicited feedback; and*
- *is emotionally attached to your company and treats the company and its products as part of his inner circle.*

So focus on developing your reservoir of trustability by doing things right, and doing the right thing proactively.

Chaos is the enemy of order and planning. But trustability is a valuable asset no matter what outcomes are produced by the chaos. Reciprocity matters, and empathy pays. You can't direct it or implement it or install it or manage it, but empathy is valuable to a business nonetheless. And remember: you are part of the system, too. Contributor, curator, freeloader, punisher—your own actions figure in someone else's feedback loop. *Your trustability is a part of the system's trustability.*

TRUSTABILITY
TEST

Think about how you'd answer these questions based on how things work at your company, institution, or government agency. Talk about your answers with your colleagues. Visit www.trustability.com to see how other visitors' responses compare with your own for these and other questions.

▶ Do you trust your employees, generally, to do the right thing for your business? If so, how far down in the hierarchy does this trust extend? What steps would you have to take to extend it even further?

▶ Can you recognize a "self-serving bias" (see p. 130) when evaluating any of your own professional accomplishments or your business's successes? Name at least two.

▶ Do you believe your business provides "above average customer service"? What portion of your customers would agree with you? And what portion of your own employees would agree with you? How often do you ask them?

▶ Do your customers trust your brand more than, about the same as, or less than they trust your competitors' brands? Products? Service? Reputation? Guarantees? The company? What makes you think so?

▶ Is your company focused more on long-term value creation, or on short-term financial targets, or on both about the same?

▶ What policies or processes do you employ now to help a budget-constrained customer better manage his or her spending on your company's products and services (i.e., to spend less, if it's in the customer's best interest)?

▶ Think of some business result—positive or negative—that you would attribute almost entirely to luck, random events, or unpredictable actions by others. What favorable or unfavorable effects did this random result have on the compensation, position, or influence of various executives at your firm?

▶ Does your business monitor social media platforms for general sentiment and specific complaints? Do you do it five days a week or 24/7?

> How does your company's behavior change based on what you learn?

> Who has responsibility for responding to problems or issues uncovered by such social media monitoring?

> What authority do they have?

▶ Has your organization ever run a social media "fire drill"?

▶ If you wanted to build your company's trustability in advance of any potential social media conflagration, what steps could you take?

▶ Is there data available to your firm that, if it were more widely disseminated, would make it easier for customers and/or employees to address their issues and solve their problems?

[7]

BUILD YOUR TRUSTABILITY
IN ADVANCE

Be prepared.
BOY SCOUT MOTTO

It's a tough world out there. Technology moves faster than ever, and the social winds of customer sentiment can build to gale force instantaneously. If you want to survive in this new world of transparent, always-on interactivity and rapid, unpredictable shifts in opinion, don't wait for the storm to hit. Get ready for it now. In this chapter we'll tell you how.

But first, here's a kind of "self-assessment" question that might indicate how well your company is prepared for trustability:

> *Do you allow customers to make comments about your products and services on your own Web site, for other customers and prospective customers to see?*

We've now asked this question of enough audiences around the world to know that the overwhelming majority of senior executives still tremble with fear at the very idea. We even put this question to a forward-thinking crowd of several hundred gathered for a "social media" conference, and fewer than a dozen hands went up. *At a conference on social media!*

[Customer Reviews Are Essential.
And Anyway, They're Inevitable.]

Hosting product reviews written by customers on your own Web site may be one of the most significant steps you can take to demonstrate trustability, and yet only a tiny minority of companies actually do. We predict, however, that in just a few years virtually every legitimate firm in any kind of business anywhere in the world will, as a matter of routine, make customer-authored product reviews widely available for the benefit of other customers and prospects. It will be one of the most essential activities any firm can undertake to build up its stock of trustability in the minds of customers.

To be proactively trustworthy, a company *must* facilitate customers' sharing their honest opinions with other customers about the problems they are trying to solve or the needs they are meeting, and this honest sharing will include, of necessity, the role that the company's own products and services play.

In the pre-Internet world, of course, customer reviews were rare. Customers had no electronically efficient capability to "talk back" to marketers or share their views with other customers. You couldn't just use your mobile phone to broadcast your customer experience to your tweeps* or Facebook friends. As a result there was no efficient way to enforce trustworthiness or to punish those who couldn't be trusted. When customers are technologically unable to spread the word about untrustworthy behavior, the control freaks responsible for managing a brand never get punished, never get corrected, never even face serious questioning—at least not by their customers, and not in public view.

This doesn't mean that companies weren't concerned with their reputations, because they were. Companies have always spent money and effort to

---

*Twitter has spawned a language. Tweets are the messages you send. Tweeps are your followers (your peeps, or people, on Twitter).

ensure that their well-crafted brand images spoke of integrity, authenticity, honesty, and respect. But in the final analysis, in the presocial era companies' brand images were still largely under their own control.

> Traditional marketing doesn't have to *be* trustworthy. It merely has to *appear* trustworthy.

As Walmart, Nestlé, Verizon, and others have discovered, however, appearances are no longer sufficient. Spin is out, trust is in, and the fact that a higher standard is being applied today by more and more consumers in a wider and wider variety of marketing and selling situations owes much to the e-social revolution.

> Monologues are totally controlled by one party—the speaker. Mass media monologues are controlled by the marketer. Anyone within earshot of a monologue will hear it, although not everyone will want to. Only those listeners who want to hear it will pay attention.
>
> By definition, however, a dialogue cannot be totally controlled by either party—not by you and not by your customer. Instead, as a free exchange of thoughts, or conversation, a dialogue will go in its own direction. You can push it and guide it, but you cannot control it.

When they engage in dialogues with you, customers just want their needs met. Most aren't all that interested in being "sold to," although sometimes they have to tolerate a sales message in order to get at the information they need. But hearing the honest opinion of another customer? That's useful. That's informative. And it's usually more objective than a sales message or a brand slogan.

Executives have lots of perfectly logical reasons to fear making their customers' actual opinions freely available. What if a customer has a complaint and goes public with it, right on our own Web site? Or what if a customer just doesn't like the product? Or what if a competitor masquerades as a customer and runs our product down?

We've heard all these complaints and more. Listen up: Get over it. If you abdicate your own role in the conversation, you are simply undermining your trustability. (Anyway, people will ask, What are you afraid of—the truth?)

The reality is that truth is more persuasive than spin, and this is one of the secret advantages of allowing customers to be honest in their opinions with other customers. Do you remember the last time you went online to evaluate a product or service by scanning its reviews? Maybe you wanted to see what people were saying about a particular hotel or vacation package, or maybe it was a new car, or a video game, or a set of golf clubs. And when you navigate to a site where 100 percent of the reviews are composed of peachy-keen, five-star glowing praises—what's your reaction? Do you really believe these terrific reviews, or doesn't this imbalance create a suspicion in your mind? You aren't alone. Glowing reviews, in isolation, don't sell as well as mixed reviews. Really.

> While the average consumer rating of products on a 5-point scale is roughly 4.5, the numbers show that a negative review actually converts to a sale more effectively than a positive review.
> *BRETT HURT, FOUNDER OF WEB ANALYTICS FIRM COREMETRICS,*
> *AND COFOUNDER AND CEO OF BAZAARVOICE*

A bit of criticism from customers assures other customers that your online product reviews are authentic. They're genuine. You are trustable. When a company hosts this kind of information exchange it is departing from the money-dominated commercial ethos of economic self-interest. Rather than unswerving (and psychopathic?) self-promotion, when you make it easy for customers to find out what other customers honestly think about your product or service you are showing a human face, and proving your trustability.

There are already a whole host of e-social places where your product or brand can be openly discussed, including all the social media sites—not just gigantic communities like Facebook or Myspace, but thousands of other, niche communities all over the Web. In addition, many sites are specifically dedicated to soliciting and compiling reviews, depending on your category, including Amazon, TripAdvisor, Trusted Opinion, Rate-ItAll, Epinions, and Minekey, for example.

None of these services, of course, involves putting a customer review directly on your own Web site. But while you may not want this, your customers will. Your customers will want the convenience of being able to read other customers' views of your product or service without having to search too hard for them. So even if they comment as well on other sites—even if they comment more on other sites—they are still likely to want to see the opinions of other customers somewhere nearby, right where they're looking at the product, if they feel like it.

> Your customers want access to your reputation at their own point of purchase.

And as technology continues to facilitate faster and easier interaction, you can bet your last Facebook page credit that customers will soon be reviewing products right on your own Web site, with or without your permission. It is technologically inevitable.

Don't believe us? Even join a service like StumbleUpon or Digg, add the iGlue plug-in to your browser. These are just a few of the applications already available to help users "annotate" the Web, collectively providing notes and comments on various pages for the benefit of users. Visit a page, make a comment about it, and depending on the service, your comment might appear in a sidebar on the site, or a kind of hot link for particular words or phrases on the original. If you like, you can review a product or post a story about a particular service experience you had with this firm, or a tip for a competitive product, or how to get better service or something you may have heard about your oil or whatever—and each of these services allows other users to see or comment on your comments as well. Similar pro capabilities come from Diigo, ReframeIt, Apture, and several other vendors.

Take one more step into the future, however, and soon (probably very soon) we'll see new and more useful ways to access Web annotations by others integrating the annotated Web with the mobile technology of augmented reality. Imagine pointing your smart phone at a restaurant across the street, or a product in a store, and seeing on your screen competitive pricing information, along with reviews and opinions of the restaurant or product posted by other customers, or by your friends, or by the friends of your friends. Services like foursquare already offer nearly this level of service. By the time you read this, your kids will be doing it.

The point is that no matter how big a gulp you have to take, *your customers will talk about your brand whether you want them to or not,* and with or without your participation. (So wouldn't you rather have the conversation happen on your own doorstep?) In the end, you have to choose: either give up control in a peaceful and orderly way, or have it taken from you forcibly.

This is a technology-fueled express train. The only decision you can make is whether to board the train or lie down on the track.

[Sockpuppeting for Fun and Profit]

But wait! What if a competitor poses as your customer and posts a negative review?

This can be a problem in an online world characterized by anonymous user IDs, where masquerading is practical and easy and registrations can be treated as disposable. Remember the old *New Yorker* cartoon? On the Internet, nobody knows you're a dog.

Here's the thing: Any competitor who stoops to this kind of dirty trick today is playing a very dangerous game himself. Even if he succeeds for a while in remaining anonymous, sooner or later he is likely to be outed by the same transparency dynamic that operates on everyone else, and technology's advances make this a more and more probable outcome. Just ask John Mackey, cofounder and CEO of Whole Foods, who got into the habit of posting anonymous comments touting his company's stock and disparaging a key competitor, only to find his cover blown and his ruse revealed to everyone in the pages of *The Wall Street Journal* and *The New York Times* (and now, this book).

A "sockpuppet" is an online anonymous persona employed to hide a person's identity, the way Mackey did. And sockpuppeting is a time-honored technique not just for protecting your own privacy but also for getting up to mischief—deceiving others, manipulating opinion, cheating on your spouse or partner, or violating trust in some other way.

While your competitor himself may be less likely to stoop to sockpuppeting these days for fear of being outed as a fake, *hiring* people to pose as customers and write fake reviews—both positive and negative—has become a cottage industry. Web sites like Yelp, TripAdvisor, and Amazon depend for their credibility on customer reviews, and they're now being inundated with fake ones, often written for a few pennies each in India. Amazon's people-for-hire service, known as Mechanical Turk, is even used to find people willing to author bogus reviews on Amazon and other sites. (eBay doesn't get many fake reviews because you can't review a seller on eBay without first buying from him.)

Fake reviews and other forms of "opinion spam" are a significant enough threat that sites depending on reviews for their credibility have often put in place complex algorithms designed to filter out fakes. These algorithms are similar to the spam filters that block out inauthentic e-mail messages. Yelp blocks a substantial number of the reviews it receives, but it also allows you to view the blocked reviews, and the company won't discuss its algorithm. One Cornell research team publicized the fact that they had developed a new set of algorithms for detecting opinion spam, and they were immediately approached by a number of firms, including Hilton Hotels, TripAdvisor, and Amazon.

But something interesting about the e-social revolution is that it is rapidly reducing the usefulness of anonymous comments when it comes to sharing and evaluating brands, opinions, products, or services. One of Facebook's biggest assets, for instance, is that it's almost impossible to pose as someone else on the service. After all, who's going to "friend" someone they never heard of? And if you do agree to be friended by someone you don't know very well, isn't it because you share some mutual acquaintances, or perhaps a school or business relationship? Chris Kelly, Facebook's onetime head of privacy, maintains that "the friend infrastructure and an identity base ultimately is the key to safety. Trust on the Internet depends on having identity fixed and known."

There have been cases reported of someone's Facebook identity being stolen or of social networking participation allowing an identity thief to gain highly private information about someone, but, strictly speaking, these cases do not really involve the hijacking of someone's "social identity" in a criminal sense. Rather, it is their personal information that is more at risk. Your *social* identity is extremely difficult to steal, because everyone's "social graph"—that is, the network of people they know, and the people that *they* know—is like a fingerprint. Your social graph can perfectly, flawlessly identify you, in a verifiable way. Unsure if someone really is who they say they are? Ask a friend. Better yet, ask a friend you have in common, or a friend of a friend. In the not-too-distant future, in fact, rather than simply believing any review you happen upon, you will instead search first for your friends' opinions, or those of your friends' friends, or (maybe) *their* friends.

The exact future of online identity and anonymity hasn't yet come into clear view, but the trends right now don't look good for sockpuppeting. For one thing, obviously, the practice has become much riskier than ever before, as Mackey and others have discovered. The fact that people everywhere are so well connected means that rumors and coincidences are pursued now with a vengeance, and there's almost always someone who has a vested interest in "punishing" this untrustable behavior. A search on Google or Bing for the term "sockpuppet" (no hyphen, all one word) turns up more than 100,000 entries, with many of them exposing various sockpuppeting fiascos. Some of the most interesting are stories of high-stakes political sockpuppeting now exposed. Just on the first page of Google's search results, for instance, one story from the political left recounts the exposure of Kevin Pezzi, a former writer for

Andrew Breitbart's BigGovernment site, as a master sockpuppeter with a coterie of Myspace identities used to promote his own right-wing views and work, while another story from the political right reveals that President Obama's single most ardent supporter, Ellie Light, is (probably) a sockpuppeter who has had nearly identical letters to the editor published in at least forty-two newspapers in eighteen different states, and has claimed to be a resident of many different locations.

But in addition to the increased risk of being outed as a sockpuppeter, there is another important reason sockpuppeting is likely to decline over the long term. More reliable, trustable user identifications play an important role in supporting the advertising and personalization services that generate a great deal of online revenue. The advertising that provides financial support for the vast majority of "free" Web information services works better, and generates more value with greater efficiency, when ads and promotional messages are directed toward individual consumers based on their own particular wants, needs, and preferences. Despite technologies designed to track IP addresses and plant cookies on people's hard drives, however, today's Internet users are often incorrectly categorized, with the result that a lot of advertising not only appears irrelevant to consumers, but represents wasted money for the advertisers. According to one Internet advertising executive, even identifying the gender of online users is subject to a 35 percent error rate.

But rapid technological progress in identifying Internet users is inevitable, if only because it will help advertisers and marketers do a better job of putting the right offer in front of the right person at the right time. It's not possible to say just what user-identifying technologies will be developed in the future or when, but it is a certainty that businesses are highly motivated to develop them, and we can expect rapid improvements. One such technology already being employed, for instance, is the quick and convenient sign-in you can do on many Web sites by using your identity from Twitter, or Facebook, or LinkedIn.

Moreover, even though some social networks are specifically configured to allow for anonymity (as Myspace is, for instance), anonymity itself does not always mean someone is untrustworthy. We will almost

certainly remain technically capable of adopting multiple online personas in order to participate in multiple roles, or to engage with different
social "circles" (business, pleasure, school, close family, etc.), but even
though these personas can provide anonymity, they will also carry their
own levels of trustworthiness. As an example, consider how Amazon's
online book reviews work. It used to be that all you saw about a reviewer
was the user name, with as much or as little additional profile information as the user chose to reveal. But now you can click to see this reviewer's other reviews, you can see how his comments have been rated by
others, and you can find out how he ranks compared with all other reviewers. So if you see a fantastic book review (or a terribly negative one)
by a one-time reviewer, how much credibility will you give it? An anonymous reviewer can keep his actual name and identity a complete secret,
but his trustworthiness in the domain of book reviews is still on display
to everyone. Sockpuppeters and paid opinion spammers can't stand up
to this kind of scrutiny.

No matter how the issue of online identity develops over time, the
simple truth remains that product or brand opinions (or any other opinions) expressed by anonymous users with no track record will not be considered trustworthy, and will have less and less of an influence. They
will be like the e-mail messages that sometimes get through the spam filters, from people we've never heard of, touting deals that are going to
make us rich. Trust is driven by interaction, and anonymity just gets in
the way.

[Workers of the World, Blog!]

It's not just customers whose honest opinions can help you build
your trustability, either. In the last chapter we discussed how you can empower employees and customers alike to improve the customer experience on their own, just by providing access to the necessary
information—product specifications and features, inventory records, delivery times, and the like. The point is that people *want* to help themselves, if you'll just let them. They'll find a way. And part of building

your trustability in advance is proving that you intend to help customers solve their problems even if (occasionally) it might make you uncomfortable.

A genuinely trustable company will take into account the fact that people have a natural urge to converse, to share, to create, and to help others. It will participate in the e-social world by sharing its own expertise with customers, and by empowering employees to engage in social interactions designed to help customers even when those interactions have little or no immediate financial benefit for the firm.

In 2003 Robert Scoble began working as a "technical evangelist" for Microsoft, with responsibility for blogging on the company's behalf. But Scoble's posts startled the online world because he often criticized Microsoft's own products. Rather than putting people off Microsoft, however, Scoble's negative comments persuaded readers that his writing was accurate and trustable. As Chris Brogan and Julien Smith relate in their book *Trust Agents,*

> *In his early career at Microsoft Scoble blogged about the good—but more important, the bad—Microsoft products at the time. When he shared his take on why Internet Explorer wasn't as good as Firefox, we (his audience of readers) felt that Scoble represented One of Us. We could believe what he said, because he was a member of our community, talked like us, spent time where we spent time, and seemed to be genuine and honest with us.*

So what is it about admitting errors that inspires trust? Probably it has to do with a combination of vulnerability and credibility. When Scoble spoke the truth about Microsoft's weaknesses as well as its strengths, (1) he was showing his company's vulnerability, and (2) his message was more credible, because we all know that no one is perfect, including Microsoft (or any other company). Fallibility is as quintessentially human as food, sex, conversations, or music. Like a bad customer review, admitting vulnerability *confirms* that a company is worthy of interaction—that it is, in fact, trustable.

In 2009 Best Buy launched Twelpforce, a Twitter program for customers, manned by hundreds of the company's sales associates and other employees contributing their thoughts and comments to solve customer problems and answer customer questions. In its first year of operation Twelpforce answered nearly thirty thousand customer inquiries, and has not only improved customer service but served as a vehicle for educating and motivating employees, and generating great publicity as well.

At a 2011 business conference Jason Sadler, one of the founders of iwearyourshirt.com and a widely respected authority on social media, related an anecdote about how Best Buy's Twelpforce had helped him. Sadler had been looking for a wall-mounted flat-screen television for his living room, and was unsure what kind of parameters might work. So he tweeted this out. *Anyone know anything about flat-screen televisions?* As he told the story, he soon received a reply from Best Buy's Twelpforce, asking him what the dimensions of his room were. After this, Twelpforce asked him where the light came from in the living room—what side of the room were the windows on, and how big were they? After a number of such questions, the helpful Best Buy employees on Twelpforce recommended a particular type of television for him.

This, Sadler said, was amazing. He had been completely sold by a series of Twitter interactions. He went into the Best Buy store and found the television that had been recommended to him. However, as he was in the store he also used his smart phone to search online for the same model, and he was able to find it on Amazon for a lower price. But this now presented a dilemma: What should he do? What would you have done?

Although his conscience pained him, Sadler elected to save the money and bought the product from Amazon. Before he did, however, he tweeted back to the @twelpforce folks to let them know. Their message back was something like "Well, we're glad we were able to help. Maybe next time . . ." Ever since, Sadler said, he has looked for every excuse imaginable to patronize Best Buy. He tells this story everywhere he goes. And now we're telling you about it.

So, did Best Buy lose or gain value from their Twelpforce

recommendation? Was it stupid or smart for Best Buy to spend time simply helping a customer find the right product to meet his need? They lost the sale in the end, didn't they?

[Trustability as a Competitive Strategy]

Yes, Best Buy may have lost the sale, and they lost it for the same reason many other brick-and-mortar retailers are losing sales to online companies—because the world has now become completely transparent to customers who are armed with smart phones and connected to the 'net. When the world is transparent, then why *shouldn't* a customer simply find the lowest price before buying a product? After all, in this kind of immediate buying situation, the products being compared are virtually identical. They are probably mass-produced by the same company at the same plant, so if one is even a dollar cheaper than the other, then that's a dollar in the customer's own pocket.

Brick-and-mortar retailers do serve an important purpose, however, beyond just inventorying products for people to walk out with. As difficult as it may be for them to compete with online retailers, it's highly unlikely we'll ever live to see the day when physical stores cease to exist. Something retail stores do that online vendors don't, for instance, is allow consumers to view, feel, or even test a product up close before buying. Like Sadler, before you buy that high-end television, computer monitor, washing machine, or automobile you're probably going to want to see it firsthand. The problem for the retailer is that once you've seen it up close you can often find it, as Sadler did, for a lower price at an online merchant who doesn't have to pay to maintain stores, showrooms, or salespeople.

In this situation the most obvious and direct competitive response for a retailer would be to supplement its regular, physical-products-in-stores business with online products delivered from warehouses, in order to try to match the lower inventorying and service costs of an online vendor. Buy the product in the store and walk out with it right now, or wait four days and we'll deliver it to you for less. Some stores have already installed kiosks to facilitate customers' browsing the stores' online offerings from within the stores. Even doing this, however, it's unlikely that a brick-and-mortar retailer will always be able to match the lower costs of a pure online vendor. They can come closer, but they'll have a hard time closing the gap entirely.

Over the past few years, therefore, retailers have attempted several strategies to compete with online vendors by emphasizing their natural differences—local presence, physical showroom, and so forth. One strategy, for instance, is to improve the customer experience within the store. When Target puts a Starbucks in front of the cashiers' stations, or when a bookstore adds a reading lounge and brings in authors for book signings, this is what they're trying to do—to create an experience worth coming into the store for. While this does make it more attractive for customers to come in, they may still choose not to *buy* the product from the store, which is one reason Borders has closed its doors and Barnes & Noble isn't doing so well, while Amazon and other online book vendors continue to grow briskly.

Another possible strategy for a retailer would be to charge admission. This is what warehouse stores like Sam's Clubs and Costco do—they charge customers an annual membership fee for the privilege of entering their stores. Other kinds of stores do this on an occasional basis. When the iPhone was first introduced, Apple stores charged admission in order to manage the crowds of customers jamming in to see it. And some independent bookstores have begun charging admission for customers who come to the store for author book signings and similar events. It isn't hard to imagine a future store with high-end products or very-low-price products charging customers a one-time fee for entry, and refunding that fee if a product is bought within, say, forty-eight hours.

Yet another strategy allowing a retailer to secure the purchase, especially for more complex products, might be to build a reputation for excellent service, including installation, maintenance, and repair. A car dealer with a great service reputation, for instance, is likely to generate better car sales, even when facing competition from no-service vendors selling the same cars for less. And where Don lives in Georgia, although he and his family could buy their electronics products from any of several "big box" retailers, he chooses to use H&H, a local retailer with slightly higher prices but a reputation for comprehensive and excellent service (this way if the home theater system gets out of whack he doesn't have to wait until one of the kids comes home from college before getting it to work again!).

There is, however, another strategy which might be the most effective of all, and this is the strategy that Best Buy is pursuing with Twelpforce—*trustability*. Yes, you can argue that Best Buy may have lost Jason Sadler's sale, *but wouldn't it have lost this sale anyway?* For this particular product, at least, its price just wasn't close enough. And even as it lost this particular sale, Best Buy still gained a tremendous amount of customer trustability, likely to generate future sales. Sadler knows, and Sadler's friends and followers know, that when they deal with this company, the company will work in their own best interest.

And if you think about it, trustability changes the entire framework of competition, because it can engage an individual customer's empathy. There's no such thing as one-way reciprocity. It was clear from the way Sadler related his anecdote to the crowd that he actually felt *guilty* about not returning the empathy and goodwill that Best Buy had shown him. He told his audience he was actively looking for other opportunities to do business with Best Buy in the future. He *wants* Best Buy to succeed, as a business. He wants *you* to buy from them.

So Best Buy lost Sadler's business to Amazon this time, but it isn't likely to lose the next time. Plus, there is the fact that Sadler has twenty-four thousand tweeps and several hundred thousand regular online viewers for the talks and the demonstrations he does on his Web site.

Trustability engages people's natural impulse to show empathy. As a result, when trustability is used as a competitive business strategy it actually transcends the commercial domain of monetary metrics and incentives, and taps into the social domain of friendship, sharing, and reciprocity. Rather than simply calculating the dollar value of product features and pricing, an empathetic customer is more likely to take into account the *feelings* of the business itself, because the business is showing its human face.

A friend of ours moved to New York during the recession. Determined to get a great apartment for a great price, she and her husband met up with a Realtor they really liked. She told the story this way:

> *Our Realtor Karen Kelley, with the Corcoran Group, showed us forty apartments. It took days. We had narrowed the choice to three, when we got a call from another friend who was selling a classic co-op "by owner." So I called Karen to ask what we should do. She suggested we go see the apartment, which turned out to be wonderful. Despite the fact that no commission was involved, Karen rushed over to join us, armed with lots of useful information about the building's history, maintenance records, tax information—the works. That was before we insisted on paying her the buyer's part of the fee she would have earned, had the apartment been listed. Even if she didn't make money this transaction, she wanted us to have the right apartment. Since then we've sent several other people to her—both buyers and sellers. We feel as though we're doing our friends a favor by helping them find a Manhattan Realtor they can genuinely trust. And of course we're thrilled to see Karen succeed too!*

Imagine how things might have developed differently for Staples' word-of-mouth marketing campaign if the company had first had its own "Twelpforce," advising customers on how to solve their problems regardless of which products they bought or even which store they bought from. If a company is trying to cultivate a reputation for trustability you could hardly do better than harnessing the honest, problem-solving capabilities of your own employees (and other customers) and making that ability available to customers, even *before* they buy from you.

[The Power of an Apology]

One of the lessons Facebook learned is that a simple apology can go a long way toward soothing the crowd. This was a lesson that would have benefited Nestlé immensely. Seeking the forgiveness of others is an action that epitomizes vulnerability. It is the ultimate form of openness.

In the e-social age, however, apologizing is also a potent competitive strategy. *Seeking forgiveness is a form of social aikido.* Rather than resisting someone else's action, you are actually using their momentum in your own cause.

Or perhaps more accurately, as we said in the last chapter, you can become more trustable *to* others by becoming more trusting *of* others. Exposing your own vulnerability is one of the fastest ways to earn someone else's trust, because you are signaling that you trust *them*. Dan Ariely designed some experiments to help explain the effects of apologies on the behaviors of the people being apologized to. As a first step, he tried to figure out the degree to which our honesty and trustworthiness are affected by irritability or being upset. His theory was that the more upset or irritated we are with any particular person (or with a store, or a company, or a government agency) the less likely it is that we'll behave in an empathetically honest way with that person or entity. That is, we won't feel a strong social obligation to respect that person's interests. Turns out Ariely's hunch was correct.

In one experiment, for instance, unsuspecting subjects were approached by a researcher in a coffee shop and asked to perform a simple "research task" in return for a nominal payment of $5 (in this particular case the task required people to scan a list of letters on several sheets of paper and to circle certain letter combinations). But the researchers fell into two categories—those who did something calculated to irritate or annoy the research subject, and those who did not. While they were explaining the task to the research subject, some researchers ("the annoyers") received a call on their cell phone and made the subjects wait while they took the call, which was obviously personal. So while both groups of research subjects were asked to do the same menial letter-identification task, one group was annoyed, and one group was not.

Now, in order to assess people's trustability, once each subject completed the task and was paid $5 by the researcher, the researcher included more money in the payment envelope than was actually due, apparently by mistake—instead of five one-dollar bills, for instance, the envelope might have included a five-dollar bill at the bottom of four one-dollar bills. What Ariely found was that those who had been instructed by the annoyers were *much* less likely to return the extra cash, with just 14 percent doing so, while 45 percent of the others did. (Moral of the story: If you want empathy from people you do have to be likable. Don't irritate them with a bad customer experience or a faulty product.)

In a subsequent iteration on this experiment, however, Ariely also tested the effectiveness of an apology. He had some of his "annoyers" take the phone call the same way as before, but then asked them simply to *apologize* for having taken it, before continuing on with the exercise. What he found was that this apology *completely offset any negative effects of the annoyance*:

> . . . *the apology was a perfect remedy. The amount of extra cash returned in the apology condition was the same as it was when people were not annoyed at all. Indeed, we found that the word "sorry" completely counteracted the effect of annoyance.*

Ariely goes on to caution his readers that this experiment shouldn't be thought of as giving anyone a license to annoy-and-apologize repeatedly. Each of the research subjects was involved in a one-time-only interaction, and none of them had any familiarity or relationship with the researchers. Still, the experiment represents an interesting comment on human nature, and probably accords with your own common sense with respect to how people behave toward others.

RECOVERING LOST TRUST

Research has shown that both your perceived concern for others (i.e., your good intentions) and your past behavior (i.e., your competence) are major factors in the degree to which others trust you. Academicians studying trust to learn what conditions promote it or discourage it, how it is broken, and how it can be restored, have found:

▶ One way to help restore trust, when it has been lost through untrustworthy behavior, is simply to apologize. Customers can forgive incompetence if you recognize and acknowledge your own boneheaded behavior as such and if you state clearly how you are cleaning up your processes to make sure it doesn't happen again. Hint: If you do apologize, just do it, without excuses. Don't say "But you have to understand . . ." or "It wasn't our fault entirely." Just say "We goofed, we're sorry, won't happen again." Include a gift, if appropriate, . . . in order to drive home the sincerity of your apology.

▶ Good behavior is the single most effective way to restore trust after an episode of bad or untrustworthy behavior. Even though a stated promise of better behavior does accelerate the growth of trust, trustworthy actions alone are every bit as effective in the long term. . . .

▶ Although trust lost through bad behavior can generally be restored after a period of good behavior, when trust is violated with both bad behavior *and* deceptive statements, it never fully recovers. Incompetence can be forgiven, in other words, but bad character is a fatal flaw. This is one of the biggest problems plaguing most firms, because the first officials on the scene of a service disaster are usually the PR folks, and no matter how good it is, spin is the opposite of straight talk.

▶ Interestingly, research has also shown that using a binding contract probably erodes the trust of a customer or business partner. People who use binding contracts make situational judgments, rather than personal judgments, when assessing how trustworthy the other party is.

While we're on the subject of apologies, please note that people will forgive mistakes or incompetence much more quickly than they will deception or selfish intentions. When you screw up, be frank and 'fess up immediately. Do not even be tempted to deny things, because inevitably the cover-up will always be worse than the crime.

Even in businesses in which serious problems are inevitable, and negotiation by lawsuit has prevailed in the past, exposing your vulnerability and talking about it openly can actually minimize the damage from customer problems. Toro, the lawnmower and snowblower company, had a long history of personal injury litigation in its business. For years, the firm's management simply accepted these lawsuits as a cost of doing business, reasoning that injuries were inevitable with the types of products they made. In the mid-1990s, however, Toro began to wonder whether litigation had to be as inevitable as the injuries were. Yes, the firm manufactured products with spinning blades, and a mistake while using a lawnmower is inherently more dangerous than a mistake made while using, say, a washing machine. And yes, many, if not most, of the mistakes are actually made by the user—the customer. But if the firm were really to take the customer's point of view—if it were actually to *empathize* with a customer's own interest—what would it do? How would a customer actually *like* to be treated?

In answer to this question, the company initiated a new policy, sending apologetic representatives to meet personally with injured customers. These representatives sympathized with customers, acknowledged their suffering, and suggested quick settlements to avoid the lengthy delays and high costs of going to court. And the results were impressive, not just for the firm's customers, but for its bottom line as well. Using "nonthreatening paralegals, experienced settlement counselors, and mediators familiar with Toro's preference for early case resolution," the company suggested that disagreements, if they arose, could be worked out with less hassle in arbitrations. In the first ten years of this new policy, Toro has not had to go to court for even a single personal injury issue, and the company estimates it saved about $100 million in litigation costs.

Now in this kind of situation we can question whether Toro's customer settlements are really in "the customer's interest" or not. After all, it's certainly possible that an injured customer could, by hiring the right attorney, achieve a higher monetary settlement in a court of law. But our argument is that trustability trumps pure self-interest. Supremely rational self-interest tells only half the story, and not even the most important half. Trustability, on the other hand, is produced by empathy, by emotion, and by the deep-seated human instinct to connect with other people and *to be social*.

Lawnmower accident victims don't sue Toro for the same reason that legitimately injured patients refuse to sue doctors who apologize, USAA members send refunds back to the company, and Jason Sadler is looking for additional opportunities to patronize Best Buy: because people value so highly what they perceive to be genuinely good intentions. We all know everybody makes mistakes. People can forgive honest mistakes, but they are slow to forgive bad intentions.

[Letting Bygones Be Bygones]

It is inevitable that mistakes will happen, so we have to deal with it. Bad things will happen, random events will confound the most well-meaning efforts of the best companies, and businesses can only put on a "human face" by letting go of the control-freak obsession with managing and directing everything. Trusting others, in order to be trusted yourself, means that mistakes can't be avoided even if your own performance is perfect. Mistakes and errors just have to be a part of your business plan.

And then, life must go on, and commerce must continue to take place. So it's very unlikely that any single mistake will cripple your company for good, unless it cascades into a crisis of trustability that is truly catastrophic and insurmountable. Ultimately, because failures are inevitable, and because transparency and openness mean that failures will be exposed to everyone's view, apologies and forgiveness are likely to become art forms in the socially networked world. This is a far cry from the way traditional public relations professionals and marketers have always operated. The hunker-down impulse is strong in the PR profession, but in today's new e-social environment, this is exactly the wrong instinct.

Unfortunately, however, "no comment" can sometimes be the unintended consequence of a rapidly moving social media environment. The social media system has its own dynamic, and it is in the nature of electronically transmitted word-of-mouth opinions that the system's feedback loops are prone to generating very significant, very rapid, and completely unpredictable waves of sentiment—oscillations that can't be foreseen, and can spring to life in days, or even hours. If you don't pay attention to what is being said about your brand on a more or less continual basis, then you will always be at the mercy of the system's capriciousness.

After the disastrously tasteless Kenneth Cole gaffe on Twitter (chapter 5) it took only a few days before much of the uproar died down and the brand's reputation seemed to return to normal. Just four days after the fiasco, an *Ad Age* commentary on the affair noted that while some observers labeled blunders like Cole's "brand suicide," the fallout isn't usually permanent, and frequently not even very severe:

> *Why? Largely because those folks who are out there looking to yuk it up with a parody account on Twitter quickly distract folks from the distasteful mistake that made people mad in the first place. We don't suspect a marketer has yet been smart enough to set one up themselves, but going forward, you never know.*

A more likely reason Cole's mistake was so quickly forgiven by the public, however, was that it was seen as a mistake of *incompetence*, rather than bad intent. Cole's good intentions were demonstrated by the immediacy of his apology. Obviously, he regretted his blurt. But back up for a second and ask yourself what might have happened had Kenneth Cole ignored the furor for several days instead of just a few hours? The general conclusion from this might well have been that his original tweet had been intentionally tasteless, designed to achieve exactly the purpose laid out by the *Ad Age* columnist, that is, generating buzz for the brand. In that case, forgiveness would have been much more difficult to come by.

In chapter 8 we'll argue that at some level competence and good intentions are actually related. If Cole's apology had been delayed for days simply because his company didn't monitor the social space, and didn't know what was going on, the conclusion could still have been "bad intentions." How good can a company's intentions really be if it doesn't go to enough trouble to pay attention?

As more and more interactions occur online, more and more mistakes will be made and exposed—mistakes not just on the part of companies and brands, but on the part of individuals as well. We all know the stories. One 2009 poll of U.S. businesses found that a third of employers had rejected job candidates based on things uncovered on social networks, including "provocative or inappropriate photographs or information."

Does this mean that people will soon become more timid, more reserved, and less spontaneous? Perhaps. On the other hand, it might mean that society, as a whole, will become a bit more forgiving and tolerant. Everyone makes mistakes. Everyone.

Many of the senior executives at Facebook have come to believe in what is often called "radical transparency." Everything will be known, because the world is inevitably evolving into a social system in which everything can be seen by everyone else. But while this might spell the end of what passed for privacy during the twentieth century, proponents of radical transparency maintain it's not at all a bad future. On the contrary, it's something we should welcome. More transparency leads to more honesty. It's exactly what your grandmother used to tell you: If you don't want people to find out you did it, don't do it. Some Facebook users suggest that the existence of Facebook makes it more difficult to cheat on your girlfriend or boyfriend, for instance.

The fact is that personal information will continue to be more and more widely disseminated, because this is simply an unintended by-product of social networks, and social networks are here to stay. This will almost certainly lead to a more tolerant and less judgmental society because, as Adam Penenberg poignantly says in his book *Viral Loop,* "shame is largely generational. If you are in your forties or older, your parents didn't talk about their feelings; today you can barely stop people from telling you their life stories."

And today's youth have their own ways of adapting to this new reality. In 2007 *New York* magazine explored how kids use the Internet, and how they deal with the increasing volume of personal, sometimes embarrassing information found online. The kids interviewed for the article almost universally subscribed to a philosophy of stoic acceptance of the fact that sometimes bad things do happen—negative comments, occasional wild accusations, bullying, and even terrible breaches of personal privacy. In general, however, they deal with all this constructively, and they recognize the utter impracticality of trying to "control" what others say and do.

One young woman, for instance, found that a racy, rather explicit video she had made for her ex-boyfriend had been posted online. Initially horrified, she tried to have it taken down every place she found it, but each time it just popped up again somewhere else. Unable to get the pee out of the swimming pool, in other words, she instead resorted to flooding the network with other references to herself—multiple videos and blog entries that portrayed her as a smarter, more mature and "together" person—in order to overwhelm the embarrassing video in search engine results. After a while, it seemed to work, and the prominence of her discomforting video diminished.

[Cultures in Transition]

The need to be transparent, open, and trustworthy is self-evident to those already involved in these new technologies, and a willingness to give up some control is the price of admission. No one who has observed the e-social revolution up close has any doubt about its dynamics. And the ones who are most successful tend to get it "in their bones." Clive Thompson, writing in *Wired* magazine, says, "Some of this isn't even about business; it's a cultural shift . . . A generation has grown up blogging, posting a daily phonecam picture on Flickr and listing its geographic position in real time on Dodgeball and Google Maps. For them, authenticity comes from online exposure. It's hard to trust anyone who *doesn't* list their dreams and fears on Facebook."

Victor Stone, the entrepreneur behind ccMixter, commented to Lawrence Lessig, "You know . . . this discussion will be over in ten or twenty years. As the boomers . . . get over themselves by dying, the generation that follows . . . just doesn't care about this discussion. They just assume that remixing is part of music, and it's part of the process, and that's it."

> The future is already here—it's just not evenly distributed yet.
> *WILLIAM GIBSON, SCIENCE FICTION AUTHOR*

We suspect Stone is correct, not just about remixing music, but about many other aspects of this technology-induced cultural shift. If you pick this book up to read it twenty years from now you will likely wonder what all the fuss was even about. By then, a completely new ethos will have emerged for governing how content is created, owned, and shared, how businesses "manage" their own image, how personal privacy is handled, and how people come together to get things done. In twenty years it will be obvious to all of us. Looking back we will say, "Of course it had to be like this; it was inevitable."

But right now, today, giving up control and wading into the "chaos of community," as Tara Hunt called it, is terrifying. It is a gut-wrenchingly scary prospect for any business manager, and represents a complete subversion of the power structure. Thompson, in his *Wired* article, summarizes the dilemma facing today's business executives like this:

> *The Internet has inverted the social physics of information. Companies used to assume that details about their internal workings were valuable precisely because they were secret. If you were cagey about your plans, you had the upper hand; if you kept your next big idea to yourself, people couldn't steal it. Now, billion-dollar ideas come to*

CEOs who give them away; corporations that publicize their failings grow stronger. Power comes not from your Rolodex but from how many bloggers link to you—and everyone trembles before search engine rankings.

Giving up control turns the "inverted social physics" of online interactivity into a tremendous asset—but it obviously can't be directed from the top down. It has to rise up from the bottom. Your Facebook "fans"— or your friends or customers or colleagues or connections—have to *want* your effort to succeed, either because they get a thrill out of it themselves, or simply because they like you and trust you. Whatever their reason, if you want them to have empathy for you, and to wish the best for you, then you have to go with what *they* want. You have to let them join the conversation themselves, realizing that the conversation itself will be changed just by their joining it.

This is a cultural transition. No matter how good you are, bad stuff could happen. Social media asteroids will inevitably crash into different companies at different times. Control won't be possible. You have to build up your reservoir of trustability in advance, *before* the asteroid strikes. John Costello, chief global marketing and innovation officer of Dunkin' Donuts, says it's like a savings account.

You make deposits by doing the right things for customers, treating employees fairly, making it work. You have to realize everything you do affects trustability, including how you handle it when things go wrong. And in the end, you have to make sure your deposits exceed your withdrawals. Promise what you deliver, and deliver what you promise. Consistently.

In the less predictable but more transparent e-social world, a company's *good intentions,* as evidenced by its decisions and actions, are the primary criterion customers use to decide whether they can trust the company, and the *competence* to deliver on those good intentions determines whether or not customers will really be able to see into the soul of that company. You can call it managing the customer experience, or delivering on customer insights, or simply the right hand knowing what the left is doing, but when you commit to trustability you have to get the basics right. Competence counts every bit as much as good intentions. And when everyone is watching, you'll have to be proactive about it.

Competence is the subject of our next chapter.

TRUSTABILITY
TEST

Think about how you'd answer these questions based on how things work at your company, institution, or government agency. Talk about your answers with your colleagues. Visit www.trustability.com to see how other visitors' responses compare with your own for these and other questions.

▶ Do you allow customers to make comments about your products and services on your own Web site, for other customers and prospective customers to see? If so,

　▷ How do you police these reviews and comments for obscenities or offensive language?

　▷ How do you handle legitimate complaints and negative ratings? (Do you take them down, or do you leave them in as part of the mix?)

　▷ What mechanism, if any, do you use to minimize the chance that a competitor will contaminate the review process?

　▷ Who at your firm takes charge of monitoring the reviews for useful feedback, systemic problems, and product improvement ideas? And who is responsible for making changes within the organization that will address the issues?

▶ Has your company tracked mentions of your brand or product on social media sites?

▶ Where else do customers make comments about your company besides your Web site?

▶ Where would they prefer to comment? To look for comments by others?

▶ How easy is it for customers to find other customers' comments on your products and services?

▶ Have you ever "mystery shopped" the Internet to try to find reviews and comments on your products?

▶ Have you or any of your employees or partners ever used sockpuppet identities to post positive reviews of your brand, or negative comments about competitors? Are you sure? What would happen inside the company if you discovered this practice?

▶ To what extent do you make it easy for visitors to authenticate themselves, even as you protect their identities? How do you balance (1) protecting visitors to the customer section of your Web site who are seeking objective information, and (2) encouraging candid comments? Does your company have a policy with respect to identified employees participating in blogs and social media? Approximately how many or what proportion of your employees blog or comment on your company's behalf? Does anyone in your public relations department monitor this? Do you personally know of, or have you heard any stories about, any of your company's customers who actively advocate on your behalf to others (as Jason Sadler does for Best Buy)?

▷ Do you have an initiative in place to identify such "advocates" on your behalf?

▷ Do you have any policies designed to promote the likelihood of customers becoming advocates?

▶ Do you currently have any competitors who have lower costs, faster delivery, or higher quality than you do? Have you ever sent a customer to a competitor because it was in the customer's best interest?

▶ Who at your firm ensures that poor service or mistakes are followed up with apologies and make-goods?

▶ What percentage of unsatisfied customers on the phone ask for "a supervisor" because the problem couldn't handled by the person who took the call?

▶ How soon after an incident is an apology rendered?

▶ If a social media disaster were to occur, causing a great deal of negative online publicity and comment, how would you plan to dispel this negative comment and deal with the damage? Have you practiced this plan? How much would your own employees volunteer to help? What about your customers?

[8]

HONEST COMPETENCE

Good-Nature and Good-Sense must ever join;
To err is human, to forgive divine.
ALEXANDER POPE

On the surface the two components of trust—good intentions and competence—would seem to be two completely different and independent qualities. Intention is a state of mind, and as we said in chapter 2, since we can't read minds, the only way we can get any indication of someone else's intent is by inferring it from their words and actions. We judge their intent by what we would intend ourselves, if we were to speak or act in a similar way. "Competence," on the other hand, is not a state of mind at all, but a demonstrable talent or capability. A competent firm executes well, has reliable and disciplined people carrying out its policies, and doesn't make stupid mistakes. Proficiency and competence are directly observable. And they are an important part of "customer experience"—how it feels to be a company's customer. Customer experience is the reason you connect your siloed databases, and send your people to seminars on mobile best practices, and increase efficiency so you can save your customers time and help them find and get what they need without any roadblocks, at a fair price.

[Competence Is Related to Good Intentions]

The truth is, however, that while competence may be visible, it is still a quality that has to be deliberately built over time. Companies don't just spring into existence fully capable of good service, high-quality production, and customer insight. To become competent requires some amount of deliberation and intent on the company's part. Without good intentions, it's doubtful that a firm would actually go to the trouble to build up enough competence to treat customers fairly, or "do things right."

Or, turning the question around, suppose you buy from a company that promises it will always respect your interest, but when dealing with their people you find that they don't understand your problem, they can't answer the phone in less than five minutes, they can't remember your specifications from last time, or they treat every customer exactly the same, you included. They screw up a lot, and even though they act nice and *mean* well, it's just too difficult to do business with them. And you can't rely on them. In this situation, you'd have to find yourself asking just how good their intentions could actually be, right? If they *really* intended to protect your interests, wouldn't they have made a little more effort?

In chapter 2 we reviewed Netflix's fumbled effort to separate the DVD and streaming video business, while also introducing a significant price increase. What aroused customers' ire was the fact that the company appeared to have disregarded customer sentiment altogether in making its pricing move. It might have been incompetence, or it might have been bad intentions, but customer trust evaporated almost overnight in any case.

In retrospect, Netflix could have done things differently, and the outcome might not have been so bad for them. In the first place, every junior marketer knows that price reductions should be dramatic and significant, while price increases should be small and incremental. It's almost a certainty that CEO Reed Hastings's own marketing people would have argued strenuously in favor of that kind of a strategy, but the technologists and engineers running the company (including Hastings, a mathematician and computer scientist himself) must have overridden this advice. Pity they didn't practice evidence-based management, which we discuss in the next chapter. More important, however, all Netflix's customers are monthly subscribers, most of whom are actively engaged in mailing DVDs back and forth to the company, or connecting directly to the company's Web site in order to schedule their streaming videos. In other words, Netflix's customers interact with the firm on a regular basis. Some had already subscribed for years, having deserted Blockbuster for a company they felt was more reasonable (and more trustable!), but Netflix never once acknowledged this loyalty or familiarity. Here was a direct-marketing business with vast details on people's movie viewing habits, behaviors, and tastes, and yet, when the change came, Netflix treated every customer exactly the same as every other customer! Instead of treating everyone the same, what if Netflix had announced its price increase with even a rudimentary amount of special treatment to provide a small benefit to the customers who had been with it the longest, or who had used it the most, or who had recommended other customers? What if the announcement from Hastings had said something like "Hey, in two months we have to increase our prices, but if you've been our customer for two years or more then we won't increase YOUR price until this time next year, and thanks for your loyalty!" Even a nominal offer like this, had it been aimed at those customers most involved with the company, would have had a dramatic impact on how Netflix was perceived by everyone.

Or, once the social conflagration flared up, Netflix could have handled it in a manner similar to the way Facebook handled the customer insurrection surrounding its change in the terms of service in early 2009 (see chapter 6). Consider what might have happened if, in his apology e-mail, Reed Hastings had said: "We want to continue the DVD-rental business economically, but our pricing for DVDs and for streaming videos needs to reflect the very real fact that our costs are quite different for providing those two types of service to you. So we're going to put off any price or service change for six months, and during that time we'd like your support in helping us to design a different business model that will be able to support both DVDs and streaming video, so our customers can continue seeing movies the way each of you wants to. If you'd like to help us work on this problem, we'd greatly appreciate your ideas. The job doesn't pay anything, but if you are the first to suggest any idea that we end up using we'll give you a lifetime membership. . . ." (Certainly cheaper than the million-dollar prize they awarded to the winning recommendation algorithm!)

Whether Netflix fumbled the ball on account of bad marketing advice, or bad planning, or simply arrogance, or most likely just getting caught up in the day-to-day interests of the company and putting that ahead of the interests of customers, customers looked at the result and just scratched their heads, many of them more mystified than irate. They didn't want to believe that this company they once loved had had selfish intentions all along. They wanted to give it the benefit of the doubt. But competence *does* matter. You can't maintain your customers' trust if you aren't even competent enough to handle a simple price increase.

Because a company's intentions can only be inferred from its actions, it has to be at least somewhat competent in its actions if it wants people to be able to see its good intentions. If it stumbles in an obvious or careless way, or if its actions show little regard for the competent serving of customers and respect for customers' needs and time and effort, then its intentions will definitely be called into question. Competence and good intentions, in other words, are not separate ideas at all; they are joined at the hip.

[Product Competence and Customer Competence]

To remain competitive today, a company needs to make and deliver a quality product or service, and it needs to understand and relate to the customer being sold to. We can call these two basic capabilities *product* competence and *customer* competence, and both are critical. Product competence means your company delivers a reasonably good product or service, on time, in such a way that it doesn't need a lot of maintenance, repair, correction, or undue attention from the customer just to meet the need or solve the problem it is designed to handle. Customer competence requires your company to understand the customer's individual needs and address them, and interact with the customer smoothly and efficiently.

Do things right.

When we talk about product competence, we're not just talking about the physical product, if there is one, but we're including whatever service is required. Fashioning the "offer" for a customer requires organizing the firm, procuring the resources, running a factory, scheduling jobs, managing and training people, keeping the books, evaluating investments, and deploying capital. There was a time, perhaps, when product quality varied so much among companies that simply delivering a quality product could often differentiate a business, and history is full of well-meaning companies that failed on account of product incompetence.

Today, however, no business can persist for long without having relatively high-quality products—that is, products that do what the firm says they're going to do, and don't break or malfunction with normal use. There are varieties in terms of quality and pricing in most categories, but competition is a great leveler. Without pricing differences, it would be impossible to remain in business with lower-than-normal quality. Instead, a company has to have product and service quality that is generally on a par with its immediate competitive set, and this standard has increased enough over the last century that it's hard today to find truly substandard products in most developed economies. Subquality products just aren't around long enough to be an issue. If you don't have at least a basic level of product competence your business won't be operating for very long and, of course, no one is going to trust you either.

Instead, the sort of competence most often lacking in a business nowadays has to do with customer competence—insight into what the customer actually needs (as opposed to what he's buying), how he sees the world, and how he's different from other customers, along with the ability to act on that insight by treating different customers differently. In short, most businesses are just not very competent when it comes to *empathizing* with their customers.

George Day, a professor of marketing at the Wharton School and an expert in customer relationships, says that to be a leader in customer competence (as opposed to a "price-value leader") a business must have three important characteristics:

1. Their relationships with their best customers are unusually tight, so there is mutual trust based on shared understanding and mutual commitments. These leaders are experts at their customers' businesses (or lives, in the case of consumers).

2. They have broadened their offering far beyond their core product to include customer information and training, complementary products, support services, and financing as required. They compete on scope rather than scale.

3. Their customers think they are getting an offering that has been tailored to their needs. It may be fully customized or simply personalized. This is not the one-size-fits-all approach of price value leaders.

(Note: Netflix doesn't have all these characteristics—not yet anyway.)

When a customer decides to buy a product or service of any kind, it's not because he is enamored with the physical product or the elements of service. It's not because he loves your store or your Web site or even your friendly people. The basis of the customer's motivation is that he has some need to be met, or some problem to be solved, and he believes you have the competence to do it. Your product or service is simply his tool for accomplishing the task. As Clayton Christensen famously suggests, your customer is simply hiring your product to do a job. Customer competence involves the skill to truly understand what job the customer is actually trying to get accomplished, *from the customer's own perspective.*

When Cigna made a commitment to become a "trusted" organization—we hadn't talked to them about the term "trustability" yet—the health care industry was not particularly in favor. So making a shift to build advocacy for and by customers promised to become a serious journey. Their first step was simply to take the customers' point of view about the language used in their communications with customers, which didn't match the vocabulary Cigna employees usually used. For example, customers like to be called "customers," and not "patients." And rather than hearing about a "health care provider," customers would rather use the words "doctor" or "nurse." There are more than two hundred terms that required this replacement overhaul, and internally Cigna employees docked each other when someone used the old terms instead of the customer-friendly ones. But the results were dramatic: The number of customers who understood how Cigna's business worked for them more than doubled, increasing in excess of 100 percent, while the volume of printed materials Cigna had to send out to members fell by more than 50 percent, reducing costs and improving the customer experience.

Compare this to the way most health care insurance companies work. Dietrich Chen, director at Peppers & Rogers Group, predicts that "payers will need to become more flexible in meeting the wide-ranging needs of customers. This includes providing the kind of support that different types of customers require based on their needs and channel preferences. That's going to require a sea change in the approach that most payers currently take towards delivering customer service. At the moment, for example, most payers only make themselves available to answer customer questions during normal business hours. That's not a convenient time for most people. Customers don't want to discuss personal and sensitive medical issues over the phone while they're at work within earshot of their colleagues. Payers need to provide customers with a variety of channels and time options that offer greater privacy."

An innovative health insurance company in South Africa, Discovery Life offers a special program called Vitality, which members purchase to get deep discounts on wellness benefits, such as free gym visits (which are only free provided the member makes a certain minimum use of the gym!). According to Kenny Rabson, deputy CEO of Discovery Life, "The positive impact of Vitality on mortality and morbidity is significant and it is in fact exceeding expectations, particularly in the first years of a policy's lifetime." Discovery encourages healthy behavior that reduces long-term health care costs by rewarding members for improving their health. It has been clinically proven that Vitality members have lower health care costs than nonmembers. Discovery has teamed up with Humana in the United States to offer a similar program, providing incentives and rewards to members in order to encourage them to maintain healthier habit and lifestyles. In essence, a trustable health care company will be expected to make recommendations to customers that will improve their health and *reduce* their premiums.

Before assembly lines and mass production, when virtually all commerce involved face-to-face interactions with merchants, the best merchants were those who maintained the strongest relationships with their customers, remembering their personal specifications and attending to their needs with care. The highly efficient mass marketing disciplines that characterized most of the last century meant that this sort of personalized service became far too expensive to be competitive, but computer technology has once again made it possible. Today we might call it customer relationship management (CRM), or one-to-one marketing, or customer experience management, or customer centricity—but no matter what you call it, the fact is that to be competitive today a company has to have some degree of customer competence, *in addition to* product competence. To be competitive today, a company needs to be able to empathize with customers more effectively, to take the customer's perspective, to know what it feels like to "be our customer." What it *should* feel like. As with product competence, competitive success doesn't require a firm to be the very best at remembering and interacting with customers individually, but it does require that it not be significantly behind its competitors.

Although we just said that simply maintaining a par performance for product and customer competence should be good enough, we should also stipulate that *most* firms could still generate a substantial financial benefit for themselves simply by improving their performance in either area. Both types of competence are required in order to satisfy customers. And consumer research shows that while improvements in customer satisfaction do generate modest improvements in customer loyalty, what *really* generates greater loyalty is reducing or eliminating customer *dissat-*

isfaction. Rather than figuring out how to do a better and better job of "surprise and delight" for customers, in other words, most firms would be better advised to concentrate simply on eliminating obstacles for the customer—nuisances, redundancies, or extra work on the customer's part. To be trustable, a company needs to empathize, take the customer's point of view, and figure out how to make it easy to be a customer.

Forget about "surprise and delight." Just don't screw up.

Most companies that customers see as being "competent"—as "doing things right"—either have already embraced customer centricity as a primary business driver or are in the process of doing so now. They recognize that customers are the only source of revenue (by definition), that customers are a scarce asset (likely the scarcest and least replaceable), and that customers create long-term value as well as short-term value. If you want to be customer-competent enough to be trustable, then you must:

- Treat different customers differently, based on what they need from you and what their value is to you;

- Rather than focusing on one product at a time and trying to find customers for that product, focus on one customer at a time and try to find products for that customer;

- Get smarter over time with customers, by building Learning Relationships—that is, by steadily enriching the context of your relationship with each individual customer;

- Ask what customers want and would be willing to pay for that they can't get from anyone for any price (not you, not your competitors); and

- Build customer-based metrics, including lifetime value, customer profitability, and customer equity, into the evaluations of employees and business units.

There's more to it than this, of course. All we're talking about in the bullet points above is the *stuff you have to do*. We haven't even addressed the issue of *how to get it done,* and that's a very big issue to address. When clients ask us difficult questions about how to get this stuff done, we often tell them that no matter how good your computer systems, analytics, and work processes are, you can't just write a line of code or a process requirement that will result in earning a customer's trust. Customers don't trust software, processes, or business rules. Customers trust people.

So one aspect of trustability is putting on a human face, as we suggested in chapter 2. But another aspect of it is having people at your firm who *want* to be trustable, who embrace the goal of being trustable and will push your organization toward it. That's why Mark Grindeland, CMO of TeleTech, says that

> *social media are important to your company. Your <u>whole</u> company. Handling "social" and "mobile" is not something you can assign to a junior team in the marketing department. Your approach has to be enterprise wide.*

[Honest Competence Requires Honestly Competent People]

You can't earn the trust of your customers with a policy statement. You can only earn trust with actions. The problem is that the "actions" your company takes are taken by employees, not by the CEO or the board of directors. As far as a customer is concerned, the ordinary, low-level customer-contact employee they interact with on the phone or at the store—that employee *is* your company.

If you want to ensure that your company treats each customer the way you'd want to be treated if you were the customer yourself, then you need to think about the way individual employees deal with and interact with customers. Obviously, policies and practices will be involved, but by themselves they won't be sufficient. What you really need is a culture within your company that celebrates earning the trust of customers. Or as Susan Whiting, Vice Chair, The Nielsen Company, says:

Connect "do good" with your brand. Make it business as usual to secure the website, be a good citizen, achieve sustainability. And do it right. For many companies, that will be even harder than doing the right thing. But it's impossible, really, to separate the importance of serving shareholders from the importance of serving the customers. How can you make life better, simpler, easier, more rewarding for clients?

The problem is that "culture" is one of those things that is very difficult to pin down exactly. A lot of management teams latch on to the idea of "culture" and try to codify it and popularize it within the firm, but writing a values statement for your company is not at all the same thing as living it, nor will it have much impact on your real-world culture. We once visited a company that had a written set of official company values, and these values were posted throughout the headquarters, along with the company's mission statement. You've probably seen stuff like this before (who hasn't?), but to protect the identity of this client, we'll just paraphrase the top line of the posted "statement of values," which went something like this:

We always do the right thing for customers.

Now doesn't that just sound terrific? That's a great attitude to take toward customers, the market, and the business's overall purpose. It's a marvelous statement of values for a forward-thinking, customer-oriented company. Yet the more employees and middle managers we met, the more it became clear to us that everyone in the organization was focused on one thing: Make this quarter's numbers at any cost. These managers' daily actions and decisions supported a different set of values—a set of values that weren't written down and posted on the wall, but which permeated the culture and dominated how the company decided which actions were right and wrong. The *real*, unwritten value statement, if it had been posted on the wall, would have read:

We always do whatever it takes to make this quarter's numbers.

So far, we haven't read about this firm being involved in any kind of scandal, industrial safety failure, or customer service meltdown. But our guess is that the only reason we haven't is that the company just hasn't encountered any serious threat to its quarterly bottom line yet. Sooner or later, however, they are likely to meet such a problem, and when they do they will fail the test. And then everyone will wonder how a company with such marvelous values could have acted in such a self-centered, uncaring fashion toward their customers, their employees, or their shareholders.

The culture at your firm will reflect how you measure success, how you reward people, what tasks you consider to be important, how quickly and effectively you make decisions, and who approves decisions. Your culture will reflect how friendly people are to others, how trusting they are, how much disagreement is tolerated, and what actions are considered out of bounds. Your company's culture will trump any rules, defeat any controls, and trample over any conflicting processes. "Culture, more than rule books, determines how an organization behaves" is how Warren Buffett put it. You can write down your firm's values, in other words, and even codify them in an employee manual, but if you want the company to live up to them then you'd better ensure not just that your systems, rules, and processes are aligned with your values, but that your *people* really believe in them, and are rewarded when they act on them. Really.

A company's culture can be either good or bad for the business, either a "long-lasting competitive advantage, difficult for your competitors to duplicate, or a giant albatross with bad breath hung around your corporate neck." It is your company's culture that maintains the permanence of your organization. People will come and go, business initiatives will thrive and perish, but the unspoken rules that permeate your company are a *social* phenomenon, passed on from employee to employee, aided and abetted by compensation formulas, expectations, and social protocols. Dov Seidman says it is through their cultures that "companies have the opportunity to grow more varied and diverse while simultaneously remaining tightly aligned in a common purpose."

Although culture permeates an entire organization from top to bottom to top, what a company's senior managers expect of employees, what they say and how they behave will have a pronounced influence. Creating a culture in which honest competence will succeed requires leading by example. If you want employees to treat customers the way they'd like to be treated if they were the customers, then treat your employees the way you'd like to be treated if you were the employee.

Company "culture" is what employees do when no one's looking.

And, as a leader, you should never shrink from an opportunity to stand up for your company's values. Consider the hypothetical effect of the alternative:

DEAR ABBY,

A colleague in my company is responsible for selling professional services to our corporate clients—usually large companies. He's very successful, and has built his division into a high growth business in just the few years he's managed it.

But there is something very unsettling to me about the way my friend deals with his clients. When I'm with him and he gets a business call on his cell phone, he has absolutely no regard for the truth when it comes to telling his own managers what to say to a client. In pricing negotiations, for instance, I've heard him suggest complete and utter lies, such as "tell the client this is absolutely our biggest possible discount, because the head office forbids us to undercut the rest of the company" (untrue), or "tell them the hourly rate can't be reduced on this contract because of our prior contractual obligation to this subject matter expert" (also untrue).

I've noticed that even in our casual discussions, when so much as a minor inconvenience is threatened, my friend might make up a totally bogus excuse for dealing with it. To overcome a scheduling conflict I've heard him tell his secretary to call the client and tell them he got delayed on his flight (he didn't), or that his boss unexpectedly convened a must-attend senior-staff phone meeting (not so). What bothers me most about these overheard comments is the complete casualness with which my friend bends, twists, and undermines the truth. Not only does he show no remorse whatsoever, but in many cases I've heard him suggest a lie when it wouldn't really have been much more trouble just to explain the truth carefully.

Am I a prude here? What should I do?

Signed, Honestly Stumped

[Self-Organization and Open Leadership]

For much of this book we've been discussing how important it is to be able to deal honestly and straightforwardly with conflicting ideas, random events, and situations in which you can't really exercise control. Roger Martin, dean of the University of Toronto's Rotman School of Management, is someone who has spent a great deal of time studying the traits of successful business leaders. His conclusion:

> . . . *most of them share a somewhat unusual trait: They have the predisposition and the capacity to hold in their heads two opposing ideas at once. And then, without panicking or simply settling for one alternative or the other, they're able to creatively resolve the tension between those two ideas by generating a new one that contains elements of the others but is superior to both. This process of consideration and synthesis can be termed integrative thinking.*

Integrative thinking is the only way to deal with the increasingly interconnected, highly complex "system" that characterizes the modern business environment. Michael Mauboussin, chief investment strategist at Legg Mason Capital Management, suggests it's time to rethink altogether how we evaluate and reward senior managers. Yes, we can reward a salesman or a factory worker based on sales made or on work completed, because the worker has some control over his or her output. But paying the CEO of a global firm an incentive based on sales figures or corporate profit or even stock price is not nearly so compelling, according to Mauboussin, because there are so many factors that just aren't under the CEO's control. Rather, in addition to some payment based on *output*, Mauboussin suggests that "in a probabilistic system" some sort of incentive for the right *input* is also appropriate—for instance, an incentive based on the quality of the process used in decision making, regardless of the actual outcome of the decision.

If a company were to do this, of course, the immediate issue would be the subjectivity of the evaluation. Profit may not be predictable in advance, and it may result from chance events, and it may not even be influenced much by an executive's own actions, but as an output it has the advantage of being precisely measurable. You can't quarrel with a company's "bottom line" profit any more than you can quarrel with a winning lottery ticket. Furthermore, the science of management has come a long way since the days when the fate of an employee was entirely in the hands of his subjective, opinionated, or biased supervisor. The whole "Management by Objectives" movement, for instance, is predicated on the idea that compensation and recognition should be more objectively provided, and more directly tied to actual business results.

However, what Mauboussin and others are advocating is not that results don't count, but that a pure results-only approach to evaluating any individual employee or business unit should no longer be considered sufficient in and of itself. In a word, such an evaluation mechanism is just not competent. Instead, executives should be evaluated based on inputs as well as outputs. The problem is that this requires someone somewhere (the manager's immediate boss, the board, the compensation committee) to make a human judgment, and human judgments are inherently tainted by subjectivity. We are placing the manager's economic livelihood in the hands of another person(s), and we are asking the manager to *trust* this other person to render a "fair" decision—that is, to demonstrate both good intentions and competence.

According to one technologist, today's economy is becoming "generative." Instead of focusing on how to optimize a fixed operation, today's businesses are constantly trying to create new combinations, or "new configurable offerings." As this happens, the job of "management" at a business will inevitably become less concerned with solving particular problems and more concerned with making sense of chaotic, undefined, transient situations, making a transition from "rationality to sense-making; from commodity-based companies to skill-based companies; from the purchase of components to the formation of alliances; from steady-state operations to constant adaptation."

Ultimately, of course, the plummeting cost of human interaction will not just change the nature of a corporation's activities, but *will call into question the need for the corporation at all*. Companies exist because they enable people to interact more efficiently for the purpose of creating value collectively. But we're already seeing that as frictionless interactivity increases, the number of tasks directly taken on by companies is declining. The dramatic upsurge in outsourcing and partnering with other firms (including, sometimes, direct competitors) is only the beginning. Over time, firms will increasingly divest themselves of tasks not directly relevant to their most central corporate missions.

The only kind of company or organization that will be able to survive in this environment is one fueled by the trust and empathy that flow among independently acting human employees. It relies less on top-down, hierarchical, command-and-control management principles, and more on bottom-up, values-based self-organization. When a customer problem occurs, and a couple of employees zero in on it, take ownership of it, and figure out on their own how to solve it with no top-down direction or management intervention—that is a self-organizing company, and mutual trust among employees is a minimum requirement. In the hyperinteractive, e-social future, this is rapidly becoming the most viable kind of firm. Whether it's Best Buy's Twelpforce honestly helping customers, or a customer service rep posting a $25 credit to your credit card on account of a missed delivery date, it won't be the company with rules, structures, and detailed compliance mechanisms that succeeds, but the one with employees who *want* their company to succeed—employees who *trust* their company, and have *empathy* for its customers.

Seidman suggests there are seven important reasons why such self-governing cultures are advantageous:

1. A horizontal world calls for a horizontal governance architecture. Self-governance minimizes organizational layers and can increase a company's resilience.

2. Self-governing organizations thrive on the free flow of information. "[T]he free flow of information makes cultures more self-governing by increasing trust."

3. A leading company needs to be a company of leaders. In a more transparent world, ordinary employees must be able to take more initiative.

4. Values-based self-governing cultures encourage employee development. Training is for dogs. Development is for leaders.

5. Self-governance builds universal vigilance. Not everyone is good all the time. A self-governing organization will enforce values, and expel violators more efficiently than a hierarchy.

6. Self-governance shifts decision making from the pragmatic to the principled. Reputation and trust come from respecting principles, not obeying rules.

7. Self-governance is a higher concept. It speaks to the "higher self," in the same way trust, belief, and values do. It is an inspiring organizational model.

Competence matters, and you can't be a trustable company if you aren't customer-competent.

Nor can you be trustable for very long if your product and service quality aren't on a par with your competitors'. You should be better, but at a minimum you should be comparable. In many business categories, simply not causing customers grief will go a long way toward making you tops in trustability.

But what if your product really isn't up to par?

[True Confessions: Domino's and the Transparent Pizza]

If the customer experience is bad, customers will still talk about it. They'll let others know. But don't expect acknowledgment from the brand. Yes, the marketing department would encourage their company to take steps to improve the experience, but no no NO—if the experience isn't good they certainly won't broadcast the fact. No sane marketing executive would ever call a flawed customer experience to anyone's attention.

In today's highly transparent world, however, an ugly fact like a bad customer experience will no longer go unnoticed just because it isn't advertised. Whether the marketing department acknowledges it or not, people will know. Immediately. Everywhere. Forever.

In April 2009, a couple of rogue Domino's Pizza employees posted a video on YouTube showing one of them doing disgusting things to prepare food, even sticking cheese up his nose before putting it on a pizza. The video was viewed more than a million times in just a few days and soon dominated Google's search results for Domino's Pizza, as well as becoming a trending topic on Twitter. But he who lives by the Tube dies by the Tube. Within hours of having posted their videos the perpetrators were identified by bloggers and others as Kristy Hammonds Thompson and Michael Setzer, employees at the Domino's outlet in Conover, North Carolina. Although the two maintained that none of the food filmed in the video was actually delivered to a customer, they were summarily fired and handed over to Conover police to face felony charges. Moving rapidly to contain the PR disaster, Domino's CEO Patrick Doyle immediately posted his own YouTube apology.

That would have marked the end of the episode, just one more social media headline for a day, except that a much bigger story was about to unfold. More than a year before this incident, Doyle and his marketing people had begun wrestling with the thorny problem of Domino's seemingly poor and outdated product quality, from the blandness of their standard pizza's taste and the processed appearance of its cheese to the sloppiness of its delivery. Domino's had developed a reputation among pizza consumers as the "pizza of last resort," the kind of food delivery you might order if you didn't have enough money to get a good pizza or if there was no Pizza Hut or Godfather's near enough. So, to celebrate the chain's fiftieth anniversary the company rolled out a completely new and revamped product. More than that, however, to publicize the upgraded product they launched a television ad campaign frankly admitting to the error of their (past) ways. One of the new commercials, for instance, played clips from focus groups in which participants lambasted their product as "the worst excuse for pizza" they'd ever had, before cutting to CEO Doyle's confession that while his company's pizza had been below standard for years, Domino's was now determined to do better.

Even though the new and improved pizza would still not be confused with a gourmet product, and Domino's certainly wasn't in the same league as some of the trendier, pricier pizza boutiques offering features such as whole-wheat crusts and all-organic ingredients, people were nonetheless intrigued by the company's candor. According to one college senior, for instance, who had himself participated in one of the focus groups panning the previous product, "those ads resonated with me in a way I didn't expect. I mean, they're right: Their pizza's bad. But to be honest like that—it makes you reconsider for a second."

And there was more to come. Six months later Domino's announced it would stop using retouched photos to promote its pizzas, relying instead on straight camera shots, honestly taken—and appealing to customers to send in their own photos for use in the ads. (*Adweek*'s story about this was headlined: "Domino's last week introduced an industry first: A transparent pizza.") The fact is that Domino's had embraced the power of social media early on, and company executives were already convinced that what customers said to one another mattered more to the brand's product reputation than what the company itself tried to say with its advertising. In the e-social era, they knew, no amount of gloss or bright paint would be able to cover up a weak product. According to Doyle,

. . . trying to spin things simply doesn't work anymore. Great brands going forward are going to have a level of honesty and transparency that hasn't been seen before.

The "Pizza Turnaround" campaign gave Domino's revenues and profitability a nice lift as well, with U.S. same-store sales increasing by nearly 10 percent in 2010, a phenomenal increase for the large chain. In fact, it was the first full year of positive growth since 2007, and for at least the first half of 2011 these higher levels of domestic same-store sales have been maintained or increased.

Importantly, Domino's was taking on a serious obligation when it decided to confess its sins. If the newly designed product had not been judged to be of higher quality, the brand's credibility would have plummeted even further and perhaps never recovered. As Doyle himself noted early on, while he was confident that the new product was good, "we also know this works once, and only if the claim is true." Good intentions are important, in other words, but competence still matters. And when you state your intent so openly, you have to be comfortable that your company has the competence to deliver on it.

As Domino's gained confidence from its policy of transparency it continued to push the envelope. In an effort to publicize its "Domino's Tracker," an online tool allowing customers to follow the progress of their pizza delivery orders, the company conjured up a unique demonstration of transparency for the summer of 2011. For a full month, from July 25 through August 23, Domino's took over a lighted billboard above Times Square in New York City and ran a near-real-time feed of candid customer comments about its pizza, taken from the online tool. In announcing the program, Domino's said simply that customer comments made the company better—so both positive and negative comments were going up on the billboard for the whole world to see. And sure enough, while a large majority of comments were positive, sprinkled among the positives were a significant number of negatives as well. Some comments pulled at random:

KATIE S, FT LAUDERDALE, FL, thanks for the great pie

VANESSA H, LAKE JACKSON, TX, Amazing!! Thanks!

ATHENA F, BILOXI, MS, You guys and gals are AWESOME

JOSE R, SAN ANTONIO, TX, Your guys pizza is always great no matter what I order

CAT C, FLAGSTAFF, AZ, James the pizza dude is super cute. :3

NADINE G, BLOOMINGTON, CA, The pizza was crushed by the box

SHARONNA Y, NORMANDY, MO, My address was not printed on the delivery sticker on the pizza box. I also did not receive a credit card receipt . . .

CRYSTAL C, HOUSTON, TX, Very good delivery

RICHARD C, CORPUS CHRISTI, TX, Better than it has been overall lately

JOHN F, IRVINE, CA, You guys are the best. Seriously.

DONALD L, CHAPEL HILL, NC, Outstanding Pizza, as usual. Never disappointed!

[Fallibility and Trust]

Domino's counterintuitive approach to marketing involves a frank admission of fallibility, along with a promise to do better. For traditional marketing professionals this seemed just crazy, but the craziness itself was something they found appealing. They liked the initiative's novelty, but they still weren't sure it made sense for any company to air its dirty laundry so publicly. In critiquing the Times Square billboard initiative, for example, a columnist for *Adweek* colorfully labeled Domino's broader marketing strategy "stridently self-flagellatory."

And one widely recognized positioning consultant's perspective perfectly illustrates how traditional marketing spin differs so substantially from trustability. Noting first that a marketing strategy promoting authenticity did have its benefits, she referenced the "Real Thing" campaign for Coca-Cola. But, she said, Domino's claim had been undercut by its own Pizza Turnaround effort. "What's more inauthentic than admitting you had a crappy recipe?" she asked. (Interesting question. How about: *not* admitting it?)

The traditional PR and marketing approach to a bad product or service accusation would be to follow the classic CIA dictum: "Admit nothing. Deny everything. Make counteraccusations." If you're a traditional marketer, the basic problem with the whole idea of publicly admitting any kind of error is that the admission undermines whatever artificial reality you've crafted with millions of dollars' worth of spin. Whether or not it's justified, it undercuts your investment. But the only reason an inauthentic—even deceptive—communications strategy has ever actually succeeded in the past is that until recently people mostly *didn't* know your product needed work. So even if *you* knew there was a problem (after all, it's your product, you have most of the research, and you're the one with the satisfaction statistics), admitting to it would simply alert a lot of otherwise in-the-dark customers. In such a world, any admission like that is damning. Deny everything. Make counteraccusations.

Today, however, the world has become so transparent that everybody will already know your product is "crappy," so refusing to admit it yourself is not just inauthentic but downright delusional. In the real world—the *non*marketing world inhabited not by business gurus and marketing experts but by ordinary people constantly interacting with other people—fallibility is the most direct route to trustworthiness. Admitting one's own vulnerability is the first step in earning someone else's trust.

The converse of this, by the way, is that admitting to errors is more acceptable in a more trusting environment. Therefore, if you want a resilient culture at your firm, making your organization capable of innovative experimentation and constant self-improvement, then you would be well advised to create a work environment in which errors are viewed not as political or personal liabilities, but as learning opportunities. Consider, for instance, the unexpected outcome of one study of U.S. nursing home practices during the 1990s. A Harvard Business School researcher found that in those nursing homes characterized by the most respected leadership and the closest, most trusting relationships among workers, the reported error rate was *ten times greater* than in other, comparable institutions with less trusting work environments. The reason, she found, was not that the quality of work was lower. In fact, the actual quality of work was *higher*, but because workers trusted management and each other they weren't afraid to report mistakes. There were almost certainly many more errors in the nontrusting work environments, but they weren't reported.

An honest work environment—a culture in which people share a unifying set of beliefs and are encouraged to share opinions and self-organize—is the secret sauce of a trustable organization. It is the primary ingredient of organizational competence, and competence is just as important as good intentions in earning the trust of customers.

TRUSTABILITY
TEST

Think about how you'd answer these questions based on how things work at your company, institution, or government agency. Talk about your answers with your colleagues. Visit www.trustability.com to see how other visitors' responses compare with your own for these and other questions.

▶ Do your company's products and services have reasonably good quality—in other words, are they on a par with or better than the quality of products and services offered at similar prices by your competitors?

▶ Does your business maintain active relationships with your highest value customers?

▶ You know that data is key. When you use data about customers, do you proactively protect their privacy?

▶ Do you treat all customers the same, or do you have different customer treatments designed for different customers or types of customers?

▶ Is your company's product-and-service offering broad enough so that individual customers' problems can be comprehensively solved, or do customers require additional products or services—that is, products or services you do not sell—in order to completely meet their needs?

▶ Do you maintain information systems capable of eliminating relatively minor customer mistakes and hassles, such as requiring a paper receipt as proof of purchase in order to complete a return or exchange? Are there areas in which small improvements in your own business processes or information flows could greatly improve the customer experience?

▶ Do you measure, track, and implement policies and initiatives to determine their effect on both customer satisfaction and customer dissatisfaction? On customer value?

▶ Does your company track customer profitability by individual customer? By segment?

> Do you have some insight into the different lifetime values of different customers or types of customers?

> Have you identified the factors that account for significant changes in those lifetime values—up or down?

▶ If a difficult customer problem was presented to two different employees at your company in isolation, would they probably approach the solution to the problem in a similar way? That is, do your employees all have a consistent view of the right way to handle customers and customer-related issues?

▶ Do you pay your managers and evaluate the performance of business units solely based on results, or do you also evaluate the *inputs* to their decision making, including processes used, information considered, and opinions consulted? What steps do you take to ensure the trustworthiness of subjective evaluations?

▶ Is your company's culture attuned to celebrating experimentation and new ideas?

> If an initiative or new idea fails, how are the executives involved evaluated?

> Would you say that being involved in a failed initiative is the "kiss of death" professionally at your firm?

▶ If an employee discovered a genuine mistake or problem in a product or service or discovered that "we did something wrong," would it be more likely to be concealed to avoid getting anyone into trouble or to be reported to management quickly so the problem could be resolved?

   ▷ Would the employee be more likely to report the problem to management or act as a whistleblower and report the problem publicly?

▶ If management finds out before social networking reveals it, how will it be handled—squelched, delayed, or reported publicly right away?

[9]

TRUSTABLE INFORMATION

Who you gonna believe, me or your own eyes?
CHICO MARX, IN THE MOVIE *DUCK SOUP*

When your customers seek the advice of others—whether they turn to your own employees, or to other customers, or to complete strangers—what they're looking for is information. They want to *know*. They want the answers to all the questions they have about you, your service, and your products. Is the service worth the price? Are you as good as your competitor? Does your product really work? How hard is it to use? If it breaks, are you going to fix it? Would you take advantage of me or even rip me off if you got the chance? Am I going to feel comfortable doing business with you?

The answers to these questions may consist of fact or opinion, but they all constitute information, and it's information that's useful, because with it customers can do a better job of solving their problems, or meeting whatever needs they have. Information is the ammunition for every decision we make—not just in buying things, but in life itself. Information is how we navigate the world.

The problem is, whether you measure it by the gigabyte or the megaflop, information today is cheap, and it's everywhere. Data being created and stored today include not just business documents, government statistics, and scientific research, but also blog posts and Web sites, status updates, photos, videos, comments, product reviews, text messages, podcasts, "like" and "share" buttons, and location check-ins. More and more today, information is generated through the individual efforts of millions of people, interacting in billions of ways, independently. For instance, every twenty-four hours Google processes more than a billion individual search requests and Facebook users generate some three terabytes of new information.

One of the key reasons for the explosive growth in data is the fact that people just want to "be social." Being social is a driving human force, generating not just increased transparency and trust but an explosion of information as well. Social media platforms are superefficient tools for sharing. Snap that picture of a rock star onstage as seen from the front row, or capture the Shuttle launch coming up through the clouds as seen from your airliner window, and you can share it with everyone, right away. That's why, even though Flickr and some other photo sites have more robust features, Facebook has rapidly become the world's largest photo repository. On Facebook you can not only display your photo, but tag your friends and share it around, and you were already there doing a bunch of other things anyway.

Current estimates are that the volume of data available to the human race doubles roughly every two years, but now that technology is beginning to connect up highly efficient networks of people, as opposed to simply streamlining the storage and processing of data itself, the speed at which new data will be generated is likely to accelerate faster than Moore's law. From a mathematical perspective, the messaging in a growing network increases at a "combinatorial" rate, faster than geometric growth, and some of the more breathless estimates are that within just a few years the volume of data and "technical information" may be doubling every few hours.

This is an almost unimaginable acceleration in new data and information. It will test the limits of human understanding, requiring us to focus ever more carefully on accuracy, reliability, usefulness, objectivity, and consistency. It may be an ocean of data, after all, but a lot of it is repetitive or banal ("the first 10 search results out of 12 million"). If you tweet that you'll be at the Starbucks on Tenth Street in thirty minutes, your friend's retweet of that message generates more data but not much new information. And lots of information is inaccurate, or fictional, or just wrong.

[Can This Information Be Trusted?]

We will have to have enough focus and discipline to ignore a great deal of this information tonnage, while becoming skilled at spotting the most useful nuggets. And the very first filter applied whenever we take on new information is trust. As individuals, that's how we decide what's worth paying attention to. Is it credible? Do we believe it? Is it useful? Do we trust the source? Whatever benefits we obtain from new information will be directly related to how trustworthy we think the information is. And when we pass information on to others, it (and we) will be judged by how skilled we are in analyzing and understanding it, handling it, and using it ourselves.

But what does it really mean to "trust" information? Circling back to the components of trust—do things right and do the right thing—we can employ a direct analogy:

> *Information that has "good intentions" is <u>objective</u> information, and "competent" information is information that is <u>accurate</u>.*

When we judge the trustability of information—the opinions of others, news, insight, or other data—we are assessing its objectivity and accuracy. Is the information slanted and biased, or is it reasonably objective? Is the information incomplete, sloppy, or mistaken, or is it correct, factual, and thorough?

We have all experienced the frustration of dealing with higher and higher volumes of data, and once again, it's easy to recognize the rising importance of trustability when it comes to handling this overload. Think about what happens when, say, you open your e-mail inbox in the morning and you see twenty-five or maybe fifty new messages. You want to sort through them fairly quickly, so one thing you look for right away is whether a message seems to have new, unusual, or unanticipated information. In a work situation, or even if you're just scanning personal messages, you know that it's really only the new or different information that merits your immediate attention.

And while you're trying to decide what's worth paying attention to, you're also judging how *trustworthy* each item of new information is. Something may look interesting (you didn't expect it, or you're surprised by it), but is it really accurate? Is it objective? Is it credible enough for you to believe it? The more interesting or unusual any particular item of information is, the more skepticism you are likely to apply to it, raising the bar for its trustworthiness. Before any piece of news or information radically changes your view of things, you have to be certain you can trust it.

Reconciling what we already know and believe with whatever new information we come across creates an immediate conflict in our minds, so before any new information can ever improve our understanding of how the world works we first have to resolve this tension. We have to let go of our illusion of control—that very helpful belief that we already understand completely what's going on around us—and we will only do this if we *trust* the new information.

When new information is predictable—when it doesn't surprise us or give us a different perspective—it's not as useful. *Unpredictable* information—information or insight that we didn't anticipate in advance—is more useful, because it can improve our understanding of how the world works, but it's also more threatening, because it conflicts with the secure feeling we all get by knowing that the world is understandable.

Still, by improving our insight, unpredictable information makes us smarter and more capable. When people say that something is "informative," what they're really saying is that it's unanticipated or surprising. It changes our view of things. We're writing this book, for example, because we think we have an informative idea—an idea no one might have thought of in quite the same way as we have, and which we hope will be helpful. It's our view that customers will demand a higher standard of trustworthiness from the companies they deal with, as social technologies continue to generate greater and greater transparency. This concept may seem intuitive once you think about it a bit (we hope so!), but it may not have been something you fully realized before you started chapter 1 with us.

Knowledge, perspective, and insight come from being exposed to unpredictable information. If everything you were exposed to were predictable, then you'd never get any wiser about the world. In an interesting parallel to this idea, sociologists who study our social connections with others have found that the best and most creative kinds of insights and new ideas are usually generated by our associations with people who are outside our closest social circles —that is, the more distant friends and colleagues whose views or insights we may be less familiar with. Quantitative studies, for instance, have shown that most people who get a new job through the recommendation of someone else do not receive that recommendation from a close friend or colleague, but from a distant one—someone they don't know as well, and whose own connections aren't as familiar. The reason this happens isn't because your best friends don't like you as much as your distant ones, but because for the most part you and the people you're closest to are already aware of all the same opportunities. The job openings known by your more distant friends, however, are more likely to be new and untried.

In the e-social world our ability to connect with friends and colleagues with whom we didn't have very close connections before has suddenly skyrocketed. Yochai Benkler maintains that we all use interactive technology to craft "limited-purpose, loose relationships" with an increasing number of our more distant friends and associates. You can see it happen all around you. A fifty-year-old mother starts an account on Facebook in order to keep up with her children now that they're in college, and soon she's corresponding with high school classmates she hasn't talked to in years. A business manager responds to a LinkedIn message from someone in a related field and suddenly the two of them are hatching a new business.

> People connected to groups beyond their own can expect to find them-
> selves delivering valuable ideas, seeming to be gifted with creativity. This
> is not creativity born of deep intellectual ability. It is creativity as an
> import-export business.
>
> *RONALD BURT*

Importantly, one of the keys to making diverse connections and gaining such new insights is simply to remain open to new or completely
strange ideas, and this kind of openness requires—you guessed it—
trusting other people. When two people don't trust each other, they're
unlikely to give much credence to each other's suggestions or ideas, and
neither will take the other's opinion very seriously.

The problem is that in our very human desire to associate with others,
we have a built-in preference for associating with others who are like
ourselves—people who share our beliefs, our values, our philosophy.
Most of us take more comfort in being with people who share our own
point of view, simply because this affirms our thinking and assuages our
ego. By contrast, we have a natural aversion to strange and unknown
things, and this aversion has an effect on whom we choose to associate
with and rely on, which in turn affects our ability to understand and in-
novate. Diversity has a lot to recommend it, but it's not a natural instinct.

The tension created in our minds between new or unanticipated
information and our own more comfortable illusion of control is a tool
that helps us understand the world. And we're all familiar with people
who seem to have gotten this tool out of whack. If someone is so open to
new information that he never worries about its trustworthiness, then we
say he's "gullible." Conversely, if someone is so averse to new information
that *nothing* passes her trustworthiness test, we call her "close minded."
Either way, you can't trust what *they* say without running their point of
view through your own trust filter.

On the other hand, when you strike just the right balance between
acceptance and skepticism, seeking out the most trustworthy new
ideas and then allowing them to change, improve, and enrich your own

perspective—this is a talent all too few of us have. You probably know people like this, though. They're called "iconoclasts."

In the end, the degree to which we trust new information has a great deal to do with whether we trust the source—the person we get the information from. Everyone reading this book probably has some relative or friend who blasts out e-mail after e-mail promoting his own political, religious, or economic point of view. It may be your uncle Charlie, and while you love him dearly, you wouldn't attempt to have a serious discussion with him about his views because they're set in stone. And have you ever bought something from a company, signed up for the e-mail updates, and then had to block the sender just to stop them from e-mailing you two or three times a day?

> Trust is the primary data filter protecting our attention span, and as the volume of data grows, this filter has to work more efficiently.

[Science, Trust, and Evidence-Based Management]

In order to benefit from the most useful information, we have to will ourselves to relish surprise and embrace the unpredictable—to be iconoclastic. For many of us, this may require a new mind-set and decision-making discipline.

The "scientific method" is designed in large part to overcome the flaws and biases in the thinking of individual scientists, ensuring that whatever new information or insight is gained from experimentation can be trusted. Valid and reliable scientific experiments are those that do a good job measuring what they purport to measure (demonstrating validity), and show results that can be replicated by others in similar experiments (demonstrating reliability). When scientific studies are published in journals, their trustworthiness is enforced by peer reviews.

But while the scientific method may work very well for science, it isn't used very often in making business management decisions. A good scientist tries hard to recognize his own biases and prejudices, but most business executives aren't so disciplined in their thinking. In fact, the higher the title, the more likely the executive is to think that she got there precisely because her way of thinking is just, well, right. (We saw a bumper sticker recently that could appear on the doors of a lot of offices: "I didn't know that when I met Mr. Right, his first name would be 'Always.'")

There are a lot of thinking habits and biases that undermine our ability to use and produce trustworthy information. For instance, we tend to place more credence in whatever facts or numbers confirm the point of view we already have, while we dismiss, minimize, or simply forget information that conflicts with our preconceived ideas. Social scientists call this the "confirmation bias," and we all have it. It flows naturally from the illusion of control we talked about in chapter 6.

The confirmation bias is particularly debilitating whenever (a) we are confronted with conflicting information, or (b) the problem we're solving is complex or subject to varying interpretations. In one social experiment, for instance, two groups of forty-eight Stanford students—one group in favor of the death penalty and the other group against it—were asked separately to read and discuss the exact same set of academic studies covering the death penalty's effectiveness. The experimenters found that both groups came away more convinced of their own views, and that the studies supported them. They remembered and noted the data from the stories that supported their own ideas, while either ignoring or finding fault with data that contradicted their views.

In the field of medicine, helping doctors to overcome their own natural human biases and shortcomings, including the confirmation bias, can be a matter of life and death, and as a result the discipline of evidence-based medicine (EBM) has been introduced. *Before* making a judgment or formal diagnosis, a doctor is encouraged to examine the actual data from epidemiological studies and quantified research. In this way, whatever judgment he or she makes will be based not just on the doctor's own perspective, but on the best available prior evidence as well. Unfortunately, this discipline is not universally applied, because not all medical professionals are equally capable of objectively balancing judgment and facts. Moreover, EBM itself constitutes a kind of belief system, and might easily conflict with a medical professional's prior beliefs (for instance, that his or her own first-impression hunch or intuition is likely to be correct).

Nevertheless, EBM is a good example for business leaders to emulate in their own decision making. In order to deal with the ever-increasing flood of data now available, and to keep personal biases and limitations in check, executives should adopt "evidence-based management." This would help them put aside their preconceived notions and natural biases, and rely more on what the numbers and data actually say. To do this properly, however, executives would also have to become more comfortable with the language and best practices of data analysis and statistics—control groups, correlation versus causation, standard deviations, confidence intervals, statistical significance, testing the null hypothesis, and so forth. Analytics can help us shape our own judgments more objectively, with better results, but it will require an effort to improve our mathematical literacy—or "numeracy"—first.

It's easy to find examples of poor mathematical thinking that are much less obvious than the innumerate lottery winner's comical superstition we cited in chapter 6. Consider, for instance, the banning of silicone breast implants in 1992. Of the 100 million American women alive at that time, roughly 1 percent of them (about a million women altogether) had had breast implants, while another 1 percent of all American women were afflicted with connective tissue disease. This meant that 10,000 of the women with implants (1 percent of a million) *also* had connective tissue disease, which led to many stories and anecdotes in the news, creating a wave of public opinion and political pressure for regulators. The result was that silicone implants were banned in the United States despite the *absolute lack of any scientific evidence at all* about a link. (They were not banned in other countries, however, and after fourteen years the FDA began to permit them in the United States again.)

One of the most infamous examples of flawed statistical reasoning came in the O. J. Simpson trial, when the prosecution maintained that because O.J. had frequently abused Nicole Simpson in the past it was more likely that he had also murdered her. The defense easily overcame this argument by telling the jury that of the 4 million women battered by their husbands the previous year, only 1 in 2,500 was actually murdered. By letting this highly persuasive argument stand, the prosecution demonstrated a complete lack of statistical knowledge (as did the press, various legal commentators, and others involved in assessing the case as it unfolded). Regardless of your own opinion about the actual verdict, the outcome might have been different had prosecutors pointed out a different and more relevant statistic: Of all the women who were battered by their husbands in the previous year and *also* murdered, 90 percent of *them* had in fact been murdered by their abusive husbands.

Understanding statistical analysis is way more important for the current generation of managers than it was for the last, not just because there is so much more information, but also because the task of performing sophisticated and complex statistical computations is so easy with today's technology. Decision science experts, economists, and other academics are all over this problem, urging business managers to come to the table and become more informed.

In his best-selling book *Super Crunchers*, for example, Yale economist Ian Ayres wrote that the best way to employ an expert opinion is to supplement and enhance whatever conclusions or implications we see in our analysis of the data. Analysis should come first, before applying intuition, hunches, or judgments, which should then be used to improve and check our understanding of the data. *Start* with the data, in other words, *then* apply judgment, and make a decision.

One customer research firm based in Sydney, Australia, for example, describes on its blog how the firm manages its own analytical process when trying to glean the right insights from massive quantities of data:

> With the rapid advances in text analytics it is very tempting at this level to stay focused on the [customer] comments but our experience is that as the feedback is aggregated, the need to rely on the numbers becomes critical. It is very easy to analyse comments and stumble over

an insight that backs up your gut-feel or pre-disposition; but without the numbers, it is also very easy to overplay the significance of your insight or, worse still, be downright wrong!

Stanford's Robert I. Sutton suggests that evidence-based management requires adopting the kinds of beliefs and settings "that enable people to keep acting with knowledge while doubting what they know, and to openly acknowledge the imperfections in even their best ideas along the way."

Suppose, for instance, that you're a board member of a company trying to align the interests of senior managers with the interests of shareholders. It's obvious to everyone on the board that such an alignment requires managers' monetary incentives to be structured so as to go up in value when share prices rise, and down when they decline. Based on this, you decide on a program of stock option awards for the senior executives who have the broadest powers to affect the company's performance. It won't be hard to find success stories that buttress this decision. But that would be the wrong way to approach it. Never assume that because something seems "intuitively obvious" it must be correct. The right way to make this kind of decision is to start with the data: Ask first what evidence actually exists demonstrating both the effectiveness and the ineffectiveness of executive stock options.

If that had been the process, you would have found some favorable evidence to support your plan, but you would also have found some disturbingly unfavorable evidence. You would have learned that numerous studies show stock options are often counterproductive, setting up a climate of gamesmanship, expectations management, and even fraud. In fact, according to Pfeffer and Sutton, one study of more than four hundred companies found that "the higher the proportion of the senior executives' pay in stock options, the more likely the company was to have restated its earnings." After considering this data you may still have elected to adopt a stock option plan, but your judgment would have been much better informed.

Unfortunately, our natural bias is to make our decisions the other way around, making a judgment first and then searching out the evidence to support it. That's just the way our psychologies are structured. But in order to see our customers' needs more clearly, and to take action more effectively, we have to dedicate ourselves to better, more objective and accurate management decisions.

Ironically, it may be the case today that the social science disciplines do a better job of preparing managers for a world of incomplete answers, randomized events, and probabilistic information. Engineers and physicists can do the higher math, but the problems they usually deal with almost always have straightforward solutions. We can precisely calculate the tensile strength of a steel girder or the escape velocity for putting a satellite in orbit, but handling a problem that incorporates poorly understood, conflicting, or unreliable inputs is likely to be more familiar to a sociologist, a psychologist, or perhaps a behavioral economist.

In any case, our trust filters have to be robust and well tuned. Failing to recognize our own biases when making decisions will call into question our competence as managers, and the customers and others who are affected by our decisions may question our good intentions as well.

[Intuition and Hunches in a Data-Rich Environment]

The fact that numbers and data are more available and should be employed more effectively in helping executives to make decisions doesn't mean that judgment and intuition aren't also important. Statistical and analytical studies should never be considered flawless, no matter how sophisticated they are. One reason for the 2008 financial meltdown, for instance, was an overreliance on flawed statistical models, coupled with a failure to exercise straightforward, reasonable judgment. According to Michael Mauboussin, empirical evidence from as far back as the 1920s shows that changes in asset prices don't have a normal, bell-shaped distribution, but the financial community still plans as if they did, using normal-curve metrics such as alpha, beta, and standard deviation. And Felix Rohatyn suggested that the kinds of financial derivatives that led to the 2008 meltdown were like "financial hydrogen bombs, built on personal computers by twenty-six-year-olds with MBAs."

Straightforward human judgment or intuition can sometimes be the last line of defense against innumerate statistical reasoning. There are many examples of the incredible power that the human mind actually possesses when it comes to cutting through immense amounts of information to make intuition-based judgments. Intuition is powerful, but the conditions under which it will triumph usually have to do with accumulated expertise—expertise that often lies dormant in our subconscious minds, but has the power to shape our conscious decisions if we just allow it to. The more "expert" you are at any given subject—the more time you've spent analyzing and discussing it, benefiting from it, categorizing it, using it—the more likely you are to have absorbed a large array of facts and patterns you may not even recognize consciously. If you've come to understand a subject intimately over several years, then your snap judgment *on this subject* can often be uncannily accurate. Malcolm Gladwell cites research showing that this level of expertise requires about ten thousand hours of practice or study, for instance.

Accumulated expertise is why an art critic's quick instinct about whether a particular piece of art is authentic or fake, or a brilliant general's intuitive decision to defy his opponent's expectations in order to win a battle partly by confusing the enemy, are examples of the proper use of judgment and "wisdom," as opposed to simply analyzing a large array of data and facts. In such cases, the expert's subconscious mind *is* relying on data and facts, by drawing on a large assortment of accumulated memories, lessons, and comparisons built up over years of study and attention to the issues. But the key words here are "expert" and "facts." Because of the expert's accumulation of facts and information over years of study, it's likely that his own subconscious mind will be able to reassemble all these miscellaneous facts and observations into a logical, insightful conclusion. (Think about it: If a twenty-six-year-old financial MBA has ten thousand hours of practice in the discipline, he or she is likely to have experienced at least one significant and unanticipated market collapse.)

On the other hand, experts can still be fooled by the illusion of control, coming to believe that their judgment is right even when confronted with contrary facts. "Isabel" is a computer program designed specifically to narrow the consideration set of medical diagnoses based on symptoms observed. According to Ayres, of the eleven thousand diseases afflicting humans, 96 percent of the time Isabel can successfully place the correct diagnosis within a relatively narrow range of between ten and thirty diseases, which is far better than the success rate of physicians relying on their own judgment and research, especially when analyzing rare or unusual diseases. Unfortunately, doctors still resist Isabel energetically. (One of Isabel's creators started learning to fly in 1999, and was struck by how much easier it was for pilots to accept flight support software than for doctors to accept diagnosis support software. "I asked my flight instructor what he thought accounted for the difference, and he told me, 'It's very simple. Unlike pilots, doctors don't go down with their planes.'")

Unfortunately, most of us also tend to make snap judgments about issues in which we *haven't* actually accumulated much expertise, and these are the kinds of decisions that get us into trouble most often. The business world is full of seemingly commonsense patterns and obvious assumptions that are just not supported by the data available. Earlier in this chapter we cited research showing that the best job referrals don't come from your own best friends but from more distant acquaintances. In chapter 5 we talked about the fact that if you try to boost your business by offering discounts or special deals in the social domain, you can sometimes (as Disney found out) generate worse results than offering nothing at all. In chapter 7 we made reference to the fact that a negative product review can actually improve the chances that a product will sell. As counterintuitive as all these facts are, the data don't lie. Moreover, in each case, if you had already been an expert—in social production or in network theory, say—then it is more likely that your initial "hunch" would have been correct, even prior to examining the data. Paying attention to the data doesn't mean ignoring your subconscious or overriding your intuition, but simply using discipline in applying it.

The fact of the matter is that we are all fallible. We are all afflicted with flawed thinking patterns that flow from the way our brains process information and threaten not just the way we interpret the mass of information now available, but the way others interpret the information we pass along and the decisions we make. If we want to be seen as trustable by our customers, employees, and others, then we have to show we can filter information for its trustability ourselves, and fashion it in a trustable way for others.

> Two forces are converging and fundamentally changing business: increasing data complexity and escalating customer expectations. Handling the former is a way to keep pace with the latter. This situation underscores the urgency of integrating companies' data sources to gain a holistic view of the customer. . . . Having this ability to analyze cross-channel data is the ultimate goal for business intelligence practitioners.
>
> JUDI HAND, PRESIDENT AND GENERAL MANAGER, DIRECT ALLIANCE,
> AND CHIEF SALES OFFICER, TELETECH

[Managing for Transparency]

We're headed for a world in which all our e-mails and phone calls will be as public as Facebook. There will be no more closed-door meetings unless the doors are made of glass. In such a world, no matter what actions we ultimately agree to take, and regardless of how we "position" ourselves in the media, our intentions are likely to become visible as well. This is the reality of transparency, and it is technologically inevitable.

> Transparency is like a disinfectant for business. It will purify things and help start the healing, but it's going to sting like hell.

Think about the process: Marketing and PR messages are carefully crafted to be as appealing as possible, and the spin put on a tagline or a press release is an important marketing asset. But inherent in the whole concept of "spin" is the idea that there is some genuine truth—presumably known to the marketer or the author of the spin—while a separate, *created* truth is meant to be conveyed by the spin. There is nothing evil here, and certainly no one can really blame a company for wanting to put its own brand or story in the best possible light. That's what any positioning strategy is supposed to do. But because they aren't stupid, and because they know that sellers have a vested interest in persuading them to part with their money, customers have learned to maintain a healthy skepticism about advertising claims in general.

In the e-social world, spin is out and customer experience is in. When one customer communicates with another, she doesn't share her impression of the brand's promise; she shares her experience.

> Your customer doesn't talk about your spin, but about his reality, which is the only reality he knows, and the only one that matters to him.

Managers at companies doing business in the e-social world already understand this, because socially connected customers won't let them get away with spinning a story in any way that might be deemed to be self-serving. According to Mitchell Baker, CEO of open-source Web browser Mozilla, for instance, "We see ourselves as part of a community, some of which is inside the organization and some that is outside it. . . . We also try to be very low spin. In fact, sometimes we joke that we're negative spin. We don't need the press or anybody else to do that; we'll do it ourselves."

Every company can benefit from this philosophy. Every company's long-term interest would be served by embracing a more authentic, transparent marketing approach. Even "dirt world" companies—companies with manufacturing plants, service personnel, delivery trucks, retail stores, and warehouses full of physical products—are coming to the realization that their social media reputation is critical. Whether a company participates in social media or not, its customers are still going to talk. So it can acknowledge the conversation and try to participate in it, or it can ignore it.

But the company's marketing executives can't "spin" it. It's not their message to spin.

TRUSTABILITY
TEST

Think about how you'd answer these questions based on how things work at your company, institution, or government agency. Talk about your answers with your colleagues. Visit www.trustability.com to see how other visitors' responses compare with your own for these and other questions.

▶ Have you ever had one story or "spin" about events for the media and the general public, while knowing that an alternative explanation was in fact more truthful?

▶ How often do you find yourself discussing a situation in an internal company meeting in ways that are different from what you say to the public?

▶ What criteria do *you* use to decide whether new information is worth your paying attention to?

▶ What criteria do *your customers* use to decide whether new information is worth paying attention to?

▶ Do you ever search out new and unusual information or perspectives from people? If so, how do you go about it? And how do you decide whether this new information is objective and accurate?

▶ How do your customers seek out information about your industry, your product category, your services, your prices, and your company? How do customers make sure that the information they seek out about you is both objective and accurate?

▶ Are the executives at your company aware of their own "confirmation bias"—the natural human tendency to interpret available information as supportive of their own point of view? What steps do they take to overcome their own confirmation bias in making decisions?

▶ How do you think confirmation bias affects the way your customers make decisions?

▶ When your customers read or hear statements from your company about your product or brand's benefits, do they trust what you say?

▶ Can you explain these statistical concepts in plain English?

 ▷ Control groups

 ▷ Correlation vs. causation

 ▷ Standard deviations

 ▷ Confidence intervals

 ▷ Statistical significance

 ▷ Testing the null hypothesis

▶ Would you be able to recognize a slant in reporting when you read research results using these statistical concepts?

▶ When your company reports survey or research results to the public to make a point to customers, do you ensure that the information is truly objective and unbiased?

▶ When was the last time one of your executives cited his or her "hunch" or "judgment" with respect to making a complex decision, and based on what you've read in this chapter, was that a correct use of intuition?

$\begin{bmatrix}10\end{bmatrix}$

DESIGNING TRUSTABILITY
INTO A BUSINESS

Once the trust goes out of a relationship, it's really no fun
lying to them anymore.
NORM PETERSON, ON THE TV SHOW *CHEERS* (1984)

As transparency continues to increase and consumers become more aware, increasing numbers of businesses are likely to find that a lot of the fun has gone out of their customer relationships. It won't be nearly so lucrative to deceive customers, or to make money through customer error, once customers begin to realize what's going on.

[Imagining the Trustable Future]

Although the vast majority of businesses today are not in fact trustable, if you've followed our argument to this point then we hope you're already convinced that it will just be a matter of time before successful companies are routinely characterized as doing things right, and doing the right thing, proactively. Trustability is already becoming a predictor for success. The standards for what constitutes acceptable, customer-oriented business activity are going up, and all businesses are bound to become more and more trustable in the long run.

Let's take some time right now to imagine how various businesses will operate in this "trustable future" that we're predicting. Even though it might be highly disruptive as a competitive strategy, it isn't overly difficult to imagine how trustability would operate in any given business category. We only need to put ourselves in the customer's shoes. We discussed what a trustable credit card company might look like in chapter 6, and in chapter 9 we reviewed how a more trustable health care company might operate. So let's just imagine how trustability would manifest itself in a few different kinds of businesses, starting with mobile phones:

Trustability in the Mobile Phone Category. Within an environment of smart phones and increasingly capable wireless services, the charges a mobile carrier assesses can be complex, and complexity presents a tempting opportunity to take advantage of customers. It might be failing to put a customer on the most beneficial or cost-efficient calling plan, or it might be tricking customers into incurring unintended data charges (as Verizon Wireless was caught doing, in chapter 4). Or it might be simple neglect (incompetence): If a customer is due to get a new phone at the end of his two-year contract, for instance, but doesn't notice when a period of two years elapses, a trustable mobile phone company would remind him, and invite him to come in to choose a new one. Most mobile operators do not, however, preferring to "let sleeping dogs lie" and to wait for the customer to request an upgrade for some other reason.

A genuinely trustable telecom operator would automatically assign customers to the most economical calling plans based on their calling, texting, and data usage. We confidently predict (you saw it here first!) that this will soon be a widely accepted "best practice" in the mobile category, as carriers proactively assign the most economical calling plans to each of their customers, even crediting customers with refunds where appropriate. Very few operators today do this, of course, and those that do often use it as an excuse to extend a postpaid contract.

While most mobile companies (and other subscription-based businesses) will make outbound calls to customers at bill-paying time to prompt payment, when appropriate, AT&T actually calls at least some of its customers before the due date by which a late fee would be assessed. A friend of ours reports having received one of these proactive service calls, and said: "Experiencing this was pretty nice. I personally feel that

AT&T is looking out for me by doing this. They're building customer trust." So at least in this arena, AT&T is not one of those me-first companies, always trying to fool customers out of their money.

A trustable telecom operator would almost certainly have an unconditional money-back guarantee available to cover any and all customer complaints. In the same way today's best online merchants offer unconditional refunds, tomorrow's telecom operator will use such a policy to ensure that customers always receive the service they expect. If a customer is about to subscribe from a home or business address prone to poor network coverage or slow broadband connectivity, a genuinely trustable telecom company would advise him in advance of this weakness in its offering, perhaps providing a discount or other benefit until such time as service in the customer's home area is improved. After all, with today's level of transparency it won't take a new customer any time at all to have the flaws in your system pointed out to him by other customers, so the best strategy for a mobile carrier with a weakness in its offering is to follow Domino's example: 'Fess up, and promise to improve soon. (And then do it.)

But untrustable policies proliferate at even the highest-quality mobile carriers. At one client of ours, for instance, an e-mail was circulated to employees and front-line staff asking them to help identify untrustable policies and practices. Some of the things identified:

- Customers often incur roaming or data charges from companies without knowing how or why, and there's no proactive initiative to inform customers regarding how these charges have been incurred.

- Poor network quality sometimes causes dropped calls and lost data, and while the carrier is working hard to improve quality, it also needs a better system for helping customers get either compensation or at least sympathy for bad experiences.

- Very few people at the company pay attention to the refund and return policy, because refunds and returns on new phones are obviously not a high-priority marketing transaction. As a result, however, no one understands the policy well, it's too complicated for customers, and it often becomes a source of conflict, all but invisible to the company's executive team.

- Marketing offers often imply a "free" service or a very low price when in fact there is a complicated mail-in rebate required, or the low price only applies under very special conditions.

- Customers like interacting with the carrier's call center reps (high satisfaction scores), but the reps regret that once they log a complaint or an issue, they never find out what eventually happens to the problem or the customer, because there's little or no follow-up.

These were just a few of the ideas volunteered by more than five hundred employees at this client, to the great surprise of our consultants and the company's executives. The large number of participants and their sheer enthusiasm for the initiative indicated a deep interest in the idea of turning the company into a more trustable operator.

Already, mobile companies in crowded retail markets around the world are trying to position themselves as more trustable. Vodafone Turkey, for instance, launched a "Customer Bill of Rights" program designed to assure customers that the company would always act in the customer's interest, whether that involved proactively assigning a customer to the right calling plan or counseling a customer on how to spend less for messaging and roaming. As Vodafone was preparing to launch the program—but before anything had been said publicly about it—Turkcell, Vodafone's primary Turkish competitor, launched its own "Customer Constitution" initiative. Turkcell's program was so strikingly similar to Vodafone's that it precipitated a legal dispute amid allegations of corporate espionage. As of this writing, the two firms are still engaged in a fierce competitive battle over just which company is more likely to act in the customer's best interest.

Trustability in Prepaid Cards. Many retailers and other marketers have adopted "stored value" cards as a marketing and promotion vehicle.

Sometimes these cards are sold as gift cards at face value, and sometimes they are distributed as rebates or refunds. Retailers like prepaid cards because studies have shown that a consumer typically spends more than the value of the card when redeeming it.

Manufacturers use prepaid cards to lower the effective price of their goods in a retail store, doing so in a way that puts them in direct touch with consumers whose identities they would otherwise perhaps never learn. Buying a new flat-screen television for $499.99 "after $100 manufacturer's rebate" means that you pay the initial purchase price of $599.99 and mail your receipt in to the manufacturer along with the UPC code clipped from the packing box, and the manufacturer sends you a $100 rebate. When the rebate comes, however, it isn't a check but a stored value card with $100 stored on it. Unlike a gift card, most rebate cards aren't limited to a particular brand or store, but can be used more generally, as a kind of debit or credit card.

So far, so good, but the problem with a prepaid card is that it can also serve as a vehicle for retailers and manufacturers to trick consumers, fool them, or profit from mistakes that consumers make. For one thing, a substantial portion of the "stored value" in prepaid cards goes unclaimed by consumers, because while accounting rules have historically required businesses to put an expiration date on a card, the customer may neglect to use it before it expires, or the card itself might get lost or misplaced before all of the stored value is claimed.

New legislation may reduce this problem for companies and consumers, but if you buy a $50 Starbucks gift card and send it to your friend for her birthday, there's still a good chance she'll lose it or forget about it before she claims the full $50 worth of value you purchased for her. In fact, of the $80 to $90 billion in gift cards issued in the United States annually, the average "breakage" (industry lingo for the amount issued to consumers but unclaimed for any reason) averages 6 to 10 percent, a loss to consumers that rivals all debit card and credit card fraud combined. In other words, when a marketer sells a gift card it is actually *better than cash* (for the marketer).

In addition to the risk of expiration, loss, or misplacement, however, customers often encounter service fees assessed by issuers on the use of prepaid cards. In response to consumer complaints, Congress passed the Credit Card Accountability, Responsibility and Disclosure Act, or "Credit CARD Act," which puts limits on these activities, banning the imposition of "inactivity fees" during the first year after a gift card's issuance, for instance, and requiring at least five years' wait time before a card can be deemed to have expired. But of course these legal restrictions were only necessary in the first place because many card issuers were using fees and expiration dates to trick unsuspecting customers out of their money.

A retailer or manufacturer that wants to be trustable with its rebate or gift card policy would link the card issuance to customers' identities in order to notify them if the card hasn't been used after some period of time, or if there is money remaining on a card that hasn't been fully claimed. It would be relatively simple and risk-free for a trustable company to offer replacements to customers who lose their cards. (Many competent retailers already keep electronic receipts so customers don't have to keep up with paper slips just to return or exchange a purchased item.)

At a minimum, a trustable company should send the customer an e-mail notice a few weeks before imposing any sort of service fee or expiration action. And any *competent* gift or rebate card issuer will have in place a convenient mechanism for capturing the customer's name and e-mail address or other contact details when the card is issued in the first place.

ONE CUSTOMER'S TAKE ON REBATES AND REBATE CARDS

As long as companies play fair, I can accept the fact that the financial return on a rebate program may depend on breakage, but three direct experiences make me think that some companies are making it even harder for consumers, especially those who buy from online retailers.

Case history one: MacMall. MacMall sells Apple products. Having bought a couple of iPods from this retailer, when it came time to buy an iMac I checked out its prices. I purchased from MacMall specifically because it offered a $50 rebate on the iMac. When you buy a rebated item from a brick-and-mortar retailer, you usually get a mail-in card or some other information about claiming the rebate. I expected to get that information from MacMall on how to redeem the rebate, either with my order confirmation or with the product, when it arrived. I finally contacted MacMall about four weeks after I received the iMac to find out how to claim the rebate. Oops—the program has expired—we're sorry, you're out of luck. Now, in fairness to retailers, rebate programs often come from the manufacturer. But, since only MacMall was offering the rebate, it probably deserves all the blame for this one. And any retailer passing a rebate offer through to customers has some obligation to tell them how to obtain the rebate. Of course, if the company doesn't care at all about losing a customer . . .

Case history two: Staples. I needed a new printer. Staples was offering a $50 rebate to anyone who recycled an old printer when purchasing a new one. No-brainer here; do something good for the environment and get a good deal on the new printer. And Staples' online rebate system was great. I had my rebate sooner than I expected. So what's the problem? The rebate came in the form of a stored-value Visa debit card with an expiration date. I made one purchase of $20 and then sort of forgot about the card for a while. When I tried to use it again, a couple of months later, I was told that it had expired. Sure, there was something in the fine print that came with the card (which I only read after this happened) about an expiration date, but revoking a rebate that you've already paid? Thumbs down to Staples on this one.

Case history three: Amazon.com. Same situation as MacMall. The product was offered with a rebate, but no information about how to claim it. When I contacted Amazon, its service rep informed me that the rebate had expired. But unlike MacMall, Amazon did the right thing by the customer and refunded the amount of the rebate.

It's easy to estimate the financial return from breakage on a rebate program. It's near impossible to estimate the future losses due to treating customers badly. Give that a thought the next time you plan a rebate program.

BLOGGER DAVID BAKKEN

Trustability in Financial Services. How would a genuinely trustable retail bank operate? What would it do differently? How would it operate if it wanted to demonstrate trustability?

While there is obviously no requirement for any financial institution to extend credit to a customer (or to cover an overdraft without charging a fee), a large proportion of "penalty" fees are incurred by customers who are in fact creditworthy. A genuinely trustable retail bank would use easily available information to assess customers automatically for their creditworthiness, eliminating many such charges and possibly offering an automatic e-transfer among accounts when such a transfer is available but just hasn't yet been elected by the customer. At present, most banks reserve this kind of service for high-balance customers only, but there's no business reason it couldn't be more generally available.

A genuinely trustable retail bank would also disclose its fees in a way that is more obvious and available to consumers. Even though U.S. banks are already required by law to disclose their fees, multiple studies show that the majority of banks make information about fees either completely inaccessible to consumers or difficult to find. Small banks and credit unions are more likely to disclose fees, but in the transparent future even the large, publicly held financial institutions that are so notoriously devious today will be forced by competitive pressure to do so.

And any genuinely trustable financial institution would allow its customers to post their own reviews of its services and products (including comparisons with other companies' offerings) on the company's own Web site, making these reviews freely and impartially available to other customers.

We once met an insurance manager whose company offered "freeze damage" insurance to contractors and homeowners. Freezing weather in the manager's Florida region is very rare, but when it hits it can ruin all the plumbing in a home and create a great deal of damage. Some customers bought the coverage, and some didn't. Nevertheless, whenever freezing temperatures were predicted, this manager had his agents call *all* the company's policyholders—even those who had not bought freeze-damage coverage—to warn them about the impending freeze and educate them about how to prevent the damage. In this way he minimized damage to the properties he would have had to pay to repair, but also helped the policyholders who hadn't even paid for the coverage, and who obviously trust him more as a result.

So here's an "Extreme Trust" idea for retail banks that might at first sound just as foolish as serving customers who haven't bought your product, but could have similarly beneficial effects in terms of securing your reputation as a trustable company: One of the hassles involved in switching banks is setting up your electronic bill payment system. Once you've gone to all the trouble of inputting dozens of business names, addresses, and account numbers for your bank's online bill paying system, the very idea of having to start over again at another bank is wearying. But if, as a bank, you were truly confident in your ability to serve customers well and always act in their interest, then you could offer a service to do just this. That is, if a customer ever decides to leave you for another bank, you could provide all the customer's bill payment files in some kind of format for the new bank to load automatically.

What you would be saying to customers with this policy is that you are always on their side, no matter what, and if for any reason they feel they'll be better served somewhere else, then doggone it, you're going to help them. Don't hold your breath for most banks to do this kind of thing, but it wouldn't be too big a surprise for Navy Federal, Ally Bank, USAA, or maybe RBC to offer a service something like it someday. *And then how will everyone else compete?*

Trustability in the Automotive Category. What would it mean for an automotive company to be trustable? This depends on which type of automotive firm we're discussing. In most countries manufacturers or importers procure the physical product and are generally responsible for its quality, while retail auto dealers sell, deliver, and service the product, having many more day-to-day interactions with consumers. As a consumer, however, you are more likely to hold the *brand* accountable for both product and service failings, as well as for its "intentions" toward you. So a genuinely trustable brand would have to involve a close, competent relationship between dealer and manufacturer. When a brand-name dealer's service doesn't live up to the car brand's advertised standard, it's a recipe for customer disappointment.

A trustable car dealership would probably try to compensate salespeople based not just on how many autos they sell, but on how much customer satisfaction is actually generated. One idea might be to pay a "lifetime commission" on new car sales. Whenever a salesperson sells a car to a customer who is new to the dealership, the dealer would tag that customer with the salesperson's name, and every time that customer spends anything with the dealer any time in the future—for service, for buying another car (new or used, even if bought from a different salesperson)—then the original salesperson would get some kind of commission. This would give the salesperson a vested interest in the continued satisfaction and loyalty of the customer, and it would also help ensure that a dealer's most productive and valuable salespeople remain loyal themselves.

There are some obviously untrustable behaviors in the auto category ("Would you buy a used car from this man?"), but increasingly we'll find that untrustable practices will be "outed" by social media commentary and online word of mouth. Even today it isn't hard to find out, for instance, whether a dealership has a reputation for unnecessarily expensive servicing, or for overly aggressive up-selling of features and options. And as transparency continues to throw light on this and every other business category, such practices are likely to prove less and less financially attractive.

A trustable car brand would e-mail or phone you thirty days before your warranty expires, so you can bring the vehicle in for any needed repairs while the warranty is still valid. And to improve its reputation for trustability during the sales process, a brand might want to consider helping customers to make direct comparisons with competitive vehicles. At a minimum, a trustable auto brand would host objective online reviews by authenticated owners and drivers of multiple brands, and it might even consider arranging test drives right at the dealership. Imagine a BMW dealer allowing a customer to test-drive a Cadillac, Infiniti, or Audi, for instance.

This is in fact exactly what General Motors did in a 2003 pilot program. One aspect of the initiative involved creating a new Web site, AutoChoiceAdvisor.com, designed to give customers completely unbiased, objective advice on the right type of car for them—from all different brands and makes, not just GM. An obvious benefit of the site for GM was that it gave the company better insight into customer preferences, including those that sometimes led customers to choose non-GM brands, enabling GM executives to develop new products and design new cars to address more specific customer needs. The company followed the launch of this Web site with a car show that allowed more than 100,000 consumers to test-drive not just GM brands but also BMW, Ford, Volvo, and other brands as well.

GM knows that consumers will explore different brands. So why not facilitate a process that will occur anyway, and in effect be "present" for a greater portion of the customer's overall shopping experience, with the opportunity to get smarter? GM was simply acknowledging what should have been obvious all along: providing objective, unbiased advice to customers will earn their trust, and trust is highly valuable for the brand.

Think about it: if a company thinks it *isn't* in its own interest to provide good, objective advice to customers, then what is the firm really saying?—that it prefers to take revenue from unknowledgeable or unsuspecting customers before they acquire enough information to make more intelligent decisions? That its business model depends on customers who don't make smart decisions?

In the event, what one car company found after a similar test-drive program was that "After the test drives [including competitive brands], vehicle consideration was increased by 20% and sales were increased by 11%."

Trustability in the Enterprise Computing Industry. When selling software or SQL server installations to large enterprise customers, it has always been Microsoft's practice to provide, free of charge, a number of vouchers allowing the customer to send key personnel to special Microsoft training courses, which are conducted through the firm's network of certified partners. Training is one of Microsoft's most important value-added services, because it is designed to appeal especially to the kind of enterprise customer more likely to want a collaborative, long-term commercial relationship. But a few years ago, Microsoft was wrestling with the challenge that fewer than 20 percent of these vouchers were being redeemed by customers. Four out of five vouchers simply languished in customers' desk drawers, never to be used. The marketing people at Microsoft had mixed emotions about the low redemption rate, however. Even though they knew that such training could help cement the firm's relationships with its largest customers and would also likely improve customer experience with the product, the fact was that high levels of voucher breakage were good for the marketing budget, because every dollar of training not redeemed was money that could be used to fund other marketing activities.

Chris Atkinson, a vice president of Microsoft, decided that customers who were not redeeming their training vouchers were just not getting the most benefit from Microsoft's products, and even though it cost money, his unit began sending out reminders to those customers. Atkinson noted,

*There were absolutely no strings to these reminders, which were sim-
ply notices to customers that they should be sure to take maximum
advantage of the training vouchers they had been provided and not
yet redeemed. This program immediately doubled the redemption
rate in the Southeast Asia region and caught the attention of Microsoft corporate product marketing in Redmond, as well, with the result that it is now standard practice around the world to send out
reminders to enterprise customers who have unredeemed training
vouchers.*

Soon redemption rates for Microsoft training vouchers around the
world soared, as did trust in the Microsoft brand. Reminding a customer
that she is due for a benefit or service she may have overlooked is certain
to build your brand's reputation for trustability, and Microsoft earned
this benefit in the same way as the homebuilder we cited in chapter 3 did,
when he began reminding his customers when their new-construction
warranties only had thirty more days to run.

Trustability in the Airline Industry. Airlines are seen by most consumers
as highly self-oriented and untrustable, partly on account of their complex and hard-to-understand pricing policies. Airlines do need pricing
flexibility because their inventory is perishable. Like a phone network, an
airline has an extremely high ratio of fixed to variable costs, and an airline seat flying empty (like network capacity that goes unused) is revenue
lost forever.

Airlines have, over the last thirty years or so, greatly improved the science of revenue management, constantly evaluating the ebb and flow of
demand for every flight as its departure time nears. When revenue management is combined with tariff rules for discount fares that require
things like Saturday-night stays, no refunds, or advance purchase restrictions, the plane will fill up with passengers who have actually paid many
different fares and are subject to many different restrictions. And, while
there is nothing overtly wrong about this type of pricing, the system is

so complex for passengers that many simply don't understand whether they're being treated fairly or not.

An airline could deal with this problem in a number of ways. It could, for instance, heavily promote a low-fare offering, and then (if the flight isn't yet filled) promote an even lower fare closer in to departure. While this might appear highly cynical on the airline's part, it is in fact the practice of at least a few airlines. But even if the initial low fare (later to be undercut) is not specifically advertised or promoted, reducing the fare at a later point to fill a plane at the last minute might still seem unfair to many of the early planners, unless the last-minute fares have some significant and rather onerous restrictions or conditions.

A genuinely trustable airline, on the other hand, would go to great lengths to try to ensure that customers didn't end up paying a higher fare just because they were unknowledgeable or unlucky. If you book a ticket at one price, and the price for a similarly restricted ticket on that flight later drops, a trustable airline would either refund you the difference automatically or offer to allow you to exchange your ticket for one at the lower price (with different restrictions). It's one thing to manage your seat capacity scientifically, but it's an entirely different proposition to make money by playing a shell game with customers.

Some travel delays are unavoidable in the airline business, for reasons that have to do with random weather patterns and maintenance issues. But different routes are subject to different patterns of delay, with some more likely to be affected than others. The FAA keeps accurate statistics with respect to the historic patterns of travel delays by airline and route, and any passenger could turn to www.fly.faa.gov to look up an itinerary she is planning, but why wouldn't the airline itself display a travel-delay likelihood score for each flight segment? In fact, it would be a relatively simple thing for an airline's online travel reservations system to tap the government's database and display a "likelihood of on-time arrival" figure for any particular itinerary booked.

Airline frequent flyer programs are useful vehicles for earning the trust of customers, provided that they aren't relegated to serving purely as marketing come-ons. If an airline promotes the fact that it "only" takes twenty-five thousand miles to make a trip, but then heavily restricts the availability of eligible seats, it's just playing the same kind of airfare shell game with passengers, only this time with mileage redemptions.

Most airlines allow their frequent flyer miles to be redeemed for car rental days, hotel stays, or merchandise, and miles have become a kind of promotional currency, bought and sold in a variety of different ways. One way an airline could immediately boost its trustability in the eyes of its frequent flyers might be to let them redeem their miles on *other* airlines, including even direct competitors. As long as Airline A can buy miles from Airline B, it wouldn't be difficult for A to allow its own frequent flyers to redeem their miles for flights on B. Such a program would provide evidence to customers that Airline A is actually on their side, and not just trying to line its own pockets with customer patronage. In addition, of course, the air carrier would also acquire valuable insights into the flying preferences and off-route travel habits of its most frequent customers, a benefit somewhat analogous to the insight a car company would get from allowing customers to test-drive a variety of different car brands.

And if something doesn't work—there's no seat light for reading on a night flight, or the entertainment system doesn't work, or the seat won't lean back—the proactive airline will not only apologize, but also make sure the flight doesn't cost the same as it would if the full value were available to the passenger.

Airlines, in the end, are just as much a high-end *personal service* business as hotels or restaurants are, where the smiling face or warm touch of a competent and caring maître d' or concierge can immediately generate a feeling of trust and confidence. If you fly frequently on United Airlines, sooner or later you may find yourself, as Don did, on a plane captained by John McFadden, a veteran pilot based in Chicago. After the passengers had boarded, and while the plane was still at the gate, Don noticed that the pilot himself came out to make an announcement to passengers, using the microphone usually handled by flight attendants. While it was unusual, he thought nothing more about it until, two hours after take-off, flight attendant Diane Johnson began distributing McFadden's business cards to about twenty different passengers in first class and coach, each with a brief thank-you note handwritten on the back:

> Dear Donald Peppers (1F):
> Thank you for your business! How can we exceed your expectations?
> *JOHN MCFADDEN*

McFadden says he began giving out these thank-you notes to high-value passengers during a period about ten years ago when United was going through a rough patch, and says he almost always gets favorable feedback for the initiative, including innumerable e-mails from passengers when they complete their trips. When Don asked him why he began doing this, he was stumped. But in a few hours he sent an e-mail:

> *As we flew to SFO [the next destination], I reflected on your question—"Why do you do what you do?" That is a question I am asked quite a bit. The simple and straightforward answer is—If I try to teach my kids (16 yr old son and 13 yr old daughter) to treat others as I would wish to be treated, it is crucial that I put that "golden rule" philosophy into action. I know that may sound somewhat simplistic. The truth is, I really believe in living my life this way.*

In the final analysis, McFadden values empathy and reciprocity above everything else. He refuses to be just an employee. He insists on being a human.

[Is Your Business Trustable?]

Okay. Let's have another go at this. Write your company's name in the blank in this sentence:

What would a trustable [your company's name here] look like?

Before you answer, you might want to take a look at what your customers are saying. Or maybe do a survey of your rank-and-file service people, the way our mobile client did. The result might surprise you as much as it surprised them.

Go back through the book and answer the "Trustability Test" questions at the end of each chapter. Here are some key summary questions:

- Do you remind customers if their warranty is up soon, or if they are due for a free upgrade or other benefit?

- Do you warn customers if they are buying too much of something, or if the product or service they're buying might not be right for them?

- Do you allow customers to post their own honest reviews of your product or service on your Web site, for the benefit of other customers?

- Do you treat all customers the same or are you capable of treating different customers differently?

- Do you count on making money from customer mistakes, omissions, or oversights?

- Do you make more money by selling to well-informed and knowledgeable customers, or to uninformed customers?

- Do you ever find it necessary to have one story inside the company, but a different story (i.e., the "spin") for outsiders?

- If a social media disaster were to happen, do you know who at your firm has responsibility for interacting with the "crowd"? Have you ever done a fire drill?

- If a social media disaster were to happen, do your own best customers trust you enough to defend you?

- Do you pay sales commissions for selling products, or pay rewards for building relationships and increasing the value of customers?

Better yet, take the customer's point of view. How many of your customers could agree enthusiastically with the following statements:

- I can depend on this company to do the right thing for me.

- I know this company will make sure I get the right deal.

- This company does things right and makes it easy for me.

- I would be willing to tell people I know how much I trust this company.

- I trust this company more than I trust their competition.

[Can a *Product* Ever Be Trusted, Really?]

This is not a trick question. Obviously, when you speed down the highway at eighty miles per hour in your car, it goes without saying that you trust the product to keep you safe.

But "trust," as we've defined it in this book, implies more than simple product quality or reliability. These attributes are synonymous with competence, but trust also implies that the entity being trusted has *good intentions*. And in chapter 2 we suggested that good intentions are a distinctly human attribute, residing in the mind. Because companies and organizations don't have minds of their own, we ascribe trustworthiness to a company by observing its actions (the same way we would observe a person's actions), and then deciding for ourselves whether these actions evidence goodwill or not. In effect, we evaluate the actions of a company as if they had been organized by some person, and then we try to infer that *person's* intentions.

The whole concept of "good intentions" presumes that we are evaluating an intelligence of some kind—a thinking, planning intelligence that could be seeking to further either your interests (good intentions) or its own interests (selfish intentions). People have intentions, but products and other inanimate objects do not. Or do they? The fact is that more and more products today are embedded with information and even decision-making capabilities. When iTunes reminds you that you already purchased a tune you were about to buy, or when Amazon reminds you that you already bought a particular book, there's no human being typing out the keystrokes to protect you from making a mistake. It's a piece of software. We may view the message as an indication of the company's good intentions, but these intentions are carried out by a few lines of computer code.

This doesn't mean, of course, that people aren't involved. The software doesn't spring into existence by itself, after all. In effect, the people responsible for programming how these Web sites respond to customer interactions have created a set of rules designed to protect individual customer interests. The programmers, or the people who directed their efforts, clearly had good intentions toward you.

And while visiting a Web site is easy to understand as an interaction with a company, the truth is that all sorts of physical products today are being embedded with information and decision-making capabilities. Information technology is permeating our existence. When a car beeps as you shut the door, reminding you that your keys are still in it, is that any less representative of the car maker's intentions than when software prompts you to avoid a mistake in ordering something on the Web? And why shouldn't a refrigerator, or a microwave oven, or even a cordless drill prompt you to remember that the warranty period expires in thirty days?

[The Technology of Trustability?]

Is trustability actually a technology? On one level, it could be. Like a technology, trustability facilitates change and innovation, and because empathy begets empathy, trustability also creates its own "network effect." The more trustable some companies become, the more attractive it will be for their competitors to be trustable, and the faster the whole idea will likely be adopted as a more general business practice.

In addition, as is the case with any new technology, early adopters can secure a first-mover advantage for themselves, competitively. No business could succeed if it failed to create and maintain a Web site once it became possible, just as no business in the early twentieth century could have succeeded for long without making use of electric power once it became available. In the end, new technologies boost all businesses.

This is where the comparison ends, however, because trustability is definitely *not* a technology. The desire to be trustable comes not from some novel combination of previous technical innovations or business processes, but from the most basic, deeply human motive: simply to associate with others. To be social. A company cannot fake trustability. It can't be purchased or installed, and you can't outsource it. Trustability either will spring from within the motives of the people who animate and direct your business, or it won't.

Nevertheless, there is still a method any business must follow if it wants to embrace trustability as a business practice. Check in at www.trustability.com to follow along with us as we develop ways to assess your company's trustability. Our goal is to help companies understand how trustable they are, relative to competitors and over time, based on whether they are seen to be doing things right, and doing the right thing, proactively.

[Start Planning for Trustability Now]

At its root, Extreme Trust is not a complicated idea, but it does require overcoming a lot of barriers. The three basic principles we outlined in chapter 1 were:

1. Doing things right,

2. Doing the right thing,

3. Proactively.

Philosophically, all we're talking about with these three central principles is ensuring that the components of trustworthiness—*good intentions* and *competence*—are *proactively* pursued, rather than just passively acknowledged. Still, this requires a company to undertake a substantial change to the way it probably does business today, even if it is already a highly trustworthy and admired brand. Doing the right thing will often be difficult to justify financially, for example, unless you are competent enough in customer analytics to be able to quantify the long-term financial value represented by customers' good opinions of your business. And being proactive about protecting customers' interests will, of necessity, require admitting mistakes when they happen, rather than hiding them—something that will almost certainly come up against stiff resistance in the legal department, not to mention PR.

So as you focus on these three principles— "Do things right," "Do the right thing," "Proactively"—you'll need to keep in mind what you've learned in this book about how the age of transparency really works. To be trustable, you need to know how to gain traction in the e-social world:

- **Think long term.** You can't be trustable if you're entirely focused on the short term. And customer relationships are the link between short-term actions and long-term value at a business. If you don't have the ability to embrace the long term, then don't even think about trying to become more trustable, because eventually your flawed arithmetic and off-center metrics will do you in. You'll never be able to build a business model focused on "doing the right thing" for customers if you can't justify it to your shareholders. Period.

- **Share.** People want to contribute and share with others. That's what human beings like to do, and if you want your business to be trustable, then you'll find ways to share, too. Your business needs to contribute, so share your ideas, your technology, and your data. Make your intellectual property more freely available, in order to stimulate faster innovation. Said another way: Trust others the way you want them to trust you. And remember that the currency of the sharing economy is trust, not money. So be careful when navigating between the social domain and the commercial.

- **Show a "human face."** Empathy is not just a business strategy for demonstrating trustability. Empathy is a basic human instinct, and if you want to show a "human face" to the world, acting as another human being would, then you have to admit your fallibility when it is appropriate. No one is perfect, and this goes double for a business. So accept your vulnerability. It will never be possible to control all outcomes.

- **Rely on evidence.** As technology promotes more and more interaction and transparency, businesses will have to figure out how to cope with a supernova of information. If you want to be trustable, then you have to be able to evaluate this information for its objectivity and accuracy. Don't ignore judgment and intuition, but pay attention to numbers and data. And take the steps required to deal with the inevitability of random events: Pay more attention to numbers and statistical best practices, measure inputs in addition to outcomes and results, and plan more carefully for alternatives and multiple scenarios.

In the final analysis, it is almost certain to be the new companies and the start-ups that employ these tactics to overturn the old way. They have less invested in the current paradigm, and less to lose by destroying it. Gradually, they will use trustability to transform our entire economic system, in the same way that interactivity itself has so dramatically transformed our lives already. They will deploy honesty as a brutally efficient competitive weapon against the old guard.

As standards for trustability continue to rise, the companies, brands, and organizations shown to lack trustability will be punished more and more severely. But the sting of the transparency disinfectant will be greatest when the wounds are new. Very soon, for competitive reasons, all businesses, old and new, will begin to respond to the increase in demand for trustability by taking actions that are more worthy of trust from the beginning—that is, actions that are more transparently honest, less self-interested, more competently executed, less controlling, and more responsive to others' inputs. More proactively trustworthy. Trustable.

ACKNOWLEDGMENTS

Our profound thanks to Amanda Rooker, who is not only a social-media-savvy researcher, but a phenomenally detailed editor, a smart writer, and a terrific, upbeat person who keeps us going as well. She has been our right arm on this project. At the risk of making her so successful she won't have time to help us in the future, we highly recommend her to any of you who need detail and research backup, and those who are working on Internet publishing.

At Penguin, we acknowledge with thanks Adrian Zackheim, who immediately saw the importance of proactivity and championed the cause of "Extreme Trust." And we thank Jillian Gray, Julia Batavia, and a host of talented designers and editors at Penguin who bore with us as the idea grew and the manuscript morphed into something better but always different. Thanks, also, to Rafe Sagalyn, our literary agent these last twenty years, not only for his constant and thoughtful insight, but especially for his very helpful advice on this particular topic and how best to put it across to our readers.

Our appreciation to Alan Fine, president of Marvel, for a thoughtful weekend spent pushing these ideas around and testing their validity in different situations. And to Eric Carrasquilla at Amdocs and Mariann McDonagh at InContact for their ideas and feedback.

It wouldn't be inappropriate to thank all our colleagues at Peppers & Rogers Group and 1to1 Media. It's a talented, brilliant, and hardworking bunch who inspire us and our clients every day. And thanks to the clients, too. It's the work in the field that makes us smarter, and leads to better learing and to better companies. Special thanks to Marji Chimes, our conscience and inspiration, who embodies what is right about corporate America. We also thank Peppers & Rogers Group top brass, who keep our business successful while we are busy speaking, writing, thinking, and meeting: Caglar Gogus, Orkun Oguz, Hamit Hamutcu, Mounir Ariss, Ozan Bayulgen, Amine Jabali, and Ivo Sarges. We have learned a lot from Tulay Idil, Marc Ruggiano, Aysegul Bahcivanoglu, Dietrich Chen, Tom Schmalzl, Michael Dandrea, Ginger Conlon, Liz Glagowski, Mila D'Antonio, and Tom Hoffman. Thanks to Annette Webb for keeping us all looking so good. And we thank the leaders of our parent company, TeleTech, who believe in the highest levels of Extreme Trust, who want to help all TeleTech clients achieve it, and who have helped us brainstorm it: Ken Tuchman, Judi Hand, Karen Breen, Mark Grindeland, Jonathan Gray, and Taylor Allis.

We couldn't have gotten this done without the cheerful and capable help and quiet dedication of Susan Tocco and Lisa Troland, who run interference and back us up.

Finally, mere words can't articulate the appreciation we feel for our own helpmates, Pamela Devenney and Dick Cavett.

NOTES

1: TRUST: NOT JUST A GOOD IDEA. INEVITABLE.

Page 1   This USAA refund-check story is referenced in Raj Sisodia, Jag Sheth, and David B. Wolfe, *Firms of Endearment: How World-Class Companies Profit from Passion and Purpose* (Pearson Prentice Hall, 2007), p. 61. Quoting the authors: "With an empathetic understanding of the difficulties that going to war poses for military families, USAA decided to do something about it after the first Gulf War. It sent refunds to policyholders who had gone to the Gulf, covering the period when they were not driving back home. Some 2,500 policyholders mailed the refunds back to USAA. They included notes of appreciation in which they said 'thanks' but were returning the refunds to help keep USAA financially sound." Stories like these are why we dedicated one of our books to the late Brigadier General Robert McDermott (USAF), who served as USAA's CEO for more than twenty years, from 1969 until he retired in 1992 (https://www.usaa.com/inet/pages/about_usaa_corporate_overview_history).

Page 4   Moore's law is named after Gordon Moore, cofounder of Intel, who pointed out in 1965 that the number of transistors that could be fit onto a square inch of silicon doubled roughly every two years.

Page 4   Mark Zuckerberg, founder of Facebook, has asserted that every fifteen to twenty years we will interact a thousand times as much with others. This is sometimes referred to as "Zuckerberg's law."

Page 6   Bill Price and David Jaffe did some pretty interesting research for their book, *The Best Service Is No Service* (Jossey-Bass, 2008), including looking at the discrepancies between how good companies think their service is and how lousy the customers think it is.

Page 10   Stephen M. R. Covey and Rebecca R. Merrill's extremely well-written book *The Speed of Trust: The One Thing That Changes Everything* (Free Press, 2006) is based on this formula: "When trust goes up, speed will also go up and cost will go down . . . When trust goes down, speed will go down and cost will go up." In their taxonomy, trust is built (and can be rebuilt) on two things: competence and character. (Fundamentally, Covey and Merrill's idea of "character" is parallel to our concept of "good intentions.") They talk about five waves of trust: self-trust (credibility), relationship trust (trust-building behaviors), organizational trust (measuring low-trust "taxes" and high-trust dividends), market trust (reputation), and societal trust (contribution). David Hutchens and Barry Rellaford wrote a short fable that succinctly illustrates the power of trust, based on the principles of Covey and Merrill's book: *A Slice of Trust* (Gibbs Smith, 2011).

You should also see David Maister, Charles H. Green, and Robert Galford, *The Trusted Advisor* (Touchstone, 2000); Charles H. Green, *Trust-Based Selling* (McGraw-Hill, 2006); and Charles H. Green and Andrea P. Howe, *The Trusted Advisor Fieldbook: A Comprehensive Toolkit for Leading with Trust* (Wiley, 2011). Green and his colleagues are highly respected for their work in helping companies build trusted relationships with their customers over the years—mostly in B2B settings. Their Trust Equation is based on the idea that self-orientation is the most influential component in building trust—and it's negative. Even if you have all the other components of trust, self-interest can neutralize them all.

$$\text{Trust} = \frac{\text{Credibility} + \text{Reliability} + \text{Intimacy}}{\text{Self-Orientation}}$$

In Chris Brogan and Julien Smith's book *Trust Agents: Using the Web to Build Influence, Improve Reputation, and Earn Trust*, 2nd ed. (Wiley, 2010), the authors emphasize that the Web should be treated as one big cocktail party, and your goal should be to humanize and not monetize the Web. The way to be a "trust agent" is to share ideas, facts, and insights freely—knowing that investing in relationships always brings a return eventually, even if you're not focusing on that return in the moment. The goal is to simply be a helpful person—generous and other-focused. This is what builds trust. They advise us never to be "that guy"—who's always trying to turn the conversation back to himself or his business, who makes you want to run when you see him coming.

In *The Economics of Integrity: From Dairy Farmers to Toyota, How Wealth Is Built on Trust and What That Means for Our Future* (HarperStudio, 2010), financial journalist Anna Bernasek profiles nine businesses whose success has been built on trust, and in our new "age of responsibility," argues that businesses must start with a "DNA of integrity," whose nucleus includes disclosure, norms, and accountability (p. 147).

Kathy Bloomgarden points out in *Trust: The Secret Weapon of Effective Business Leaders* (St. Martin's Press, 2007) that recent corporate scandals have decimated public trust in global companies and in the office of the CEO in particular. Bloomgarden emphasizes that CEOs must actively earn the trust of a company's stakeholders if they want to keep their jobs in this highly skeptical environment.

Also see Peter Firestein, *Crisis of Character: Building Corporate Reputation in the Age of Skepticism* (Sterling, 2009). Firestein, a corporate reputation risk consultant, presents a variety of case studies from some of the best-known brands in the world, illustrating how companies with behind-closed-doors strategies end up doing lasting harm to their reputations and thus their existence. Alternatively, he presents the Seven Strategies of Reputation Leadership to help corporations build a trustable reputation right into the core of their decision-making structures.

Joe Healey is a consultant and banking executive who has been speaking on the importance of trust in business leadership for twenty years. In *Radical Trust: How Today's Great Leaders Convert People to Partners* (Wiley, 2007), Healey uses four case studies to show how trust is no longer merely a moral choice, but a requirement for competitive advantage. According to Healey, trust requires four competencies: execution, character, communication, and loyalty.

Also see Geoffrey A. Hosking, *Trust: Money, Markets, and Society* (London: Seagull Books, 2010). Hosking argues that the stability of a global economy depends on trust, which includes a robust understanding of exactly how trust is developed, how it's broken, how it's maintained, and how it's repaired. Key to this is understanding where to place trust, as he cites misplaced trust in financial sectors and state welfare systems as precursors to the global economic crisis in 2007.

John Kador, *Effective Apology: Mending Fences, Building Bridges, and Restoring Trust* (Berrett-Koehler, 2009) explains why, as transparency grows and everyone seems to be apologizing for something, we don't necessarily need more apologies, but more effective ones. And if trust is a renewable asset that needs to be developed consciously, broken, and then rebuilt, an effective apology becomes a vital skill to master.

Roderick M. Kramer, a social psychologist and Stanford professor, argues that despite overwhelming evidence of corporate deceit, and despite the many books and articles that promote trust as if it's a hard sell, we still tend to trust too readily. He examines common human trust activators, such as physical similarities and the presence of touch, and after showing how easily we're fooled, he argues for "tempered trust." See "Rethinking Trust," *Harvard Business Review* 87 (June 2009): 68–77. Kramer also authored *Organizational Trust* (Oxford University Press, 2006), and *Trust and Distrust in Organizations* (Russell Sage Foundation, 2004) with Karen Cook.

Consider Robert Solomon and Fernando Flores, *Building Trust: In Business, Politics, Relationships, and Life* (Oxford University Press, 2003). Solomon and Flores argue that although trust is an important precursor to any interaction, it should be neither a static quality nor a knee-jerk reaction. Trust is a skill to be developed, and the authors explain how to go from simple or naïve trust to authentic, fully conscious trust in a number of contexts, including business.

Page 10   The Edelman Trust Barometer, available at http://www.edelman.com/trust, has been surveying the attitudes of the educated toward institutions in twenty-three countries for more than a decade, and it's a crucial source for understanding global and national trends in public trust of institutional sectors such as business, government, NGOs, and the media.

Page 11   See Elizabeth Hass Edersheim and Peter F. Drucker, *The Definitive Drucker* (McGraw-Hill Professional, 2007), p. xi.

Page 11   This idea of the "sharing economy" has been floating around for several years now, most clearly presented in Lawrence Lessig's *Remix: Making Art and Commerce Thrive in the Hybrid Economy* (Penguin Press, 2008), pp. 116–18. But the term seemed to galvanize at the March 2011 South-by-Southwest Conference in Austin, Texas, where a panel of presenters talked about "The New Sharing Economy." The following month, *Fast Company* published an article by Danielle Sacks titled "The Sharing Economy," which profiled many of the thinkers and practitioners in this new industry.

Page 12   Peter Walker, "Amnesty International Hails WikiLeaks and Guardian as 'Catalysts' in Arab Spring," *The Guardian* (UK) online, May 13, 2011, available at http://www.guardian.co.uk/world/2011/may/13/amnesty-international-wikileaks-arab-spring, accessed September 9, 2011.

Page 12   "A Comcast Technician Sleeping on My Couch," available at http://www.youtube.com/watch?v=CvVp7b5gzqU, accessed September 9, 2011.

Page 12   Since Dave Carroll and Sons of Maxwell posted their legendary YouTube video "United Breaks Guitars" in July 2009, which has generated a keynote speaking career and case study materials, a genre of luggage-mishandling videos has cropped up on YouTube. For just one example, see "Mistreating Luggage," available at http://www.youtube.com/watch?v=lzmJr1a-BHU, accessed September 9, 2011.

Page 13   Here is just a sampling of how business how-to books dealing with social media emphasize transparency and honesty:

Paul Gillin, *The New Influencers: A Marketer's Guide to the New Social Media* (Quill Driver Books, 2007), p. 14: "transparency is key to working in this medium."

Mitch Joel, *Six Pixels of Separation: Everyone Is Connected. Connect Your Business to Everyone* (Business Plus, 2009), p. 15: "Throughout this book you will be able to underscore all of the information and tactics and weave them through one long thread of authenticity." Also see chapter 2, "The Trust Economy."

Gary Vaynerchuk, *The Thank You Economy* (Wiley, 2011), p. 233: "Being authentic—whether online or offline, say what you mean and mean what you say."

Larry Weber, *Marketing to the Social Web: How Digital Customer Communities Build Your Business* (Wiley, 2007), p. 170: "bloggers are a community bound together by trust." And see p. 56 for the story of how "[t]rust is another major reason to allow critical comments on your site." A woman cited by Weber reports that after her negative review of a product was not displayed on Overstock.com's Web site she never trusted any of the other reviews she saw on that site.

Chris Brogan and Julien Smith, *Trust Agents: Using the Web to Build Influence, Improve Reputation, and Earn Trust* (Wiley, 2009), p. 15: "Trust agents have established themselves as being non-sales-oriented, non-high-pressure marketers. Instead, they are digital natives using the Web to be genuine and to humanize their business."

Charlene Li, *Open Leadership: How Social Technology Can Transform the Way You Lead* (Jossey-Bass, 2010), p. xvi: "Leadership will require a new approach, new mindset, and new skills. It won't be enough to be a good communicator. You will have to be comfortable sharing personal perspectives and feelings to develop closer relationships. Negative online comments can't be avoided or ignored. Instead, you will come to embrace each openness-enabled encounter as an opportunity to learn." On pp. 5–6 Li talks about the "culture of sharing" now springing up because of new technologies for interacting.

Darren Barefoot and Julie Szabo, *Friends with Benefits: A Social Media Marketing Handbook* (No Starch Press, 2009), p. 10: "With the culture of sharing comes two key concepts we always cite when discussing social media and specifically blogs: authenticity and transparency. A cult of honesty has developed in tandem with technical innovation."

Charlene Li and Josh Bernoff, in Groundswell: *Winning in a World Transformed by Social Technologies*, revised edition (Harvard Business Press, 2011), made many references to the requirement for honesty and authenticity, for instance: "Authenticity was crucial. Dell couldn't get anywhere in the groundswell until it honestly admitted its flaws" (p. 229). And from page 117: "Tips for successful blogging . . . 10. Final advice: be honest."

Francois Gossieaux and Ed Moran, *The Hyper-Social Organization: Eclipse Your Competition by Leveraging Social Media* (McGraw-Hill, 2010), also has numerous references to the need for honest, participatory collaboration with customers, and the importance of frank authenticity. For instance, p. 25: "Reciprocity is one of the key factors that allow communities to work—you scratch my back, I'll scratch yours. . . ." And p. 92: "Becoming human-centric also creates new knowledge flows for the company that may not have existed in the past. For instance, if everyone at your company began receiving daily reports on the top social media opinions expressed about your company, its brands, and its executives, instead of just monthly market share or sales data, wouldn't this transparency profoundly affect decision making across various groups?" And p. 39: "So the key to success in this new economic reality is to move from a transactional world to a long-term trust-based world." And of the authors' "Eight Characteristics of Hyper-Social Leaders," two are "They Trust Their People and Create Trusted Environments" and "They Embrace Transparency" (pp. 320–24).

Tara Hunt, *The Power of Social Networking: Using the Whuffie Factor to Build Your Business* (Crown Business, 2010), p. 2 : "First and foremost, the reason people are on these networks is to connect and build relationships. Relationships and connections over time lead to trust. And trust is the basis of whuffie—aka credibility." And p. 82: "Responding effectively to feedback expands your whuffie because when you respond correctly, you demonstrate to your customers that you are truly listening and responding to what they are saying, building trust. That trust will lead to more feedback and conversation, which leads to a deeper relationship."

Page 13   The quote about transparency being a disruptive innovation is from Paul Gillin, *The New Influencers* (Linden, 2007), p. 24.

Page 14   There's a lot of information out there about spam. See, for instance, http://www.barracudacentral.org/index.cgi?p=spam, which calculates spam percentages daily, or http://www.spam-o-meter.com/stats, which calculates spam percentage over time. On October 18, 2011, this site calculated the percentage of spam worldwide as 89.9 percent, measured over the previous three years.

Page 14   Ironically, the more open and trustable you are, the more likely your inevitable foibles will be discovered. If you seek out complaints on social networking sites and host reviews and comments on your own site, some of those reactions may get publicized. So—for a while anyway—you may look less trustable as you are becoming more trustable.

Page 18   Tara Hunt's definition of whuffie comes from *The Power of Social Networking: Using the Whuffie Factor to Build Your Business* (Crown, 2009), p. 33.

Page 18   Tara Hunt's quote about the gift economy and whuffie is from *The Power of Social Networking*, p. 5.

Page 18   Whitney MacMillan, chairman emeritus of Cargill, makes the case for the critical value of building social capital within your company and offers a proven formula for how to do it. See Whitney MacMillan, "The Power of Social Capital," *Harvard Management Update* 11, no. 6 (June 2006): 1–4.

Page 18   The comparison of annual Gallup surveys from 1970 to 2010, showing that American trust in institutions was at an all-time low in 2010, was found in Betsey Stevenson and Justin Wolfers, "Trust in Public Institutions over the Business Cycle," Federal Reserve Bank of San Francisco Working Paper Series, available at http://www.frbsf.org/publications/economics/papers/2011/wp11-11bk.pdf, accessed May 20, 2011.

Page 18   You can find the full 2011 Edelman Trust Barometer Findings at http://www.edelman.com/trust/2011/uploads/Edelman%20Trust%20Barometer%20Global%20Deck.pdf, accessed September 8, 2011. Also see Richard Edelman's Key Findings address, 2011 Trust Barometer Findings: Global & Country Insights, available at http://www.edelman.com/trust/2011/, accessed September 8, 2011.

Page 19   John Hagel discusses the paradox of trust in "Resolving the Trust Paradox," blog post, June 27, 2011, http://edgeperspectives.typepad.com/edge_perspectives/2011/06/resolving-the-trust-paradox.html, accessed August 13, 2011.

Page 19   More on the trust paradox can be found at John Hagel, "Resolving the Trust Paradox."

Page 20   The global survey that indicated consumers' rising expectations for good service was found here: "Customer Service Quality Falling Short of Rising Expectations Across the Globe, Accenture Study Finds," January 2008, http://newsroom.accenture.com/article_display.cfm?article_id=4630, accessed June 11, 2011.

Page 25   Yochai Benkler lists the reasons why human beings are experiencing a permanent change in how they organize themselves in *The Wealth of Networks* (Yale University Press, 2006).

2: SERVING THE INTERESTS OF CUSTOMERS, PROFITABLY

Page 27   Stephen M. R. Covey and Rebecca R. Merrill, *The Speed of Trust: The One Thing That Changes Everything* (Free Press, 2006).

Page 29   John R. Patterson and Chip R. Bell wrote about AOL's attempt to spin customer cancellations as sales leads in *Wired and Dangerous: How Your Customers Have Changed and What to Do About It* (Berrett-Koehler, 2011), pp. 51–52.

Page 29   Many sources, from a variety of angles, have documented AOL's storied practice of making money by fooling or manipulating its customers. For example, Ed Maxell reports that the phone rep at AOL would not cancel his deceased brother's account and would not give the cancellation number until after the complete do-not-cancel pitch, claiming that it was an FCC requirement. Maxell wrote a letter to AOL, "suggesting that a more sensitive method be used for death cancellations—like faxing a death certificate" (*PC Magazine*, May 18, 2004, p. 55). AOL financials and other facts were found in Robert A. Burgelman and Philip E. Meza, "AOL: The Emergence of an Internet Media Company, SM-75," case study (Stanford Graduate School of Business, 2003), p. 24, available at: https://gsbapps.stanford .edu/cases/documents/SM75.pdf, accessed September 14, 2011; "Meet the Market's Biggest Losers," CNN Money, February 5, 2010, available at: http://money.cnn.com/galleries/2010/ fortune/1002/gallery.biggest_losers.fortune/8.html, accessed September 13, 2011; Jessica E. Vascellaro and Emily Steel, "AOL Shifts Emphasis, Bit by Bit," *Wall Street Journal* online, September 29, 2010, at http://online.wsj.com/article/SB10001424052748703882404575519 831320838198.html, accessed September 13, 2011; "AOL," Wikipedia, available at en .wikipedia.org/wiki/AOL, accessed September 13, 2011; Hoovers online, www.hoovers.com, accessed September 13, 2011; Ken Auletta, "You've Got News," *New Yorker*, January 23, 2011, p. 32; Shelley Dubois, "Can Tim Armstrong Survive AOL?," CNN Money, September 13, 2011, http://management.fortune.cnn.com/2011/09/13/tim-armstrong-aol/?section= magazines_fortune, accessed September 22, 2011; Mike Musgrave and David A. Vise, "Arresting News for AOL," *Washington Post*, June 25, 2004, p. E01.

Page 29   The quote about AOL's "dirty little secret" is from Ken Auletta's "You've Got News," *New Yorker*, January 23, 2011, p. 32.

Page 30   The retail banking discussion is based largely on *Gotcha Capitalism* (Ballantine, 2007) by Bob Sullivan, an MSNBC blogger and commentator, pp. 62–70. According to Sullivan, some banks charge a $30-plus overdraft fee and then another $5 per day for every day the account remains overdrawn. Some offer automatic transfers from a credit card to the bank account to cover the fee, but cash advance charges apply, and the minimum amount of transfer is sometimes $100 (p. 62). When consumers get their bank balance at an ATM, the "available balance" often automatically includes the courtesy overdraft cushion, encouraging overdrafts. "Here's how it works. When a customer with an $80 balance and $200 courtesy overdraft protection asks for a balance, the ATM indicates '$280 available balance'" (p. 63). Thus Sullivan's advice to consumers, found on p. 70, is to "opt out of courtesy overdraft protection!" Continuing, Sullivan notes that debit card swipes and ATM withdrawals now account for the majority of "bounced check" fees (p. 64). And the biggest checks clear first out of an account, so that overdrafts are maximized. "Here's an example: If you have $500 in your account and you write checks for $72, $98, $28, and $410 on the same day, you'll bounce the first three checks, and pay about $100 in fees" (p. 65).

Page 32   The general consensus is "Courtesy overdraft: bad for customers" (Laura Bruce, Bankrate.com, December 19, 2007, http://www.bankrate.com/finance/exclusives/ courtesy-overdraft-bad-for-customers-1.aspx, accessed June 11, 2011). See also Connie Thompson, "The Downside to Debit Cards," KCBY News, March 23, 2009, http://www .kcby.com/news/consumertips/41468757.html, accessed June 11, 2011.

Page 32   Sullivan, *Gotcha Capitalism*, p. 60.

Page 33   The documentation of Netflix's new business model is from "NETFLIX.com Transforms DVD Business Eliminating Late Fees and Due Dates From Movie Rentals," press release from Netflix.com, December 16, 1999, available at http://netflix.mediaroom .com/index.php?s=43&item=231, accessed October 26, 2011.

Page 34   We've written about Blockbuster's decision to drop late fees, albeit late in the game, in Don Peppers and Martha Rogers, *Rules to Break and Laws to Follow* (Wiley, 2008), pp. 31–32.

Page 34   For more about how Netflix "throttled" their highest-volume customers with longer turnaround times, see "Frequent Netflix renters sent to back of the line: The more you use, the slower the service, some customers realize," Associated Press, February 10, 2006, http://www.msnbc.msn.com/id/11262292/ns/business-us_business/t/frequent -netflix-renters-sent-back-line/#.Tn8aCezjuuI, accessed September 25, 2011.

Page 35   For Dr. Natalie Petouhoff and Jennifer Tyler's robust research on customer social media responses to Netflix's restructuring and price increase, see Natalie Petouhoff, "Could Social Media Monitoring Have Saved Netflix and Blockbuster from Themselves?," September 23, 2011, at http://www.drnatalienews.com/blog/could-social-media-monitoring-have -saved-netflix-blockbuster-from-themselves#, accessed October 14, 2011.

Page 36   Our source for Netflix outsourcing its movie-recommendation algorithm was Steve Lohr's "Netflix Awards $1 Million Prize and Starts a New Contest," *New York Times* Bits blog, September 21, 2009, at http://bits.blogs.nytimes.com/2009/09/21 /netflix-awards-1-million-prize-and-starts-a-new-contest/, accessed September 26, 2011.

Page 36   Nick Wingfield, "Netflix Market Value Shrivels," *New York Times,* October 25, 2011, http://bits.blogs.nytimes.com/2011/10/25/netflix-market-value-shrivels/, accessed October 26, 2011.

Page 37   We found the Stimson quote at http://www.goodreads.com/author/quotes/ 3180556.Henry_Stimson, accessed June 6, 2011.

Page 37   Seth Godin has repeatedly and provocatively made the point that only human beings (not companies) can have relationships, from his classic *Permission Marketing* (Simon & Schuster, 1999) to *Linchpin* (Portfolio, 2010) to *Poke the Box* (The Domino Project, 2011).

Page 38   If you're looking for a copy of *The Trusted Advisor,* here's the full citation: David H. Maister, Charles H. Green, and Robert M. Galford, *The Trusted Advisor* (Free Press, 2000).

Page 38   Charles H. Green explains his trust equation in detail in "The Trust Equation: Generating Trust," in our revised textbook, Don Peppers and Martha Rogers, *Managing Customer Relationships: A Strategic Framework,* 2nd ed. (Wiley, 2011), pp. 83–84.

Page 39   A Forrester report has shown that 83 percent trust friends, more than 50 percent trust online reviews, and just 14 percent trust advertising ("The Analog Groundswell," Forrester Research, Inc., September 11, 2009, available at www.forrester.com, accessed September 13, 2011). But although most of us remember the Edelman Trust Barometer's famous 2006 finding that "a person like me" was the most trusted source of information (http://www.edelman.com/news/showone.asp?id=102), more recently the Trust Barometer has shown that people now trust experts more than peers. How can both be true? The key may be in the difference between online and offline. A study by Razorfish indicates that offline friends are more influential than online friends. Forrester has broken its results down to examine face-to-face friends as well as online friends, whereas Edelman's survey doesn't differentiate between face-to-face friends and online peers. Amanda Rooker wonders whether this is likely a result of our talking to our online peers way too much about minutiae. After experiencing how little of import our peers actually have to say (if they're talking and we're listening constantly), maybe experts aren't as overrated as we thought. See her blog post, "Too Much Communication Just Isn't Trustworthy," in *Sustainable Communication*, December 15, 2011, http://amandarooker.wordpress.com, and see Charles Green's comment at http://trustedadvisor.com/trustmatters/can-you-trust-the-data-on-trust about how Edelman measures trust on its home page at http://www.edelman.com/trust/2011/.

Page 42   The Peapod example comes from Ian Ayres, *Super Crunchers: Why Thinking-by-Numbers Is the New Way to Be Smart* (Bantam, 2007), p. 170.

Page 42   According to Synovate Mail Monitor, the world's consumers received 2.73 billion credit card solicitations in 2010. See Mark Huffman, "Credit Card Offers on the Increase," ConsumerAffairs.com, January 27, 2011, at http://www.consumeraffairs.com/news04/2011/01/credit-card-offers-on-the-increase.html, accessed October 17, 2011. Also see Becky Yerak, "Credit Card Offers and Incentives Expected to Pick Up in 2011," *Los Angeles Times* online, January 1, 2011, available at http://articles.latimes.com/2011/jan/01/business/la-fi-credit-cards-20110101, accessed September 14, 2011.

Page 42   We did the research on Royal Bank of Canada for our textbook revision, Don Peppers and Martha Rogers, Ph.D., *Managing Customer Relationships: A Strategic Framework*, 2nd ed. (Wiley, 2011).

Page 43   Adam Smith's quote about how the butcher, the brewer, and the baker are ultimately driven by self-interest can be found in *An Inquiry into the Nature and Causes of the Wealth of Nations*, Pennsylvania State University Electronic Classics Series (The Pennsylvania State University, 2005), p. 19, available at http://www2.hn.psu.edu/faculty/jmanis/adam-smith/Wealth-Nations.pdf, accessed September 14, 2011.

Page 44   The story about U.S. Army brigadier general S. L. A Marshall's survey of troops in combat was reported in Jonah Lehrer, *How We Decide* (Houghton Mifflin Harcourt, 2009), p. 179.

Page 44   The quote about *Homo economicus* is from Joseph Henrich, Robert Boyd, Samuel Bowles, Colin F. Camerer, Ernst Fehr, and Herbert Gintis, eds., *Foundations of Human*

Sociality: Economic Experiments and Ethnographic Evidence from Fifteen Small-Scale Societies (Oxford University Press, 2009), Oxford Scholarship Online, http://oxfordscholarship .com—as cited in John A. List, "On the Interpretation of Giving in Dictator Games," *Journal of Political Economy* 115, no. 3 (2007), available at http://expecon.gsu.edu/jccox/ reading/519249.pdf, accessed July 16, 2010.

Page 45 The details about the dictator game experiments can be found in Henrich et al., *Foundations of Human Sociality*. Note: There is some disagreement over how purely the dictator game illustrates actual altruism or kindness on the part of the research subjects, as opposed to "self-regarding" self-interest. Depending on the configuration of the game, for instance, a "dictator" may simply be fearful of appearing to be greedy in the eyes of the researcher. If so, then the motivation for giving to the second person would not be generosity or altruism, but a selfish desire to *appear* altruistic. But researchers have experimented with the dictator game in many different configurations, and it almost certainly demonstrates that the average person does genuinely feel an urge to be kind to other people—to share, rather than simply take.

Page 45 Lehrer's quote about the dictator game can be found in his *How We Decide*, p. 184.

Page 46 Kevin Kelly, *What Technology Wants* (Penguin, 2011), Kindle edition, Loc. 1170–76. "The third piece of evidence for small, steady, long-term advance resides in the moral sphere. Here metrics for measurement are few and disagreement about the facts greater. Over time our laws, mores, and ethics have slowly expanded the sphere of human empathy. Generally, humans originally identified themselves primarily via their families. The family clan was 'us.' This declaration cast anyone outside of that intimacy as 'other.' We had—and still have—different rules of behavior for those inside the circle of 'us' and for those outside. Gradually the circle of 'us' enlarged from inside the family clan to inside the tribe, and then from tribe to nation. We are currently in an unfinished expansion beyond nation and maybe even race and may soon be crossing the species boundary."

Page 46 Borderline personalities and true psychopaths are the subject of Barbara Oakley's fascinating book *Evil Genes: Why Rome Fell, Hitler Rose, and My Sister Stole My Mother's Boyfriend* (Prometheus, 2008), pp. 137, 321.

Page 49 Our source for the facts about how victims of the 2011 Japanese tsunami tended to return property to its rightful owner rather than loot it was Akiko Fujita, "Honest Japanese Return $78 Million in Cash Found in Quake Rubble," August 17, 2011, ABC News, http://abcnews.go.com/International/honest-japanese-return-78-million-cash-found -quake/story?id=14322940, accessed September 22, 2011.

Page 49 Trust in the social collective: Roderick M. Kramer, in his *Harvard Business Review* article "Rethinking Trust" (*Harvard Business Review* 87 [June 2009]: pp. 68–77), reminds us that humans do tend to trust inherently as a part of the human condition, despite the fact that sometimes our judgment is poor, obscured by untrustables who look like us. He offers rules for being cautious in the marketplace.

Page 49 Imitation is just the beginning. Many scientists believe that the ability to unconsciously share another's pain is a building block of empathy, and through that emotion, morality. See David Brooks, *The Social Animal: The Hidden Sources of Love, Character, and Achievement* (Random House, 2011), Kindle edition, Loc. 849–52.

Page 51   Michael Schrage, "Should Your Best Customers Be Stupid?," HBR Blog Network, November, 19, 2010, available at http://blogs.hbr.org/schrage/2010/11/should-your -customers-be-stupid.html, accessed September 14, 2011. In a full-page ad run in *USA Today* on March 28, 2007, for the Community Financial Services Association of America (CFSA), an "assistant manager" says in large letters, "There are right ways and wrong ways to use payday advances. I want my customers to know the difference." The ad lists four pointers for correct use of payday advances to prevent customers from being taken advantage of.

Page 51   John R. Patterson and Chip R. Bell, *Wired and Dangerous: How Your Customers Have Changed and What to Do About It* (Berrett-Koehler, 2011), p. 50. The average post is read by forty-five people, and 62 percent of customers who hear about a bad experience on social media stop doing business with, or avoid doing business with, the offending company.

Page 51   "Customer Experience Report: North America 2010," commissioned by Right-Now and conducted by Harris Interactive, available at: http://www.rightnow.com/resource -ra-customer-experience-impact-north-america-2010.php, accessed September 14, 2011. The survey illustrates how, despite skyrocketing Internet interactions, face-to-face is still the most powerful.

Page 52   We learned about Ally Bank's "three pillars of customer service" in a phone interview with Sanjay Gupta, CMO at Ally Bank, May 23, 2011.

Page 52   Based on a chat session with the authors, September 22, 2011. This service, called "Ally eCheck Deposit," was launched in October 2011.

Page 52   We learned about Ally Bank's testing out check scanning through a chat session with them on September 22, 2011.

Page 52   Ally Bank's customers can read and submit reviews directly on their product pages. See "Rave Reviews for the 2-Year Raise Your Rate CD," Ally Straight Talk blog, at http://community.ally.com/straight-talk/category/customer-spotlight/, accessed September 22, 2011.

Page 52   See, for instance, Ally Bank's customer reviews of its interest checking account at http://www.ally.com/bank/interest-checking-account/#tabs=customer-reviews, accessed October 17, 2011.

Page 52   James R. Hood, "More Banks Blink, Cancel Debit-Card Fees," consumeraffairs .com, November 1, 2011, at http://www.consumeraffairs.com/news04/2011/11/more-banks -blink-cancel-debit-card-fees.html, accessed November 2, 2011. See also Robin Sidel and Dan Fitzpatrick, "Debit-Fee Retreat Complete," *Wall Street Journal*, November 2, 2011, at http://online.wsj.com, accessed November 2, 2011. While there is little doubt that the banks caved in on their debit card fees due to consumer outrage, one commentator's perspective is that consumer temper tantrums like this may not be such a healthy development. See Bob

McTeer (former president of the Dallas Fed), "Debit Card Fees: Sending the Wrong Message," *Forbes* blog, November 1, 2011, at http://www.forbes.com/sites/bobmcteer/2011/11/01/debit-card-fees-sending-the-wrong-message/, accessed November 2, 2011. The debit card fee fiasco has provided hilarious material for comics, including Andy Borowitz's November 2, 2011, newsletter conveying a mock "apology" letter from Bank of America, proposing all sorts of other fees (like a $10 fee to collect the $5 refund in cash, for instance), and ending with:

"Again, accept our apologies for instituting the debit card fee. We have learned our lesson, and we make this solemn promise: next time we squeeze money from you, we'll do it in a way you won't notice.

Sincerely,

Bank of America"

Page 53   You can find out more about what drives customer loyalty in the banking and insurance industries (and what doesn't) in the report "Customer Advocacy 2011: How Customers Rate Banks, Investment Companies, and Insurers," Forrester Research, Inc., March 8, 2011, available at www.forrester.com, accessed June 9, 2011.

Page 54   You can read more about "strategic vulnerability" in Rajendra S. Sisodia, David B. Wolfe, and Jagdish N. Sheth, *Firms of Endearment: How World-Class Companies Profit from Passion and Purpose* (Pearson Prentice Hall, 2007), pp. 59–60.

3: TRUSTABILITY: CAPITALIST TOOL

Page 59   The bank fee statistic is cited in Bob Sullivan, *Gotcha Capitalism* (Ballantine, 2007), p. 58.

Page 60   You can learn a lot from "Prepaid Cards: Second-Tier Bank Account Substitutes," a Consumers Union report by staff attorney Michelle Jun, September 2010, at http://www.defendyourdollars.org/Prepaid%20WP.pdf, accessed June 14, 2011.

Page 61   Here's the source for the CFO survey that found 78 percent of them would sacrifice "economic value" to make this quarter's numbers: Emery P. Dalesio, "Executives Sacrifice Shareholder Value to Please Street," Associated Press State & Local Wire, February 9, 2004. "Three-quarters of business executives admit they massage earnings reports to meet or beat Wall Street expectations and would sacrifice shareholder value to keep earnings on a smooth upward slope, according to a survey released Monday. The study of 401 senior financial executives by researchers at Duke University and the University of Washington found that 55 percent would delay starting a project to avoid missing an earnings target. Four out of five executives said they would defer maintenance and research spending to meet earnings targets. The preference for smooth earnings growth instead of even slight variations is so strong that 78 percent of the surveyed executives would give up economic value in exchange, the study said."

Page 61   "As the economist and Nobel laureate Elinor Ostrom has shown, when we assume people are basically selfish, we design economic systems that reward selfish people." Clay Shirky, *Cognitive Surplus* (Penguin Press, 2010), p. 111.

Page 62   Most companies report and reward based on historic numbers, and leave prediction and projection to others. Steven Pinker suggests that our *understanding* of time is severely limited, psychologically, and that this is evident purely from the structure of language itself. After all, when time is expressed grammatically in most languages, there are only three real tenses: the here and now, the future unto eternity, and the history of the universe before now. Moreover, he says, because the human experience of time is entirely subjective, "it speeds up or slows down depending on how demanding, varied, and pleasant an interval is." Pinker, *The Stuff of Thought: Language as a Window into Human Nature* (Viking, 2007), p. 190.

Page 62   Orkun Oguz, "Finding Your Place on the Customer Measurement Grid," *Strategy Speaks* blog post, July 20, 2011, accessed at http://www.peppersandrogersgroup.com/blog/2011/07/customer-strategist-orkun-oguz-8.html.

Page 62   If you want to extend your examination of how KPIs are often used, see Gretchen Morgenson and Joshua Rosner, *Reckless Endangerment: How Outsized Ambition, Greed, and Corruption Led to Economic Armageddon* (Henry Holt/Times Books, 2011), for an outstanding narrative of the entire mortgage mess that led to the recession of 2008.

Page 64   The discussion about owners versus agents as one contributor to short-termism came from Alfred Rappaport, *Saving Capitalism from Short-Termism* (McGraw-Hill, 2011), pp. 7, 11, 16.

Page 65   Michael Lewis tells the story of the investors who bet against housing prices and mortgage bonds in *The Big Short* (Norton, 2010), p. 147.

Page 66   The facts about how Google operates were found in Ken Auletta, *Googled: The End of the World as We Know It* (Penguin Press, 2009), p. 111. Please note: The point we're making here is generally true, but ads are ranked according to an AdRank, which is a complex formula that also includes relevance to search keywords and other ads in the list. It's not purely based on user clicks, but is primarily so. Confirmed from Google's Investor Relations page, available at http://investor.google.com/corporate/faq.html and accessed on September 22, 2011. Regarding ads and how they're ranked, see http://adwords.google.com/support/aw/bin/answer.py?hl=en&answer=6111.

Page 67   The quote about Facebook came from David Kirkpatrick, *The Facebook Effect: The Inside Story of the Company That Is Connecting the World* (Simon & Schuster, 2011), p. 258.

Page 67   Launched in 1994, Amazon.com posted its first quarterly profit on December 31, 2001. "Amazon Posts First Profit," *Communications Today* 8, no. 16 (January 24, 2002): 1.

Page 69   As of 2011, only some U.S. states (including Connecticut, Louisiana, Georgia, New Jersey, and Mississippi) legally required homebuilders to provide a structural warranty, although most homebuilders voluntarily offer some kind of limited warranty in their sales contracts. Typical coverage is a one-year warranty for labor and materials, two-year warranty for mechanical defects, and a ten-year warranty for structural defects.

(Ilona Bray, "Holding Your Builder Responsible for New-Home Defects," Craig T. Matthews & Associates, available at: http://www.ctmlaw.com/articles/holding-your-builder-responsible-for-new-home-defects.html, accessed September 22, 2011. Also see "Special Problems in New Home Construction," available at: http://real-estate.lawyers.com/residential-real-estate/Special-Problems-in-New-Home-Construction.html, accessed September 22, 2011.)

Page 71   In their book *Analytics at Work: Smarter Decisions, Better Results,* Thomas H. Davenport, Jeanne G. Harris, and Robert Morison emphasize the importance of evolving more and more sophisticated and discerning analytical capabilities that provide deep insight based on facts and defensible predictions (Harvard Business Press, 2010).

Page 72   V. Kumar and Denish Shah, "Can Marketing Lift Stock Prices?" *MIT Sloan Management Review,* Summer 2011, pp. 24–26, determined that lifetime-value-increase marketing activities lift stock prices. Also see the research by Janamitra Devan, Anna Kristina Millan, and Pranav Shirke, "Balancing Short- and Long-Term Performance," Research in Brief, *The McKinsey Quarterly,* 1 (2005): 31–33, for a discussion of the characteristics of S&P 500 companies that performed well in both the long term and short term from 1984 to 2004, compared with those companies that performed well in only one or the other.

Page 73   Shaw Wu's comment about Apple is reported in http://www.appleinsider.com/article.php?id=1687.

Page 74   We talked with John Stumpf, CEO of Wells Fargo & Company, about trust and banking on June 23, 2011.

Page 74   Your competitors will have to make a profit, but we already see strong, viable companies determined to make a profit this quarter that are *not necessarily determined to make the biggest profit they can this quarter.* How will your company compete when other firms routinely balance their long- and short-term success by doing the right thing for customers, doing things right, proactively? The Fourth Sector Network in the United States and Denmark is promoting the "for-benefit organization"—a hybrid that it says represents a new category of organization that is both economically self-sustaining and animated by a public purpose. One example: Mozilla, the entity that gave us Firefox, is organized as a "for benefit organization." And three U.S. entrepreneurs have invented the "B Corporation," a designation that requires companies to amend their bylaws so that incentives favor long-term value and social impact instead of short-term economic gain. See Mohammad Yanus, *Creating a World Without Poverty: Social Business and the Future of Capitalism* (PublicAffairs, 2007), p. 23; and see Aspen Institute, Fourth Sector Concept Paper (Fall 2008); and "B Corporation," *MIT Sloan Management Review,* December 11, 2008; and http://www.bcorporation.net/declaration.

Page 76   "Trust in Mobile Services," Peppers & Rogers Group original research, 2011, summary available at www.peppersandrogersgroup.com.

Page 76   Tom Lacki's additional insights about the research on trustability and mobile carriers were sent via e-mail to the authors, October 24, 2011, and November 3, 2011.

Page 77 We've said that customers are different. Sometimes that doesn't show in social media, but we need to remember the principle. See Duncan Simester, "When You Shouldn't Listen to Your Critics," *Harvard Business Review,* June 2011, p. 42, which reminds us that trust is an important part of *business* decisions. Simester believes you shouldn't just trust feedback from some social networking sites (e.g., Yelp) willy-nilly if the participants aren't your ideal customer. Simester describes how he and two partners started a "grab-and-go food business," and obsessed over Yelp reviews—only to attend an event that hosted several hundred elite Yelp users, and realized they were mostly in their twenties and looked nothing like their customers, who were mostly professionals over age thirty. So even though there's a lot of online feedback saying their restaurant isn't very good or is overpriced, he now knows those vocal customers aren't really his ideal customers anyway. His lesson for social media is the same lesson as for pre-social-media: Don't aim to please everybody without understanding who is saying what and why, because this may undermine your sincere and legitimate customer differentiation efforts.

Page 78 Laura Blue, "Better Bedside Manners," *Time*, September 5, 2007, accessed at http://www.time.com/time/health/article/0,8599,1659065,00.html on September 27, 2010. See also: Dr. Manoj Jain, "Viewpoint: Good doctor-patient relationship reduces lawsuits," *The Commercial Appeal* (Memphis), online version, September 6, 2010, available at http://www.commercialappeal.com/news/2010/sep/06/good-doctor-patient-relationship-reduces/, accessed June 10, 2011. While we're on the subject, ABC News reported that a majority of letters from Toyota customers, in response to ABC's reporting on the recent widespread mechanical failures and vehicle recalls, defended the brand rather than detracted from it. See Alice Gomstyn, "Toyota Recalls More Cars, But Customers Stay Loyal," ABC News (online), February 9, 2010, available at http://abcnews.go.com/Business/toyota-customers -defend-brand-recalls/story?id=9781832, accessed June 10, 2011.

Page 78 See our more comprehensive discussion of the difference between behavioral loyalty and attitudinal loyalty in Don Peppers and Martha Rogers, Ph.D., *Managing Customer Relationships: A Strategic Framework* (Wiley, 2011), pp. 64–68.

Page 78 Full disclosure: TeleTech is the parent company for Peppers & Rogers Group.

Page 79 We talked with Ken Tuchman, founder and CEO of TeleTech, and other members of TeleTech's management team about the difference between attitudinal and behavioral loyalty on January 12, 2011.

Page 79 We've realized we've been writing about USAA Insurance as a paragon of customer relationships and reciprocity for fifteen years. You'll find mentions of USAA in our books *Rules to Break & Laws to Follow* (Wiley, 2008), *Return on Customer* (Currency/Doubleday, 2005), *Managing Customer Relationships: A Strategic Framework,* 2nd ed. (Wiley, 2011), *One to One Manager* (Currency/Doubleday, 2000), *One to One Fieldbook* (Currency/Doubleday, 1999), and *Enterprise One to One* (Currency/Doubleday, 1997).

Page 79 See Forrester's report "Customer Advocacy 2011: How Customers Rate Banks, Investment Firms, and Insurers," Forrester Research, Inc., March 8, 2011, available at www.forrester.com, accessed June 9, 2011.

Page 80   Peter Merholz discusses what makes Amazon, Zappos, and USAA particularly trustworthy in "What Trust Brings to Amazon, Zappos, and USAA," HBR Blogs: *The Conversation*, April 27, 2010, at http://blogs.hbr.org/cs/2010/04/what_trust_brings_to _amazon_za.html, accessed May 24, 2011.

Page 80   Market capitalization figures for Barnes & Noble and Amazon are from UBS Financial Services, Inc., as of October 12, 2011. And Robert Spector notes the role reversal of the two companies in "Yesterday's Goliath, Today's David; Barnes & Noble's Positioning Itself as the Plucky Underdog to Its Giant Competitor Amazon.com Is a Complete Role Reversal from the mid-1990s," *Wall Street Journal*, accessed via Factiva.com on September 23, 2011.

Page 80   Facts about Zappos came from Peter Merholz, "What Trust Brings to Amazon, Zappos, and USAA"; and "Zappos.com," Wikipedia, at http://en.wikipedia.org/wiki/ Zappos.com, accessed September 26, 2011.

Page 82   The classic study on how facial expression affects mood is C. L. Kleinke, T. R. Peterson, and T. R. Rutledge's "Effects of Self-Generated Facial Expressions on Mood," *Journal of Personality and Social Psychology* 74 (1998): 272–79.

4: SHARING: NOT JUST FOR SUNDAY SCHOOL

Page 87   London Science Museum's survey of adults was reported in *The Week,* September 23, 2011, p. 6.

Page 87   Technorati detail from Heather Havenstein, "Blogs Becoming Entrenched in Mainstream—and More Profitable," *Computerworld*, September 23, 2008, available at http://www.computerworld.com/s/article/9115367/Blogs_becoming_entrenched_in _mainstream_and_more_profitable, accessed July 13, 2010.

Page 88   We learned about Folding@home at http://www.answers.com/main/ ntquery?s=folding%40home&gwp=13#Wikipedia_.

Page 89   Definitions of social production abound. Yochai Benkler calls it "commons-based peer production" (*The Wealth of Networks,* Yale University Press, 2006, p. 60). Lawrence Lessig has framed it as an entirely new kind of economics—a "sharing economy" as opposed to a "commercial economy" (*Remix: Making Art and Commerce Thrive in the Hybrid Economy,* Penguin Press, 2008, pp. 116–18). And for Clay Shirky, social production is "how most picnics happen": "the creation of value by a group for its members, using neither price signals nor managerial oversight to coordinate participants' efforts" (*Cognitive Surplus,* Penguin Press, 2010, p. 118).

Page 89   One of our sources about Linux is Yochai Benkler's *The Wealth of Networks*, p. 64. Another is Eric von Hippel's *Democratizing Innovation* (MIT Press, 2006), p. 80. "Free software has played a critical role in the recognition of peer production, because software is a functional good with measurable qualities. It can be more or less authoritatively tested against its market-based competitors. And, in many instances, free software has prevailed. About 70 percent of Web server software, in particular for critical e-commerce sites, runs on the Apache Web server—free software. More than half of all back-office e-mail functions are run by one free software program or another. Google, Amazon, and CNN .com, for example, run their Web servers on the GNU/Linux operating system. They do this, presumably, because they believe this peer-produced operating system is more reliable than the alternatives, not because the system is inexpensive" (p. 64). "Contributors to the many open source software projects extant . . . also routinely make the code they have written public" (von Hippel, p. 80).

Page 89   Our source for the number of current open-source projects was http://sourceforge.net/about, accessed September 27, 2011.

Page 89   For more about the potential behind our "cognitive surplus," see Shirky, *Cognitive Surplus*, p. 10.

Page 90   See these and other examples of social production in Lessig, *Remix*, pp. 166–69.

Page 90   It took bloggers only three hours after the Lens Blog of *The New York Times* along with "Eines Tages," a site run by the German magazine *Der Spiegel*, ran some photos requesting information from readers. The photographer was identified as Franz Krieger, a military photographer and driver who joined and then quit a Nazi propaganda unit. James Barron and David W. Dunlap, "In Hours, Online Readers Identify Nazi Photographer," *New York Times*, June 25, 2011, pp. C1, C4.

Page 90   Eric von Hippel says "employees of a firm may wish to experience [enjoyment and other] intrinsic reward in their work as well, but managers and commercial constraints may give them less of an opportunity to do so. Indeed, 'control over my own work' is cited by many programmers as a reason that they enjoy creating code as volunteers on open source projects more than they enjoy coding for their employers for pay." See *Democratizing Innovation*, p. 61.

Page 91   Lessig describes Red Hat in *Remix*, pp. 181–83: "Robert Young saw early on the value of an open system. He described a conversation with some engineers from Southwestern Bell at a conference at Duke. Young was surprised to learn that they were using Linux to run the central switching station for Southwestern Bell. He asked why. Their response, as Young recounts it, is quite revealing: 'Our problem is we have no choice. If we use Sun OS or NT and something goes wrong, we have to wait around for months for Sun or Microsoft to get around to fixing it for us. If we use Linux, we get to fix it ourselves if it's truly urgent. And so we can fix it on our schedule, not the schedule of some arbitrary supplier.' . . . Young said, 'Red Hat is thus a "hybrid."' Young was not in it to make the world a better place, though knowing the man, I know he's quite happy to make the world a better place. Young was in it for the money. But the only way Red Hat was going to succeed was if thousands continued to contribute—for free—to the development of the GNU/Linux operating system. He and his company were going to leverage value out of that system. But they would succeed only if those voluntarily contributing to the underlying code continued to contribute. One might well imagine that when a for-profit company like Red

Hat comes along and tries to leverage great value out of the free work of the free-software movement, some might raise 'the justice question.' Putting aside Marc Ewing (who had great coder cred), who was Robert Young to make money out of Linux? Why should the free-software coders continue to work for him (even if only indirectly, since anyone else was free to take the work as well)? . . . [There] was a general recognition that free software would go nowhere unless companies began to support it. Thus, while there was whining on the sidelines, there was no campaign by the founders of key free software to stop these emerging hybrids. So long as the work was not turned proprietary—so long as the code remained 'free' in the sense of 'freedom'—neither Stallman nor Linus Torvalds was going to object. This was the only way to make sure an ecology of free software could be supported. It was an effective way to spread free software everywhere. And indeed, the freedom to make money using the code was as much a 'freedom' as anything was."

Page 91   Yochai Benkler notes that IBM "has obtained the largest number of patents every year from 1993 to 2004, amassing in total more than 29,000 patents. IBM has also, however, been one of the firms most aggressively engaged in adapting its business model to the emergence of free software . . . [noticeable in] what happened to the relative weight of patent royalties, licenses, and sales in IBM's revenues and revenues that the firm described as coming from 'Linux-related services.' Within a span of four years, the Linux-related services category moved from accounting for practically no revenues, to providing double the revenues from all patent-related sources, of the firm that has been the most patent-productive in the United States." From *The Wealth of Networks*, p. 46.

Page 91   According to Lawrence Lessig, other profit-making firms serving GNU/Linux users include "CodeWeavers [1996], TimeSys Corp. [1996], Linuxcare [1998], Mandriva [1998], LinuxOne [1998], Bluepoint Linux Software Corp. [1999], Progeny Linux Systems Inc. [1999], MontaVista Software [1999], Win4Lin [2000], Linspire [2001], and Xandros [2001], to name a few . . ." From *Remix*, p. 183.

Page 91   We checked in on http://lostpedia.wikia.com/wiki/Special:Statistics on July 13, 2010.

Page 92   Charlene Li talks about Solar Winds in *Open Leadership* (Jossey-Bass, 2010), p. 26.

Page 92   eBay thrived because it figured out an efficient way for total strangers to trust one another. See Shirky, *Cognitive Surplus*, p. 177.

Page 93   You can find the fascinating story of the rise of craigslist in Lessig, *Remix*, pp. 187–91.

Page 93   "Of course, craigslist was not the only Internet response to Katrina. Neither was it the most important. David Geilhufe's PeopleFinder Project probably earns that title; it was built exclusively by volunteers in an extraordinary demonstration of a sharing economy that ultimately hosted more than 1 million Katrina-related searches in the 'immediate aftermath of the hurricane.' But Geilhufe's success is not a complaint about craigslist. The significance of craigslist was that it was the place to start." See Lessig, *Remix*, p. 191.

Page 93   You can find more about the civic-minded young Pakistanis in Sabrina Tavernise, "Young Pakistanis Take One Problem into Their Own Hands," *New York Times*, May 19, 2009, cited also in Shirky, *Cognitive Surplus*, p. 126.

Page 93   You can learn more in Poornima Weerasekara, "How the Twittersphere Helped Keep Oakland Safe," in New America Media, cited at http://newamericamedia.org/2010/07/how-the-twittersphere-helped-keep-oakland-safe.php, on July 11, 2010. See Shirky, *Cognitive Surplus*, pp. 15–17, for more on Ushahidi as well.

Page 93   You can read more about helping the medical patient in Israel at http://www.jpost.com/Home/Article.aspx?id=178577, accessed July 13, 2010, and about gift giving in "Beyond the Buzzword, How Crowdsourcing Can Disrupt Brazil," TNW Latin America, August 2011, at http://thenextweb.com/la/2011/08/24/beyond-the-buzzword-how-crowdsourcing-can-disrupt-brazil/, accessed on August 24, 2011. See also the gift-giving Web site Vakinha, http://www.vakinha.com.br/ (Portuguese).

Page 94   Read more about how DemandTec enables collaboration between its employees, partners, and vendors with their customized internal social media platform at Don Peppers, "Enterprise Social Media: Getting Social Inside the Firm," Strategy Speaks, May 25, 2011, at http://www.peppersandrogersgroup.com/blog/2011/05/enterprise-social-media---gett.html, accessed September 23, 2011.

Page 95   Imitation is just the beginning. "Many scientists believe that the ability to unconsciously share another's pain is a building block of empathy, and through that emotion, morality." See David Brooks, *The Social Animal: The Hidden Sources of Love, Character, and Achievement* (Random House, 2011), p. 41.

Page 95   Alyssa Bonk, "Flash Mob Violence in Philadelphia and Throughout America: A Multi-faceted Social & Cultural Issue," August 18, 2011, available at http://www.philly2philly.com/politics_community/politics_community_articles/2011/8/18/47608/flash_mob_violence_philadelphia, accessed August 22, 2011.

Page 95   You can watch motionless people at http://www.youtube.com/watch?v=jwMj3PJDxuo, accessed August 24, 2011, and the tribute to Michael Jackson at http://www.youtube.com/watch?v=lVJVRywgmYM, accessed August 24, 2011.

Page 96   You can watch unruly behavior at http://matei.org/ithink/2011/08/17/smart-mobs-turn-violent-as-flash-mobs-rob-store-after-store-in-the-united-states/, accessed August 24, 2011.

Page 96   The story about the man without arms can be found in the *Cleveland Plain Dealer,* cited in "Dumb Human Behavior to Avoid," *Reader's Digest* online, June–July 2011, available at http://www.rd.com/family/dumb-human-behavior-to-avoid/, accessed September 14, 2011.

Page 97   You can watch the YouTube video of the elaborate prank against the Belgian telecom provider at http://operationsroom.wordpress.com/2011/01/28/customer-service-revenge/.

Page 98   Umair Haque, in a blog post for the *Harvard Business Review*, tells how "just regular folks" in Holland had the orneriness and motivation to self-organize and forced their Parliament to tax bailed-out bankers' bonuses 100 percent—and "not just going forward—but retroactively, since the beginning of the crisis." ("When Customer Rebellion Becomes Open Rebellion," HBR Blog Network, April 1, 2011, at http://blogs.hbr.org/haque/2011/04/when_customer_rebellion_become.html, accessed October 19, 2011.)

Page 98   The punishing primates story came from Dan Ariely, *The Upside of Irrationality: The Unexpected Benefits of Defying Logic at Work and at Home* (HarperCollins, 2011), pp. 126–27.

Page 98   "The monkey mind" is described in Clay Shirky, *Here Comes Everybody* (Penguin Press, 2008), p. 15. "Monkey mind" is also a term sometimes used in the Far East to describe the tendency of Westerners to allow their brains to jump frantically from one subject to another.

Page 98   The idea that jealousy and envy help society is found in Mark D. Hauser, *Moral Minds: How Nature Designed Our Universal Sense of Right and Wrong* (New York: Ecco, 2006), cited in Barbara Oakley, *Evil Genes* (Prometheus, 2008), p. 269.

Page 99   The idea of pro-social behaviors is found in Surowiecki, *The Wisdom of Crowds* (Anchor, 2005), citing Samuel Bowles and Herbert Gintis, "Prosocial Emotions," Santa Fe Institute working paper, 2003, p. 116.

Page 100   One cross-cultural study from the American Economic Association found that ". . . the higher the degree of market integration and the higher the payoffs to cooperation, the greater the level of cooperation in experimental games." (Joseph Henrich, Robert Boyd, Samuel Bowles, Colin Camerer, Ernst Fehr, Herbert Gintis, and Richard McElreath, "In Search of Homo Economicus: Behavioral Experiments in 15 Small-Scale Societies," *The American Economic Review* 91, no. 2 (May 2001), Papers and Proceedings, p. 74, and at http://tuvalu.santafe.edu/~bowles/InSearchHomoEconomicus2001.pdf). Herbert Gintis also wrote "Strong Reciprocity and Sociality," *Journal of Theoretical Biology* 206 (2000): 169–79, and at http://www.umass.edu/preferen/gintis/strongr.pdf. We also discuss "strong reciprocity" in *Rules to Break and Laws to Follow* (John Wiley & Sons, 2008), p. 126.

Page 100   The "un-Google" quote came from Linda Kaplan Thaler, CEO and chief creative officer of Kaplan Thaler Group (who brought us the Aflac duck), quoted in "What's Next?," *Fortune*, February 5, 2007, p. 28: "People are fed up with greed and opportunism. . . . I think the Internet is a very big part of it. You can't un-Google yourself. Gone are the days when snappy campaigns could mask bad behavior." Kaplan Thaler also coauthored *The Power of Nice: How to Conquer the Business World with Kindness* with Robin Koval (Crown Business, 2006).

Page 101   One of the best things about having a robust Web site is hearing from the bloggers and readers who exchange ideas right in front of us. This quote is one of our favorite gems, sent in by Grant Robertson, blog post, May 1, 2007, available at http://www.downloadsquad.com/2007/05/01/hd-dvd-key-fiasco-is-an-example-of-21st-century-digital-revolt/, accessed August 31, 2010.

Page 101   Dave Carroll and Sons of Maxwell, "United Breaks Guitars," July 6, 2009, available on YouTube at http://www.youtube.com/watch?v=5YGc4zOqozo, accessed September 27, 2011.

Page 101   "A Comcast Technician Sleeping on My Couch," available on YouTube at http://www.youtube.com/watch?v=CvVp7b5gzqU, accessed September 9, 2011.

Page 101   We followed *Bruno*'s brutal demise on http://www.boxofficemojo.com/movies/?page=daily&id=bruno.htm, accessed September 28, 2010.

Page 101   We listen to NPR all the time. (And yes, we contribute during the pledge drives. It's the social thing to do.) We heard the facts about box office windows on NPR, and you can hear the story at http://www.npr.org/templates/transcript/transcript.php?storyId-106742097. We accessed it on September 28, 2010, and if you listen, too, please contribute to your local NPR station!

Page 101   The reason Wikipedia works so surprisingly well is that social networks emerge around each topic. In *Connected: The Surprising Power of Our Social Networks and How They Shape Our Lives* (Back Bay Books, 2011, p. 280), Nicholas A. Christakis and James H. Fowler point out that "we do not cooperate with one another because a state or a central authority forces us to. Instead, our ability to get along emerges spontaneously from the decentralized actions of people who form groups with connected fates and a common purpose."

Page 103   According to Viktor Mayer-Schonberger, the "reputation on eBay is not as accurate a reflection of transactional satisfaction as the economic argument of signaling suggests. Researchers have discovered that sellers on eBay strategically time their rating of the buyer. Many of them rate buyers highly even before the transaction has concluded (when they would have the relevant information to rate buyers)—not because they are satisfied with a transaction, but because they hope to elicit an equally good rating in return. It is but one of the many ways in which eBay's customers have been trying to influence eBay's digital memory of transactional reputation. By the spring of 2008, the widespread behavior of gaming reputation memory led eBay to a dramatic reversal of its information policy. It announced that sellers would no longer be able to rate buyers except positively." From *Delete: The Virtue of Forgetting in a Digital Age* (Princeton University Press, 2011), p. 95.

Page 103   In many ways, we like what we've seen in Verizon's approach to building customer value. There are a lot of executives at Verizon working hard to exhibit goodwill and competence. So this story about making money on customer mistakes disappointed us. See David Pogue, "Is Verizon Wireless Making It Harder to Avoid Charges?," *New York Times,* June 17, 2010, available at: http://www.nytimes.com/2010/06/17/technology/personaltech/17pogue-email.html?_r=1, accessed July 7, 2011. Here's more on the story: David Pogue wrote an earlier blog about how you could call Verizon to block all data charges, and you could go online and change your own settings (very possible to do, although not intuitive—one forum shows you how at http://www.dslreports.com/forum/r23507198-How-to-block-Verizon-Wirelesss-data-services). But although any user was able to block data services online, Verizon still charged you $1.99 each time you accidentally accessed the Internet, because even to get the message "you don't have this service" it still took 0.06 MB of data, and they still charged a minimum of $1.99 for 1 MB. So even blocking it officially

For more of Dr. Moorman's surveys, see The CMO Survey, available at: http://cmosurvey
.org/, which reports findings from a biannual survey of CMOs from leading U.S. corporations on topics such as marketplace dynamics, firm growth strategies, marketing spending,
and marketing organization.

Page 132   See Lee Simonson on hindsight bias, quoted in Robert R. Prechter, Jr., *The Wave
Principle of Human Social Behavior* (New Classics Library, 1999), p. 100.

Page 132   Bill Miller, the fund manager, was touted in leading money magazines, as reported in http://en.wikipedia.org/wiki/Bill_Miller_%28finance%29, accessed October 19,
2010.

Page 132   See Jonah Lehrer's "The Truth Wears Off," *New Yorker* 86, no. 40, p. 52. But
not everybody agrees about this statistical discussion. You may want to see Mauboussin's
critique of the 1-in-250,000 issue, cited in Duncan J. Watts, *Everything Is Obvious: Once
You Know the Answer* (Crown Business, 2011).

Page 133   The six selling techniques are reciprocation, social proof, authority, scarcity, liking, and commitment and consistency. See Robert Cialdini, *Influence: The Psychology of Persuasion* (HarperCollins, 1984).

Page 134   You can find the story about the Celtics tickets in Jonah Lehrer, *How We Decide* (Mariner Books, 2010), p. 86.

Page 134   Thanks to Stewart Barret, of Hollard Insurance in Johannesburg, for the idea
about how banks could help you stick to a budget.

Page 135   Discover's Motiva Card offers a "Pay-On-Time Bonus," with the following
terms: "Pay-On-Time Bonus® is a type of Cashback Bonus® that you earn for making your
payments on time. Each time you pay at least the Minimum Payment Due by the Payment
Due Date, you'll earn 5% of your interest charges as a Cashback Bonus. If your payment is
late, you pay less than the Minimum Payment Due (or make no payment at all), or your
payment is returned unpaid, you will not earn a Pay-On-Time Bonus. The amount of your
Pay-On-Time Bonus will be included on your statement in the Cashback Bonus Summary
section, along with any Cashback Bonus you may have earned on purchases." Found at
https://www.discover.com/credit-cards/get-discover/motiva-card/faqs.html#q12, accessed
October 29, 2011.

Page 135   See Becky Carroll, *The Hidden Power of Your Customers: Four Keys to Growing
Your Business Through Existing Customers* (Wiley, 2011).

Page 136   Prechter, *The Wave Principle of Human Social Behavior and the New Science of
Socionomics*, p. 385, citing T. Harman, "Economists look for moderate growth in second
half . . . ," *Wall Street Journal*, July 6, 1993, p. A2.

Page 136   Unintended consequences abound in companies with overlapping business systems (i.e., most of them). For example, perfectly accurate financial reports can have the unintended consequence of encouraging managers to make poor strategic decisions, simply

because managers don't fully understand what assumptions or data lie behind the numbers on the page. Jonathan Hornby of SAS Institute discusses these common "cascading consequences" throughout his book *Radical Action for Radical Times: Expert Advice for Creating Business Opportunity in Good or Bad Economic Times* (SAS Institute, Inc., 2009).

Page 137   When we read Prechter, *The Wave Principle of Human Social Behavior*, p. 153, we got to thinking about stock markets fluctuating no matter what. In 1987, for instance, some social scientists from the University of Arizona and Indiana University conducted sixty lab simulations using as few as a dozen volunteers in each, typically economics students but sometimes also professional businesspeople. The researchers gave all participants the same perfect knowledge of coming dividend prospects and then an actual declared dividend at the end of the simulated trading day, which could vary more or less randomly but which would average a certain amount. *But the subjects in these experiments repeatedly created a boom-and-bust market profile.* The extremity of that profile was a function of the participants' lack of experience in the speculative arena. More experienced subjects did produce bubbles, but they were less pronounced. These experiments suggest that in the real world, bubbles and crashes might be less pronounced if the same traders were in the market all the time, but in reality novices are always entering the stock market.

Page 137   Also see James Gleick, *Chaos: Making a New Science* (Penguin, 1988, 2008), for an excellent tutorial on fractals. Benoît Mandelbrot first showed that self-similar mathematical functions involving recursive growth or development, called "fractals," characterize not just cloud formation and the jaggedness of a mountain range or coastline, but the structure of trees and the patterns in cotton prices as well. Also, Robert R. Prechter, in *The Wave Principle of Human Social Behavior,* analyzes the implications of the "Elliott Wave," named after the early twentieth-century accountant Ralph Nelson Elliott. Prechter and others maintain this distinctive wave pattern underlies all movements of free-market securities markets, and it is a pattern still used by stock market technical analysts to attempt to forecast stock price peaks, valleys, and plateaus. It can be shown that this and other, similar recursive oscillation patterns exhibit behaviors that are all related to the mathematical constant *phi* (roughly 1.62), a number known to the Greeks as the "Golden Ratio," and an important factor in the Fibonacci series, a mathematical time series that is found frequently in nature, particularly in organic structures such as flower petal counts and seed pods. So patterns do exist, even in chaotic systems. But patterns do not necessarily lead to predictability.

Page 138   We quoted Professor Donella H. Meadows from her book *Thinking in Systems: A Primer* (Chelsea Green Publishing, 2008), p. 166.

Page 138   The remarkable story about Adam Fuhrer was pulled from Don Peppers and Martha Rogers, Ph.D., *Rules to Break and Laws to Follow* (Wiley, 2008), pp. 136–37.

Page 139   Fascinating stuff, this idea of uncomputability. In *The Future of Everything: The Science of Prediction* (Basic Books, 2008), Dr. David Orrell points out that "we cannot accurately predict systems such as the climate for two reasons: (1) We don't have the equations. In an uncomputable system, they don't exist; and (2) The ones we have are sensitive to errors in parameterization. Small changes to existing models often result in a wide spread of different predictions. We cannot accurately state the uncertainty in predictions . . . [f]or the same two reasons" (p. 311).

Page 140   You can read more about Motrin's ad for new moms that missed the mark in "Offended moms get tweet revenge over Motrin ads," *USA Today*, November 19, 2008, cited at http://www.usatoday.com/tech/products/2008-11-18-motrin-ads-twitter_N.htm, accessed on September 10, 2010.

Page 140   Darren Barefoot and Julie Szabo tell their story about the Motrin debacle in *Friends with Benefits* (No Starch Press, 2009), pp. 142–44. The quote is from page 143.

Page 140   Barefoot and Szabo share the tip on sharing-friendly online apologies in *Friends with Benefits*, pp. 143–44.

Page 142   Alana Semuels reported on Staples' Speak Easy program in "Friendly advice or secret ad? Customers get freebies to join word-of-mouth marketing campaigns," *Los Angeles Times,* August 17, 2007. Also see Don Peppers and Martha Rogers, Ph.D., *Rules to Break and Laws to Follow* (Wiley, 2008), pp. 146–47.

Page 144   Randall Rothenberg was quoted in David Kirkpatrick's *The Facebook Effect: The Inside Story of the Company That Is Connecting the World* (Simon & Schuster, 2011), p. 264.

Page 145   Kirkpatrick, *The Facebook Effect*, p. 16. "Facebook already operates in seventy-five languages, and about 75 percent of its active users are outside the United States. About 143 million Americans are active on Facebook, or 46.8 percent of the entire population, according to the *Facebook Global Monitor*, published by InsideFacebook.com."

Page 145   Also in Kirkpatrick, *The Facebook Effect*, p. 275: "In thirty countries around the world, more than 30 percent of all citizens—not Internet users but *citizens*—are on Facebook, according to the *Facebook Global Monitor*. They include Canada (50.5 percent), Norway (50.1 percent), Hong Kong (49.2 percent), the United Kingdom (45.7 percent), Chile (43.9 percent), Israel (41.6 percent), and the Bahamas (40.7 percent). In tiny Iceland, 58.2 percent of people are on the service. Facebook is the number-one social network in Brunei, Cambodia, Malaysia, and Singapore, among other countries. It surpassed MySpace in global visitors in May 2008, according to comScore."

Page 145   Kirkpatrick, *The Facebook Effect*, p. 275. "And in mid-2008 the word Facebook passed sex in frequency as a search term on Google worldwide." Also see pp. 180–200. The News Feed crisis was the most serious Facebook has ever faced. Only one in one hundred messages to Facebook about News Feed was positive. You can read more about the rise and fall of Facebook's Beacon on pp. 246–51. And see p. 359. "Zuckerberg quickly surrendered, less than three days after the original article appeared. At 1 a.m. on Wednesday, he announced on the blog that Facebook was temporarily reverting to the old terms of service while it decided what to do next. He had said even in his earlier note that he agreed that much of the language in the terms seemed overly formal and needed to be simplified. In this late-night note, he invited Facebook's users to join a newly formed company group to discuss what the terms ought to say, and promised 'users will have a lot of input in crafting these terms.'"

Page 150   Greenpeace's "Take Action" campaign in September 2011, for instance, was against Chicken of the Sea for "barbaric fishing methods," complete with adulterated logo. Available at www.greenpeace.org, accessed September 29, 2011.

Page 153   Frank Eliason's Comcast Cares program is covered in Rebecca Reisner, "Comcast's Twitter Man," *Businessweek*, January 13, 2009, http://www.businessweek.com/managing/content/jan2009/ca20090113_373506.htm, accessed October 29, 2011.

Page 153   Frank Eliason told us about the difficulty of finding out who was really in charge of a customer problem area in his telephone interview with Don, February 22, 2010.

Page 153   You'll find good advice about social media crisis protocols in Jay Baer, "4 Brand-Saving Recommendations for Social Media Crisis Management," July 16, 2009, at http://www.convinceandconvert.com/social-media-marketing/4-brand-saving-recommendations-for-social-media-crisis-management/, accessed on July 16, 2011.

Page 154   Henry Ford's quote came from "The Most Neglected Fact in Business," Peak: Transforming the Way Business Is Done, March 28, 2011, at http://www.peakorganizations.com/category/blog/role-of-a-leader/, accessed on July 7, 2011. (Originally posted at *The Huffington Post*, March 28, 2011.)

Page 155   Charlene Li's "culture of sharing" is from *Open Leadership* (Jossey-Bass, 2010), p. 31.

Page 155   For a full discussion about Learning Relationships, see B. Joseph Pine II, Don Peppers, and Martha Rogers, Ph.D., "Do You Want to Keep Your Customers Forever?," *Harvard Business Review* 73 (March 1995): 103–14, available to online subscribers at http://hbr.org/1995/03/do-you-want-to-keep-your-customers-forever, accessed October 6, 2011.

Page 155   The story of how Best Buy shared its customer data with all its partners is in Li, *Open Leadership*, pp. 31–32.

Page 156   Tara Hunt cites the APA's inclusion of autonomy as one of the four principal elements of psychological well-being in *The Power of Social Networking: Using the Whuffie Factor to Build Your Business* (Crown, 2009), p. 195.

Page 156   Leonard Mlodinow, *The Drunkard's Walk: How Randomness Rules Our Lives* (Vintage, 2009), p. 186. "Ellen Langer [is] now a professor at Harvard. Years ago, when she was at Yale, Langer and a collaborator studied the effect of the feeling of control on elderly nursing home patients. One group was told they could decide how their rooms would be arranged and were allowed to choose a plant to care for. Another group had their rooms set up for them and a plant chosen and tended to for them. Within weeks the group that exercised control over their environment achieved higher scores on a predesigned measure of well-being. Disturbingly, eighteen months later a follow-up study shocked researchers: the group that was not given control experienced a death rate of 30 percent, whereas the group that was given control experienced a death rate of only 15 percent."

Page 156   Daniel H. Pink, *Drive: The Surprising Truth About What Motivates Us* (River-head, 2009), Kindle edition, Loc. 1163–69. "While the idea of independence has national and political reverberations, autonomy appears to be a human concept rather than a Western one. Researchers have found a link between autonomy and overall well-being not only in North America and Western Europe, but also in Russia, Turkey, and South Korea. Even in high-poverty non-Western locales like Bangladesh, social scientists have found that autonomy is something that people seek and that improves their lives. A sense of autonomy has a powerful effect on individual performance and attitude. According to a cluster of recent behavioral science studies, autonomous motivation promotes greater conceptual understanding, better grades, enhanced persistence at school and in sporting activities, higher productivity, less burnout, and greater levels of psychological well-being."

Page 156   Paul P. Baard, Edward L. Deci, and Richard M. Ryan, "Intrinsic Need Satisfaction: A Motivational Basis of Performance and Well-Being in Two Work Settings," *Journal of Applied Social Psychology* 34 (2004), cited in Pink, *Drive*, Kindle edition, Loc. 1174–76.

Page 157   Henry Sauerman and Wesley Cohen, "What Makes Them Tick? Employee Motives and Firm Innovation," NBER Working Paper No. 14443, October 2008. Cited in Pink, *Drive*, Kindle edition, Loc. 1559.

Page 157   Andy Hunt and Dave Thomas are authors of *The Pragmatic Programmer: From Journeyman to Master* (Addison-Wesley, 1999).

Page 157   See the discussion with Hunt and Thomas about autonomy and a sense of ownership at http://www.artima.com/intv/fixit.html, accessed July 7, 2011.

Page 157   If you haven't seen it yet, take a look at Bill George, with Peter Sims, *True North: Discover Your Authentic Leadership* (Jossey-Bass, 2007).

Page 157   See chapter 13 in Don Peppers and Martha Rogers, Ph.D., *Rules to Break and Laws to Follow* (Wiley, 2008), for more about the competitive advantage of organizations with a flatter, more collaborative structure.

Page 157   Don Tapscott and Anthony Williams's quote about the changing nature of work can be found in *Wikinomics: How Mass Collaboration Changes Everything* (Portfolio, 2006), p. 246.

Page 157   Pink, *Drive,* Kindle edition, Loc. 1313–14. "If the billable hour has an antithesis, it's the results-only work environment of the kind that Jeff Gunther has introduced at his companies. The first large company to go ROWE was Best Buy—not in its stores, but in its corporate offices."

Page 158   Seth Godin, *Linchpin: Are You Indispensable?* (Portfolio, 2010), Kindle edition, Loc. 3669–72. "In a story so good that it should be apocryphal, Zappos offers graduates of their two-week paid training school $2,000 if they will quit their new jobs. Why would Zappos offer to pay great people to quit? Tony Hsieh, CEO, does this because he wants to be sure that every person at the company is there for the right reasons, not because she's getting paid. If you're willing to leave for a few thousand bucks, good riddance."

Page 159   The quote about how an open mind-set is the best predictor of success is from Charlene Li, *Open Leadership* (Jossey-Bass, 2010), p. 7.

Page 159   We quoted Tara Hunt, who's the brain behind *The Power of Social Networking: Using the Whuffie Factor to Build Your Business* (Crown Business, 2010), p. 205.

Page 160   Raj Sisodia, Jag Sheth, and David B. Wolfe, *Firms of Endearment: How World-Class Companies Profit from Passion and Purpose* (Pearson Prentice Hall, 2007), p. 42. "The consciousness that has ruled business enterprise over the past two centuries is rooted in classical notions that reason is superior to emotions in the affairs of people. This has reduced stakeholders (including shareholders) to largely bloodless statistical entities . . . Right brain emotionality deserves no less than equal attention with left brain rationality in business analysis, planning, and operations. Recent research resoundingly confirms the primacy of the emotional over the purely rational . . . [I]n an overwhelming majority of cases, top performers are not those executives with the highest level of intellectual intelligence but those with the highest level of emotional intelligence."

Page 160   For the strategy based on using analytic techniques that don't require high accuracy, we read *Dance with Chance* (Oneworld, 2009), by Spyros Makridakis, Anil Gaba, and Robin Hogarth, p. 256.

Page 161   See the book *Little Bets* (Free Press, 2011), by Peter Sims, for an excellent overview of the strategy of placing many small bets on a variety of options.

Page 162   We were brainstorming about trustability with Joe Bellini, executive vice president and chief sales officer at TeleTech, who coined the term "trustproof" to designate the kind of company that has built up so much trust equity that it can survive a publicized mistake.

Page 162   Frank Eliason's quote about deciding to use his own picture on Comcast's Twitter account is from Rebecca Reisner, "Comcast's Twitter Man," *Businessweek*, January 13, 2009, http://www.businessweek.com/managing/content/jan2009/ca20090113_373506.htm, accessed October 29, 2011.

Page 163   According to Rebecca Reisner's *Businessweek* article: "Thanks to the friendly Twitter network Frank has built up, customers occasionally help one another, as he discovered a few weeks earlier when he mentioned in a Tweet that he had an important family event during the day and would be unavailable. Once the event ended that evening, he logged onto Twitter at home to see which customers in the Twitt-o-sphere needed help that day.
   "I found that people who didn't work for Comcast were responding, saying: 'Let Frank have his day. Can I help?'" he recalls. "They were saying: 'Here, try this.' And it was the most amazing thing. That day I understood the effectiveness of what we do."

Page 163   Thanks to Matthew Rhoden for his insights in his blog in *Harvard Business Review*, http://blogs.hbr.org/cs/2011/create_brand_superfans.html, accessed September 29, 2011.

7: BUILD YOUR TRUSTABILITY IN ADVANCE

Page 168   Don Peppers and Martha Rogers, Ph.D., *The One to One Future: Building Relationships One Customer at a Time* (Currency/Doubleday, 1993), pp. 212–16.

Page 169   The quote about ratings and negative references is paraphrased in Mitch Joel, *Six Pixels of Separation: Everyone Is Connected. Connect Your Business to Everyone* (Business Plus, 2010), p. 82.

Page 170   For more about how customers are leaving comments wherever they want, see Martin Bryant, "iGlue Makes Any Web Page More Informative with Rich Annotations," The Next Web, at http://thenextweb.com/apps/2011/06/23/iglue-makes-any-web-page-more-informative-with-rich-annotations/, accessed July 8, 2011.

Page 171   This classic "no one knows you're a dog" cartoon first appeared in *The New Yorker* (July 5, 1993, p. 61) and can be accessed here: http://www.unc.edu/depts/jomc/academics/dri/idog.html.

Page 171   One source for Whole Foods CEO John Mackey's anonymous comments promoting his own company is Andrew Martin, "Whole Foods Executive Used Alias," *New York Times*, July 12, 2007. Cited at http://www.nytimes.com/2007/07/12/business/12foods.html, accessed August 12, 2010.

Page 172   Our source for how some companies are hiring fake reviewers is David Segal, The Haggler: "A Rave, a Pan, or Just a Fake?," *New York Times*, May 22, 2011, Business, p. 7.

Page 172   The detail about five-star reviewers peddling their wares via many e-commerce sites is from David Streitfeld, "In a Race to Out-Rave, 5-Star Web Reviews Go for $5," *New York Times*, August 19, 2011, http://www.nytimes.com/2011/08/20/technology/finding-fake-reviews-online.html, accessed August 26, 2011.

Page 172   The Cornell study is "Finding Deceptive Opinion Spam by Any Stretch of the Imagination," by Myle Ott, Yejin Choi, Claire Cardie, and Jeffrey T. Hancock, published in *Proceedings of the 49th Annual Meeting of the Association for Computational Linguistics*, pp. 309–19, Portland, Oregon, June 19–24, 2011. The paper itself can be found at http://aclweb.org/anthology/P/P11/P11-1032.pdf, accessed November 2, 2011, and is referenced in Streitfeld, "In a Race to Out-Rave, 5-Star Web Reviews Go for $5." See also Ben Kunz's insightful Google+ post "You're Lying," August 20, 2011, https://plus.google.com/113349993076188494279/posts/Pcew2kqRLUe, accessed September 24, 2011.

Page 173   Chris Kelly is quoted in David Kirkpatrick, *The Facebook Effect: The Inside Story of the Company That Is Connecting the World* (Simon & Schuster, 2011), p. 13.

Page 173   On identity theft through social networking, see, for instance, Tom Rawstorne, "My identity was stolen on Facebook," Mail Online, July 27, 2007, http://www.dailymail.co.uk/femail/article-471321/My-identity-stolen-Facebook.html, accessed September 22, 2011.

Page 173   Another source for identity theft through social networking is Ron Shulkin, "How I'm going to use social networking to steal your identity!," examiner.com, June 29, 2009, http://www.examiner.com/social-networking-in-chicago/how-i-m-going-to-use-social-networking-to-steal-your-identity, accessed September 22, 2011.

Page 173   Anonymous reviews are still the norm, but signed reviews have more credibility, and some companies are moving to encourage reviewers to identify themselves, even though the identity doesn't show up on the review or the site. It is, however, verifiable. See http://www.powerreviews.com/.

Page 173   We accessed the story about Kevin Pezzi at http://mediamatters.org/blog/201008050034 on September 12, 2010.

Page 174   We accessed the story about Ellie Light on http://bigjournalism.com/fross/2010/01/23/ellie-light-indefatigable-letter-writer-or-axelrodplouffe-sock-puppet/, on September 12, 2010.

Page 174   This quote from the anonymous ad executive came from Kirkpatrick, *The Facebook Effect*, p. 142.

Page 176   Chris Brogan and Julien Smith wrote about how Microsoft's Robert Scoble developed trustability by being willing to criticize his company in *Trust Agents* (John Wiley & Sons, 2010), p. 29.

Page 177   Drew Neisser, "Twelpforce: Marketing That Isn't Marketing," *Fast Company*, May 17, 2010, http://www.fastcompany.com/1648739/marketing-that-isn-t-marketing, accessed August 26, 2011.

Page 177   Jason Sadler told this great story about Best Buy when Sadler appeared at the Promotional Products Association International conference in Denver, August 9, 2011.

Page 179   We read about brick-and-mortar stores charging admission fees for significant product launches in Brian Briggs, "Apple Store to Begin Charging Entrance Fee," BBspot .com, July 23, 2007, http://www.bbspot.com/News/2007/07/apple-store-to-being-charging -entrance-fee.html, accessed September 22, 2011, and Julie Bosman and Matt Richtel, "Come Meet the Author, but Open Your Wallet," *New York Times*, June 21, 2011, http://www.nytimes.com/2011/06/22/business/media/22events.html?pagewanted=all, accessed September 22, 2011.

Page 181   Karen Kelley, Corcoran Group, is our number-one recommendation for help with real estate in the New York City area. We mean it.

Page 182   Dan Ariely, *The Upside of Irrationality: The Unexpected Benefits of Defying Logic at Work and at Home* (Harper, 2010), Kindle edition, Loc. 2103–15. "Again, we sent Daniel to ask coffee shop customers if they would complete our letter-pairing task in exchange for $5. This time, however, we had three conditions. In the control (no-annoyance) condition, Daniel first asked the coffee shop patrons if they would be willing to participate in a five-minute task in return for $5. When they agreed (and almost all agreed), he gave them the same letter sheets and explained the instructions. Five minutes later, he returned to the table, collected the sheets, handed the participants four extra dollars (four $1 bills and one

$5 bill), and asked them to fill out a receipt for $5. For those in the annoyance condition, the procedure was basically the same, except that while going over the instructions, Daniel again pretended to take a call. The third group was basically in the same condition as those in the annoyance group, but we threw in a little twist. This time, as Daniel was handing the participants their payment and asking them to sign the receipt, he added an apology. 'I'm sorry,' he said, 'I shouldn't have answered that call.' Based on the original experiment, we expected the annoyed people to be much less likely to return the extra cash, and indeed that is what the results showed. But what about the third group? Surprise!—the apology was a perfect remedy. The amount of extra cash returned in the apology condition was the same as it was when people were not annoyed at all. Indeed, we found that the word 'sorry' completely counteracted the effect of annoyance. (For handy future reference, here's the magic formula: 1 annoyance + 1 apology = 0 annoyance.)"

Page 184   For more on how binding contracts can undermine trust, see Maurice E. Schweitzer, John C. Hershey, and Eric T. Bradlow, "Promises and Lies: Restoring Violated Trust," *Organizational Behavior and Human Decision Processes* 1, Issue 101 (September 2006): 4, downloaded at http://knowledge.wharton.upenn.edu/papers/1321.pdf.

Page 184   The list on how to restore lost trust came from Don Peppers and Martha Rogers, Ph.D., *Rules to Break and Laws to Follow: How Your Business Can Beat the Crisis of Short-Termism* (Wiley, 2008), pp. 156–57.

Page 185   The Toro story details came from Rajendra S. Sisodia, David B. Wolfe, and Jagdish N. Sheth, *Firms of Endearment: How World-Class Companies Profit from Passion and Purpose* (Pearson Prentice Hall, 2007), pp. 111–12. "Toro, the giant lawn mower and snowblower maker, discovered that by delivering better on the emotional contract, it could decrease personal injury litigation. Toro's leadership once believed personal injury litigation was inevitable given the nature of its products. However, in the mid-1990s, it abandoned that belief. Company representatives began making personal contact with injured customers. They apologetically extended the company's sympathy and suggested that if an immediate settlement could not be arranged, arbitration might be better and less of a hassle than going to court. Since adopting this emotionally sensitive approach in 1994, Toro has not been in court for a single personal injury case. This is a truly amazing record for a company that builds dangerous equipment that falls into countless careless hands every weekend of the year. Toro says that by mid-2005, it will have saved an estimated $100 million in litigation costs since it kicked off its nonaggressive approach to avoiding litigation in 1991."

Page 186   In his very insightful and intricately argued book *The Beginning of Infinity: Explanations That Transform the World* (Viking, 2011), quantum physicist David Deutsch persuasively argues that the essence of all human civilization and progress is our constant need for better and better "explanations," even though every explanation we devise (for the physical world, for our social relationships, or for life in general) is inevitably mistaken. Because it is mistaken it can be made better with more knowledge. There is an infinite amount of knowledge and explanation to be had, however, and so we are always at the "beginning" of this infinity of understanding, no matter how advanced we become. In a very real sense, he says, we can only advance tomorrow by overturning the mistaken explanations that were good enough for yesterday. Overcoming mistakes by devising better and better explanations is how creativity is applied.

Page 187   You can find the *Ad Age* commentary on the Kenneth Cole gaffe on Twitter at Rupal Parekh, "The Seven Stages of Committing a Social-Media Sin: Kenneth Cole's Cringe-Worthy Tweet on Egypt Offers a Case Study," *Ad Age*, February 7, 2011, available at http://adage.com/digital/article?article_id=148706, accessed February 14, 2011.

Page 188   The U.S. poll that found a third of employers rejected job candidates based on information uncovered on social networks was cited in Kirkpatrick, *The Facebook Effect*, pp. 204–5.

Page 188   The belief that Facebook makes it harder to cheat on your significant other is substantiated in Kirkpatrick, *The Facebook Effect*, p. 210.

Page 189   The quote "shame is generational" comes from Adam L. Penenberg, *Viral Loop: From Facebook to Twitter, How Today's Smartest Businesses Grow Themselves* (Hyperion, 2009), p. 229.

Page 189   The discussion about how kids deal with the amount of information about themselves available online was attributed to Emily Nussbaum, "Say Anything: Kids, the Internet, and the End of Privacy: The Greatest Generation Gap Since Rock and Roll," *New York*, February 12, 2007, cited in Tara Hunt, *The Whuffie Factor: Using the Power of Social Networks to Build Your Business* (Crown Business, 2009), p. 46.

Page 189   Clive Thompson writes about the cultural shift of authenticity coming from online exposure in his article "The See-Through CEO," *Wired*, March 2007, http://www.wired.com/wired/archive/15.04/wired40_ceo.html, accessed September 29, 2011.

Page 190   Victor Stone is quoted in Lawrence Lessig, *Remix: Making Art and Commerce Thrive in the Hybrid Economy* (Penguin Press, 2008), p. 97.

Page 190   Gibson is quoted in "Books of the year 2003," *The Economist*, December 4, 2003, available at http://www.economist.com/books/displaystory.cfm?story_id=E1 _NNGVRJV, cited at "William Gibson," Wikipedia, available at http://en.wikipedia.org/wiki/William_Gibson, accessed September 29, 2011.

Page 190   Clive Thompson's quote about how "the Internet has inverted the social physics of information" is from his article "The See-Through CEO," *Wired*, March 2007, http://www.wired.com/wired/archive/15.04/wired40_ceo.html, accessed September 29, 2011.

Page 191   We love the way Harvey Mackay thinks. See his book *Dig Your Well Before You're Thirsty* (Currency, 1999).

Page 191   John Costello's quote likening trustability to a savings account came from a phone interview with the authors, November 1, 2010. John Costello is chief global marketing and innovation officer of Dunkin' Brands.

8: HONEST COMPETENCE

Page 195   The quote that opens this chapter came from "An Essay on Criticism," a poem by Alexander Pope (1688–1744).

Page 195   See Christopher Meyer and Andre Schwager, "Understanding Customer Experience," *Harvard Business Review*, February 2007, pp. 117–26.

Page 196   Some companies that have every intention of treating customers fairly still create hassles and waste a customer's time. First they make a mistake. Then they make you wait on hold when you call, or wait days after you contact them. When they finally answer you, they make it *your* responsibility to set things up so they can fix the problem they caused. (This is usually where we say, "You want me to bring it in? That will take me about an hour. Since I'm not on your payroll, who will pay my hourly fee to do that work?" Why do companies think customers' time is worth nothing?)

Page 196   Here's a great idea: "Becoming human-centric also creates new knowledge flows for the company that may not have existed in the past. For instance, if everyone at your company began receiving daily reports on the top social media opinions expressed about your company, its brands, and its executives, instead of just monthly market share or sales data, wouldn't this transparency profoundly affect decision making across various groups? Wouldn't it provide customer support with insights into how that function could be improved? Wouldn't such knowledge improve the planning, pricing, and promotion of your next product? Wouldn't it give your salespeople new ideas on new segments (think 'tribes') that they should be targeting?" For more on this, see Francois Gossieaux and Ed Moran, *The Hyper-Social Organization: Eclipse Your Competition by Leveraging Social Media* (McGraw-Hill, 2010), Kindle edition, Loc. 1272–76.

Page 196   Julianne Pepitone and Aaron Smith reported on Netflix customers' mass exodus in their CNN Money article "Netflix Stock Plunges as Subscribers Quit," September 15, 2011, at http://money.cnn.com/2011/09/15/technology/netflix/index.htm, accessed October 6, 2011. But except for what we could find in public records, a lot of this is pure speculation on our part—we have no inside source at Netflix.

Page 200   George Day's list about customer competence is quoted in Don Peppers and Martha Rogers, Ph.D., *Managing Customer Relationships: A Strategic Framework,* 2nd ed. (Wiley, 2011), p. 384.

Page 200   Clayton M. Christensen, Scott Cook, and Taddy Hall, "Marketing Malpractice: The Cause and the Cure," *Harvard Business Review* 83 (December 2005): 74–83, is just one of the places you can hear this group talk about a product being hired to do a job.

Page 200   The story about how Cigna improved customer experience with a clearer, customer-friendly communication is from Tom Hoffman, "Speaking to Customers in Their Language," *1to1 Magazine,* October 19, 2011, available at http://www.1to1media.com/view .aspx?docid=33187, accessed November 27, 2011.

Page 201   Dietrich Chen first wrote about how health insurance companies are going to need to change in his *Customer Strategist* blog post, "Segmentation in Healthcare—A

Prescription for Survival," August 10, 2011, available at http://www.peppersandrogersgroup
.com/blog/2011/08/customer-strategist-dietrich-c-1.html#more, accessed December 28,
2011.

Page 201   Discovery is considered one of the global leaders in the area of health and wellness and is held out as an example of a uniquely successful model in this regard. An article
in *The Economist* (October 8, 2011) profiled Discovery as "[a] South African company that
has some bright ideas for promoting health." The article reported that the Vitality model is
recognized as a pioneer in the fight against chronic diseases of lifestyle and in rewarding
people for living healthier lives. See Discovery's October 19, 2011, press release at http://
www.discovery.co.za/discovery_za/web/logged_out/about_discovery/media/press_releases
_content/2011/2011_content/discovery_life_gives_clients_more_cover_with_cover
booster.xml, accessed December 28, 2011.

Page 202   Matthew Dixon, Karen Freeman, and Nicholas Toman, "Stop Trying to Delight Your Customers," *Harvard Business Review* 88 (July 2010): 116–22. The subtitle added
by the magazine's editorial department was "Stop Trying to Delight Your Customers: To
Really Win Their Loyalty, Forget the Bells and Whistles and Just Solve Their Problems."
The authors note that "Loyalty has a lot more to do with how well companies deliver on
their basic, even plain-vanilla, promises than on how dazzling the service experience might
be" (p. 116).

Page 203   For more on customer-centricity, see our books *Rules to Break and Laws to Fol-
low* (Wiley, 2008), *Return on Customer* (Currency/Doubleday, 2005), *Managing Customer
Relationships: A Strategic Framework* (2nd ed., Wiley, 2011), *One to One Manager* (Cur-
rency/Doubleday, 2000), *One to One Fieldbook* (Currency/Doubleday, 1999), *One to One
B2B* (Doubleday Business, 2001), *Enterprise One to One* (Currency/Doubleday, 1997), and
The One to One Future (Doubleday Business, 1993).

Page 203   For a full discussion on Learning Relationships, see B. Joseph Pine II, Don Peppers, and Martha Rogers, Ph.D., "Do You Want to Keep Your Customers Forever?," *Harvard Business Review* 73 (March 1995): 103–14, available to online subscribers at: http://
hbr.org/1995/03/do-you-want-to-keep-your-customers-forever, accessed October 6, 2011.

Page 204   To learn more about our customer-based metric Return on Customer®, see our
book *Return on Customer: Creating Maximum Value from Your Scarcest Resource* (Currency/
Doubleday, 2005).

Page 204   The quote from Mark Grindeland of TeleTech is from a telephone interview
with the authors in August 2011. TeleTech is the parent company for Peppers & Rogers
Group.

Page 205   Susan Whiting's quote about connecting doing good with your brand is from a
telephone interview with the authors on June 23, 2011.

Page 206   Warren Buffett is quoted by Dov Seidman in *How: Why How We Do Anything
Means Everything . . . in Business (and in Life)* (Wiley, 2007), p. 178.

Page 206   We first wrote about the albatross with bad breath in *Rules to Break and Laws
to Follow*, p. 101.

Page 206   You can find Dov Seidman's quote in *How*, p. 251.

Page 208   Roger Martin told us about integrative thinking in "How Successful Leaders Think," *Harvard Business Review* 85, no. 6 (June 2007): 60–67.

Page 208   For more on rethinking how we evaluate and reward senior managers, see Michael Mauboussin, *Think Twice: Harnessing the Power of Counterintuition* (Harvard Business School Press, 2009), p. xx. If a company were to do this, of course, the immediate issue would be the subjectivity of the evaluation. Profit may not be predictable in advance, it may be largely due to chance, and it may not even be influenced much by an executive's own actions, but as an output an accounting number is rock-solid. You can't quarrel with a company's "bottom line" profit any more than you can quarrel with a winning lottery ticket. Evaluating an executive based on "input" instead of output inherently implies that someone somewhere (the manager's immediate boss, the board, the compensation committee) will be making a human judgment, and human judgments are inherently tainted by subjectivity. We are placing the manager's economic livelihood in the hands of another person(s), and we are asking the manager to *trust* that the judgment will be fair.

But what's the alternative to extending this trust? Should we expect just to continue getting paid based on how the lottery numbers turn up? One action both Mauboussin and Dan Pink (*Drive: The Surprising Truth About What Motivates Us* [Riverhead, 2009]) recommend is creating more reliable and immediate feedback mechanisms for executives, so they can at least learn how good (or bad) their decision-making powers have actually been. When we judge ourselves based solely on outcomes our biases become more obstructive in a more randomized environment. For your own personal improvement, Mauboussin suggests, you ought to keep a "decision-making journal," in which you write down today the thoughts behind your current decisions. This way, in coming months or years—once the outcome of any particular decision becomes clear—you can better and more objectively assess your own performance in terms of your actual a priori assessment of the situation (p. 35). *Think Twice* has a lot of good ideas about how the most obvious managerial measurements don't always help us make the right decisions, including "number of errors made at nursing homes," where, ironically, more may be better.

Page 209   W. Brian Arthur writes about how technology is causing management to shift from problem solving to "sense-making" in his book *The Nature of Technology: What It Is and How It Evolves* (Free Press, 2009), pp. 209–10.

Page 210   Lawrence Lessig, *Remix: Making Art and Commerce Thrive in the Hybrid Economy* (Penguin Press, 2008), Kindle edition, Loc. 2119–22. "It follows from this insight that as transaction costs fall, all things being equal, the amount of stuff done inside a firm will fall as well. The firm will outsource more. It will focus its internal work on the stuff it can do best (meaning more efficiently than the market). LEGO-ized innovation is simply the architectural instantiation of this economic point."

Page 211   You can find Dov Seidman's seven reasons why self-governing cultures are advantageous in Seidman, *How*, pp. 259–63.

Page 212   Stephanie Clifford reports on the Domino's Pizza employees' stomach-turning YouTube video in "Video Prank at Domino's Taints Brand," *New York Times*, April 16, 2009, cited at http://www.nytimes.com/2009/04/16/business/media/16dominos.html, accessed August 4, 2011.

Page 213   The college senior struck by the authenticity of Domino's Pizza's self-flagellating marketing campaign was quoted in Chistopher Borrelli's article titled "Domino's Pizza, you stand accused of being boring, bland and flavorless. Of bearing cheese that tastes grainy and processed. Of having sauce like ketchup and crust like cardboard. What say you? 'Guilty as charged,'" *Chicago Tribune,* January 19, 2010, cited at http://articles.chicagotribune.com/2010-01-19/entertainment/1001180400_1_pizza-hut-domino-s-pizza-free-pizza, accessed August 4, 2011.

Page 213   *Adweek*'s story on Domino's "transparent pizza" was Todd Wasserman, "As Domino's Gets Real, Its Sales Get Really Good," *Adweek,* July 11, 2010, http://www.adweek.com/news/advertising-branding/dominos-gets-real-its-sales-get-really-good 107532, accessed August 4, 2011.

Page 214   More facts about how Domino's Pizza's transparent marketing campaign paid off can be found in "The Importance of Being Straightforward with Customers," Ocean Capital, March 21, 2011, available at http://www.ocean-capital.com/the-real deal/the -importance-of-being-straight-forward-with-customers/, accessed August 4, 2011; "Domino's Pizza Announces 2010 Financial Results," at http://www.prnewswire.com/news -releases/dominos-pizza-announces-2010-financial-results-117142383.html, accessed August 4, 2011; "Domino's Pizza Announces First Quarter 2011 Financial Results," at http:// www.hospitalitybusinessnews.com/article/10530/dominos-pizza-announces-first-quarter 2011 financial-results, accessed August 4, 2011; "Domino's Pizza Announces Second Quarter 2011 Financial Results," at http://finance.yahoo.com/news/Dominos-Pizza-Announces-prnews-3655095181.html?x=0&.v=1, accessed August 4, 2011; "Domino's Pizza Runs Unfiltered Customer Comments on Times Square Billboard," available at: http:// mashable.com/2011/07/25/dominos-comments-times-square/, accessed August 5, 2011; Tim Nudd, "Domino's Posts Customer Reviews, Good and Bad, in Times Square," *Adweek,* July 25, 2011, at http://www.adweek.com/adfreak/dominos-posts-customer-reviews -good-and-bad-times-square-133650, accessed August 5, 2011; Todd Wasserman, "As Domino's Gets Real, Its Sales Get Really Good," *Adweek,* July 11, 2010, at http://www .adweek.com/news/advertising-branding/dominos-gets-real-its-sales-get-really-good -107532, accessed August 5, 2011. And the random customer comments we quoted came from http://more.dominos.com/wp/2011/07/times-square/, August 5, 2011.

Page 216   We've all heard this CIA dictum. In his book *How,* Dov Seidman attributes it to Larry Johnson, interviewed on MSNBC by Alex Witt, August 27, 2004 (*How,* p. 146).

Page 217   The Harvard Business School study of nursing home practices and how reporting more errors actually signifies a more trustworthy environment can be found in Jeffrey Pfeffer and Robert I. Sutton, *Hard Facts, Dangerous Half-Truths and Total Nonsense: Profiting from Evidence-Based Management* (Harvard Business Press, 2006), pp. 105–6.

9: TRUSTABLE INFORMATION

Page 221   We love this opening quote from the Marx Brothers. We found it at http://www .marx-brothers.org/info/quotes.htm, accessed August 28, 2011.

Page 222   Julie Pitta, "Google and Facebook by the Numbers," *IEEE Spectrum*, June 2011, p. 38.

Page 222   We heard the Facebook numbers from Mike Saylor, CEO of MicroStrategy, at MicroStrategy World in Monte Carlo, July 12, 2011.

Page 222   The estimate that the world's data is doubling every two years is a conservative one. See "World's Data More Than Doubling Every Two Years—Driving Big Data Opportunity, New IT Roles," EMC Press Release, June 28, 2011, available at: http://www.emc .com/about/news/press/2011/20110628-01.htm, accessed October 5, 2011.

Page 222   See James Gleick, *The Information: A History, a Theory, a Flood* (Pantheon, 2011), Kindle edition, Loc. 1372–75. The lexis is a measure of shared experience, which comes from interconnectedness. The number of users of the language forms only the first part of the equation: jumping in four centuries from 5 million English speakers to a billion. The driving factor is the number of connections between and among those speakers. A mathematician might say that messaging grows not geometrically, but combinatorially, which is much, much faster.

Page 222   A 2007 academic article cited at http://www.educause.edu/ EDUCAUSE+Quarterly/EDUCAUSEQuarterlyMagazineVolum/BecomingNet Savvy/161827 says the volume of technical information will be doubling every seventy-two hours in the year 2010, and cites I. Jukes, "From Gutenberg to Gates to Google (and Beyond): Education for the Online World," version edited July 2006 for NECC San Diego, http://web.mac.com/iajukes/iWeb/thecommittedsardine/Handouts_files/fgtgtg.pdf (no longer accessible), and another 2007 reference to an IBM report says data will be doubling every eleven hours by the year 2010, http://www.zdnet.com/blog/btl/2010-data-doubling -every-11-hours/4497. Even a conservative estimate of data doubling every two years ("World's Data More Than Doubling Every Two Years—Driving Big Data Opportunity, New IT Roles," EMC Press Release, June 28, 2011, available at http://www.emc.com /about/news/press/2011/20110628-01.htm, accessed October 5, 2011) indicates that data is certainly expanding fast. Most sources we found assert that world data is doubling every two years, and lest you be underwhelmed by this rate, here are some examples of how much data that is (1.8 zettabytes in 2011—or 1.8 trillion gigabytes):
  • Every person in the United States tweeting three tweets per minute for 26,976 years nonstop
  • Every person in the world having over 215 million high-resolution MRI scans per day
  • Over 200 billion HD movies (each two hours in length)—it would take one person 47 million years to watch every movie 24/7

Page 223   When we think about "objective" information, we are reminded of scientific findings that are *valid*, and when we think of "competent" data, we are reminded of scientific findings that are *reliable*.

Page 225   This principle is sometimes known as the "strength of weak ties," after the title of a landmark 1973 paper by Mark Granovetter published in *The American Journal of Sociology* 78, Issue 6, pp. 1360–80. Granovetter maintained, based on research, that new information and insight are simply more likely to come from the people in your social network with whom you don't interact very frequently—that is, your "weak ties."

Page 225   Yochai Benkler, *The Wealth of Networks: How Social Production Transforms Markets and Freedom* (Yale University Press, 2006), p. 357. "We are seeing two effects: first, and most robustly, we see a thickening of preexisting relations with friends, family, and neighbors, particularly with those who were not easily reachable in the pre-Internet-mediated environment. Parents, for example, use instant messages to communicate with their children who are in college. Friends who have moved away from each other are keeping in touch more than they did before they had e-mail, because e-mail does not require them to coordinate a time to talk or to pay long-distance rates. However, this thickening of contacts seems to occur alongside a loosening of the hierarchical aspects of these relationships, as individuals weave their own web of supporting peer relations into the fabric of what might otherwise be stifling familial relationships. Second, we are beginning to see the emergence of greater scope for limited-purpose, loose relationships. These may not fit the ideal model of 'virtual communities.' They certainly do not fit a deep conception of 'community' as a person's primary source of emotional context and support. They are nonetheless effective and meaningful to their participants. It appears that, as the digitally networked environment begins to displace mass media and telephones, its salient communications characteristics provide new dimensions to thicken existing social relations, while also providing new capabilities for looser and more fluid, but still meaningful social networks. A central aspect of this positive improvement in loose ties has been the technical-organizational shift from an information environment dominated by commercial mass media on a one-to-many model, which does not foster group interaction among viewers, to an information environment that both technically and as a matter of social practice enables user-centric, group-based active cooperation platforms of the kind that typify the networked information economy."

Page 226   The "creativity as an import-export business" quote is from Ronald Burt, "The Social Origins of Good Ideas," quoted in Clay Shirky, *Here Comes Everybody* (Penguin, 2008), p. 231.

Page 228   We all have a natural bias to ascribe more credibility to facts and stories that confirm what we already believe, while discounting information that conflicts with our preconceived ideas. The "confirmation bias" runs strong and deep in our psyches. Perhaps, when we are bombarded with more facts and information this natural bias perversely leads us to harden our opinions, undermining our willingness to compromise and reducing the general level of "trust" we say we have in the institutions and organizations around us.

Page 228   For more about the confirmation bias, see Sam Wang and Sandra Aamodt, "Your Brain Lies to You," *New York Times*, June 27, 2008, accessed at http://www .nytimes.com/2008/06/27/opinion/27aamodt.html?em&ex=1214971200&en=459ddfe82 2c8236d&ei=5087%0A, and see also Leonard Mlodinow, *The Drunkard's Walk: How Randomness Rules Our Lives* (Pantheon, 2008), Kindle edition, Loc. 3061–65: "In one study that illustrated the effect rather vividly, researchers gathered a group of undergraduates, some of whom supported the death penalty and some of whom were against it. The researchers then provided all the students with the same set of academic studies on the efficacy of capital punishment. Half the studies supported the idea that the death penalty has a deterrent effect; the other half contradicted that idea. The researchers also gave the subjects clues hinting at the weak points in each of the studies. Afterward the undergraduates were asked to rate the quality of the studies individually and whether and how strongly their attitudes about the death penalty were affected by their reading. The participants gave higher ratings to the studies that confirmed their initial point of view even when the studies on both sides had supposedly been carried out by the same method. And in the end, though everyone had read all the same studies, both those who initially supported the death penalty and those who initially opposed it reported that reading the studies had strengthened their beliefs. Rather than convincing anyone, the data polarized the group. Thus even random patterns can be interpreted as compelling evidence if they relate to our preconceived notions."

Page 228   It occurs to us that a doctor practicing perfect evidence-based management (EBM) but who has a bad bedside manner would be more trustable but less trusted, and although she may make fewer mistakes, she'd likely be sued more. EBM is more akin to competence, but having competence without good intentions is still not trustable. Bedside manner is the "signal" a patient interprets to understand the doctor's intent.

Page 229   The implants details came from Dan Gardner, *Risk: The Science and Politics of Fear* (Virgin Books, 2008), p. 110, and http://www.yourplasticsurgeryguide.com/breast-implants/implants-fda.htm, accessed July 31, 2011.

Page 229   For more about how to de-distort statistics such as the ones about the correlation between murder and spousal abuse, see Mlodinow, *The Drunkard's Walk*, pp. 104–23.

Page 230   The quote from the customer research firm emphasizing how numbers, rather than gut reactions to individual comments, should drive insight gleaned from large amounts of data is from Jeff Carruthers, "Net Promoter Programs: Separating Signal from Noise," Resonate Solutions company blog, October 2, 2011, http://www.resonatesolutions.com.au/blog/net-promoter-programs-separating-signal-noise.html, accessed October 19, 2011.

Page 231   The quote from Jeffrey Pfeffer and Robert I. Sutton about how evidence-based management keeps us acting with knowledge while doubting what we know is from their book *Hard Facts, Dangerous Half-Truths and Total Nonsense* (Harvard Business Press, 2006), Kindle edition, Loc. 1113–15.

Page 231   The study that linked the proportion of senior executives' pay in stock options and the likelihood of the company to restate its earnings is cited in Pfeffer and Sutton, *Hard Facts*, Kindle edition, Loc. 255–60.

Page 232   The point about how the financial community still plans as if changes in asset prices have a normal, bell-shaped distribution despite long-term empirical evidence to the contrary is from Michael Mauboussin, *Think Twice: Harnessing the Power of Counterintuition* (Harvard Business School Press, 2009), p. 109.

Page 233   The quote about the "financial hydrogen bombs" that led to the 2008 collapse was cited in Gillian Tett, *Fool's Gold: How the Bold Dream of a Small Tribe at J.P. Morgan Was Corrupted by Wall Street Greed and Unleashed a Catastrophe,* Kindle edition, Loc. 573–75.

Page 233   Malcolm Gladwell's "10,000 hours" principle was popularized in his book *Outliers: The Story of Success* (Little, Brown, 2008), and the power of intuition is something he highlighted in *Blink: The Power of Thinking Without Thinking* (Little, Brown, 2005).

Page 233   See stories of the Getty Museum's evaluation of an ancient Greek statue and of Lee's strategy against Hooker at the Battle of Chancellorsville (from *Blink*'s cutting room floor at Malcolm Gladwell's Web site, http://www.gladwell.com/blink/biblio/chapter4 .html, accessed October 6, 2011.

Page 234   The quote about how doctors don't go down with their planes is from Ian Ayres, *Super Crunchers: Why Thinking-by-Numbers Is the New Way to Be Smart* (Bantam Books, 2007), pp. 98–99.

Page 235   The quote from Judi Hand came from her article "The Art & Science of Customer Experience Management," *Customer Strategy*, Vol. 3, Issue 3 (October 2011), available at http://www.peppersandrogersgroup.com/view.aspx?DocID=33152.

Page 236   Mitchell Baker is quoted in Lenny Mendonca and Robert Sutton, "Succeeding at Open Source Innovation: An Interview with Mozilla's Mitchell Baker," *McKinsey Quarterly*, January 2008, available at http://www.mckinseyquarterly.com/Succeeding_at_open -source_innovation__An_interview_with_Mozillas_Mitchell_Baker_2098, accessed October 6, 2011. Also see James H. Gilmore and B. Joseph Pine, *Authenticity: What Customers Really Want* (Harvard Business Press, 2007).

10: DESIGNING TRUSTABILITY INTO A BUSINESS

Page 240   The *Cheers* quote came from http://www.movietvquotes.com/t/trust_quotes .html.

Page 242   Our understanding of the difficulties of operating a mobile carrier in a more trustable way came from an interview we did with Peppers & Rogers Group consultants responsible for this client, Ozan Bayulgen and Zeynep Manco, Peppers & Rogers Group Istanbul office, August 2011.

Page 243   For more on Vodafone and Turkcell's dueling customer bills of rights, see the article in *Customer Strategist* by Liz Glagowski, March 2012 (http://www.peppersan drogersgroup.com/issues.aspx?publication=28030).

Page 243   You'll learn more about uncashed gift cards by checking out Melody Warnick, "Don't Be 'Breakage': 8 Tips to Avoid Losing Gift Card Value," Creditcards.com, http:// www.creditcards.com/credit-card-news/8-tips-losing-gift-card-funds-breakage-spillage -1271.php, accessed August 16, 2011.

Page 244   Because current accounting regulations count a gift card sale not as income but as a "liability for deferred revenue," something (like an expiration date) must clearly establish a basis for removing the gift card liability from the books (otherwise it could remain indefinitely). But the Credit CARD Act of 2009 has made this practice complicated: See Charles Owen Kile Jr.'s "Accounting for Gift Cards: An Emerging Issue for Retailers and Auditors," available at: http://www.giftcardpartners.com/pdfs/accounting-for-gift-cards .pdf, accessed October 10, 2011. Also see Richard Shevak's "Treatment of Gift Card/ Certificate Sales: No Answers, More Questions," *Journal of Accountancy*, February 26, 2009, available at: http://www.journalofaccountancy.com/Web/TreatmentofGiftCard Sales.htm, accessed October 10, 2011.

Page 244   Before the recent recession, breakage rates got as high as 20 percent, but Tower Group predicts a U.S. gift card breakage rate of only 3.1 percent, due to the Credit CARD Act's restriction of expiration dates. See Jim Karrh's "Procrastination and Profit in 2011," *Arkansas Business* 27, Issue 48 (December 6, 2010): 7. For more on gift card breakage, see *Freakonomics* authors Stephen J. Dubner and Steven D. Levitt's article "The Gift-Card Economy," *New York Times*, January 7, 2007, at http://www.nytimes.com/2007/01/07/magazine/07wwln_freak.t.html, accessed August 16, 2011.

Page 244   At the time of this writing, twenty U.S. jurisdictions (nineteen states plus the Virgin Islands) include gift cards in their state escheat laws, which require retailers to account for unclaimed assets like this and turn the cash over to the state government, assumedly to "unite lost or abandoned property with its owner." But the complex regulations and the fact that gift card owner information is rarely recorded mean that even if the retailer complies with the regulations and escheats the value of unclaimed gift cards to the state, the majority only ends up in the state's general fund. See Charles Owen Kile Jr. and Patricia S. Wall, "States Bite Into Broken Gift Cards," *Journal of Accountancy*, December 2008, at http://www.journalofaccountancy.com/Issues/2008/Dec/StatesBiteIntoBroken GiftCards.htm, accessed October 10, 2011.

Page 245   Other sources for gift card expiration dates and the Credit CARD Act were "Fed Issues Final Rules on Gift Card Fees, Expiration Dates," *Journal of Accountancy*, March 25, 2010, available at http://www.journalofaccountancy.com/Web/20102734.htm, accessed October 10, 2011; and Warnick, "Don't Be 'Breakage': 8 Tips to Avoid Losing Gift Card Value."

Page 245   David Bakken is chief operating officer of KJT Group, a research consultancy, and author of "The Customer Knowledge Advantage" blog, found at http://davidgbakken .wordpress.com/. He wrote this post as a guest blogger at http://www.1to1media.com/ weblog/2010/04/guest_blogger_david_bakken_a_t.html, accessed September 1, 2011.

Page 247   The information about banks making their fee information inaccessible to consumers is from Bob Sullivan, "Study: Banks hiding fee info, skirting law," http://redtape .msnbc.msn.com/_nv/more/section/archive?date=2011/4, accessed May 11, 2011.

Page 250   For more on how big brands in a variety of industries have used individualized customer strategies to fuel growth, see J. B. King, "Big Business Bets on Its Customers," *1to1 Magazine*, October 2003, pp. 18–19.

Page 250   The GM AutoChoiceAdvisor program is no longer in operation.

Page 251   The statistics from the car company that offered test drives in competitors' cars as well as their own were from John Hauser and Glen Urban, "Lessons from the automotive world: Building trust to boost sales," MIT blog post, April 5, 2011, http://mitsloan experts.com/2011/04/05/lessons-from-the-automotive-world-building-trust-to-boost-sales/, accessed September 21, 2011. (Note: Hauser and Urban do not specifically reference GM in conjunction with these success statistics, but an unnamed automotive program virtually identical to the GM program.)

Page 252 We pulled the Microsoft training-voucher story from our book *Rules to Break and Laws to Follow: How Your Business Can Beat the Crisis of Short-Termism* (Wiley, 2008), pp. 160–61.

Page 252 Microsoft's brand soon became the world's *most* trusted brand in the Edelman Survey. *Rules to Break and Laws to Follow,* p. 162.

Page 252 See our discussion of airlines in chapter 2 of *Return on Customer: Creating Maximum Value from Your Scarcest Resource* (Currency/Doubleday, 2005), on which much of this discussion is based.

Page 253 The authors did in fact meet personally with executives at one major airline in 2006 who said this pricing strategy is what their firm and several other airlines do. They were unhappy about it, sensing that it creates mistrust among customers, but didn't know what else to do to fill planes.

Page 253 See our discussion of airline trust in *Return on Customer,* pp. 31–33.

Page 253 In his *Customer Strategist* blog, "Revenue Management and Customer Centricity: Imperatives in an Era of Consolidation," October 12, 2010, http://www.peppers androgersgroup.com/blog/2010/10/customer-strategist-dietrich-c.html, Dietrich Chen, director of Peppers & Rogers Group, makes this point:

> "In simple terms, revenue management algorithms today manage inventory controls for the myriad of fare classes that exist for any given flight. Do we shut off lower fares because our forecasts and competitive analyses lead us to believe that demand for higher fares will materialize? Or will we be too restrictive, which will lead to seats going empty? These algorithms manipulate an enormous amount of data and are complex and computer-intensive. However, today, these algorithms optimize matching inventory to demand for a given route. This transaction-focused approach does not take into account the value of repeat business that airlines' most valuable customers—frequent fliers—contribute to the business.
>
> "Loyalty programs that have been launched with great success do recognize that fact. Loyalty programs not only serve as a way to identify an airline's most valuable customers, but also provide a way to balance short-term revenue management goals with long-term optimization of frequent fliers' lifetime value."

Page 254 Don interviewed John McFadden on October 1, 2011, at the conclusion of this flight segment.

Page 255 John McFadden's response about handwriting thank-you notes to his passengers is from his e-mail to Don Peppers, October 1, 2011.

INDEX